# The Cambridge Companion to Sylvia Plath

The controversies that surround Sylvia Plath's life and work mean that her poems are more read and studied now than ever before. This *Companion* provides a comprehensive and authoritative overview of Sylvia Plath's poetry, prose, letters and journals and of their place in twentieth-century culture. These newly commissioned essays by leading international scholars represent a spectrum of critical perspectives. They pay particular attention to key debates and to well-known texts such as *Ariel* and *The Bell Jar*, while offering original and thought-provoking readings to new as well as more experienced Plath readers. The *Companion* also discusses three recent additions to the field: Ted Hughes's *Birthday Letters*, Plath's complete Journals and the 'Restored' edition of *Ariel*. With its invaluable guide to further reading and chronology of Plath's life and work, this *Companion* will help students and scholars understand and enjoy Plath's work and its continuing relevance.

THE CAMBRIDGE COMPANION TO
# SYLVIA PLATH

EDITED BY
JO GILL

CAMBRIDGE
UNIVERSITY PRESS

CAMBRIDGE UNIVERSITY PRESS
Cambridge, New York, Melbourne, Madrid, Cape Town, Singapore, São Paulo

Cambridge University Press
The Edinburgh Building, Cambridge CB2 2RU, UK

Published in the United States of America by Cambridge University Press, New York

www.cambridge.org
Information on this title: www.cambridge.org/9780521844963

First published 2006

*A catalogue record for this publication is available from the British Library*

ISBN-13 978-0-521-84496-3 hardback
ISBN-10 0-521-84496-7 hardback

ISBN-13 978-0-521-60685-1 paperback
ISBN-10 0-521-60685-3 paperback

Transferred to digital printing 2007

# CONTENTS

# NOTES ON CONTRIBUTORS

STEVEN GOULD AXELROD is Professor of English at the University of California, Riverside. He is the author of *Sylvia Plath: The Wound and the Cure of Words* (1990) and *Robert Lowell: Life and Art* (1978) and has co-written or edited many other books including *Robert Lowell: Essays on the Poetry* (1986), *Critical Essays on Wallace Stevens* (1988) and *Critical Essays on William Carlos Williams* (1995). He has published more than forty articles and is now researching a book-length study of Cold War poetry.

JANET BADIA is Assistant Professor of Twentieth-Century American Literature at Marshall University, Huntington, West Virginia. Her research interests include confessional poetry, autobiography and book history, especially the study of readers and reception. She is co-editor of *Reading Women: Literary Figures and Cultural Icons from the Victorian Age to the Present* (2005). She is currently completing a book manuscript on Plath, Anne Sexton and women readers.

TRACY BRAIN is Senior Lecturer in English and Creative Writing at Bath Spa University, where she runs the PhD in Creative Writing Programme. She is the author of *The Other Sylvia Plath* (2001). In addition to the essay in the present volume, Tracy Brain has recently written on Plath in Jo Gill (ed.), *Modern Confessional Writing: New Critical Essays* (2005) and in Anita Helle (ed.), *The Unravelling Archive: Essays on Sylvia Plath* (2006).

CHRISTINA BRITZOLAKIS is Senior Lecturer in English at the University of Warwick. She is the author of *Sylvia Plath and the Theatre of Mourning* (1999) and has published articles on modernist poetry, fiction and drama, including James Joyce, T. S. Eliot and W. H. Auden. Her current research is concerned with visuality and technology in international modernist culture.

LYNDA K. BUNDTZEN is Herbert H. Lehman Professor of English at Williams College in Williamstown, Massachusetts. She is the author of two books on Sylvia Plath: *Plath's Incarnations: Woman and the Creative Process* (1983) and *The Other Ariel* (2001). Her other writings include several essays on film and feminist theory and on other women poets.

ALICE ENTWISTLE is Senior Lecturer in English at the University of the West of England, Bristol. She has published widely on late twentieth-century Anglo-American poetics, concentrating in recent years on poetry written by women. She is the author, with Jane Dowson, of *A History of Twentieth Century British Women's Poetry* (Cambridge University Press, 2005).

JO GILL is Lecturer in American Literature at Bath Spa University. She is the editor of *Modern Confessional Writing: New Critical Essays* (2005) and the author of a new study of the work of Anne Sexton. She has published extensively on modern British and American poetry.

DIANE MIDDLEBROOK is a professional writer and Professor of English Emerita at Stanford University, California. Among her books are *Anne Sexton – A Biography* (finalist for the 1991 National Book Award in the USA); *Suits Me: The Double Life of Billy Tipton* (1998) and *Her Husband: Hughes and Plath – A Marriage* (2003). Middlebrook is an Honorary Member of Christ's College, University of Cambridge.

DEBORAH NELSON is Associate Professor of English and Gender Studies at the University of Chicago where she has taught since 1996. Her first book, *Pursuing Privacy in Cold War America* (2001), examines confessional poetry in relation to Supreme Court privacy doctrine. She is currently working on a book called *Tough Broads* on women artists and intellectuals in the postwar era.

SUSAN R. VAN DYNE is Professor and Chair of Women's Studies at Smith College, Massachusetts. She is the author of *Revising Life: Sylvia Plath's Ariel Poems* (1993) and co-editor of *Women's Place in the Academy: Transforming the Liberal Arts* (1985). She is currently working on a book titled *Proving Grounds: The Politics of Reading Contemporary Women Poets*.

LINDA WAGNER-MARTIN is Hanes Professor of English at the University of North Carolina-Chapel Hill and has published fifty books on modern and mid-century American writers. She has held Guggenheim, Rockefeller, NEH, and other fellowships. Recent biographies are of Barbara Kingsolver and Zelda Sayre Fitzgerald. Her work on Plath includes her 1987 book, *Sylvia Plath: A Biography*, available in many languages; *Sylvia Plath: A Literary Life* (1999, 2nd edition 2003); and several collections of essays on Plath's work.

# PREFACE

*The Cambridge Companion to Sylvia Plath* offers a critical overview of Plath's writing (predominantly the poetry, but also fiction, letters and journals) and of its place in twentieth-century literature and culture. The eleven specially commissioned essays in the collection are the work of leading international scholars in the field and represent a spectrum of critical perspectives and practices.

The book is divided into two sections. The first section discusses Plath's writing in relation to relevant contexts and perspectives (exploring the temptations and limitations of reading her work biographically, the insights to be gained by examining its historical and ideological contexts, the difficulties and rewards of adopting a psychoanalytic perspective and the influence of her writing on contemporary American and British poetry). The aim here is to show that Plath's work is not entire unto itself; that it emerged in particular historical, ideological, literary and personal contexts, and, moreover, that the figure of Plath we may think we know is a product of a complex, mutable and contested tissue of discourses. These essays combine a critical awareness of key issues and debates in Plath studies with incisive readings of the poetry and prose; their intention is to inform and to stimulate the reader's own engagement with the writing.

The second section discusses a range of Plath texts in turn – from her earliest collection *The Colossus* to the poems of the *Ariel* period to *The Bell Jar* and the manuscripts of *Letters Home* – raising a number of important and challenging issues, and proposing a variety of reading positions. This section is interested in both the diversity and the detail of Plath's work, in its richness, its craft and its technical complexity, and it focuses on Plath's concentrated and ambitious use of poetic form. It draws attention to its sometimes overlooked variety and it alerts readers to Plath's sustained manipulation of a range of genres and voices and her development of a sophisticated and linguistically self-aware poetics. It reflects on the publishing history of specific volumes and the construction of a Plath 'canon' and highlights recent critical debates about agency and ownership, about the politics of editing and the ethics of criticism. The essays in both sections are informed by an awareness of gender as a factor in the production and reception of Plath's work.

Like others in the series, the *Companion to Plath* draws on and – implicitly or otherwise – assesses previous scholarship in the field. This critical heritage is examined in detail, where relevant, in the chapters which follow (and a comprehensive list of sources is provided at the end of the book). Nevertheless a brief survey of the field of Plath studies is useful at this point as a way of setting the scene and of demonstrating, first, that approaches to Plath's work change over time and second, that there is no orthodoxy of critical opinion. Some of the earliest studies of Plath's writing – for example, C. B. Cox and A. R. Jones's 1964 article 'After the Tranquillized Fifties' and Al Alvarez's 1967 'Beyond all this Fiddle' – considered it in the context of the newly emergent 'confessional mode' of poetry (the name was coined by M. L. Rosenthal in a review of Robert Lowell's 1959 *Life Studies*) with which Plath – rightly or wrongly – was typically associated. Plath was an acquaintance of Lowell's, had studied alongside poet Anne Sexton in his Boston University writing workshops and seemed, particularly in the poems which culminated in *Ariel*, to belong within this frame. Such an association seems now to be rather limiting, although recent revisions of confessionalism in the light of, say, Michel Foucault's work and in the context of Deborah Nelson's reading of the mode as a product of Cold War anxieties about privacy and surveillance suggest the potential value of revisiting Plath's work in the light of a revised definition of the term.

Contemporaneous with this (and perhaps an inevitable consequence both of the turn to the personal and private in this period, and of the particular circumstances of Plath's death) were early and persistently influential biographical accounts. Memoirs by family and friends featured in Charles Newman's 1970 collection *The Art of Sylvia Plath* (which reproduced articles originally published in a 1966 special issue of the journal *Tri-Quarterly*). This was followed by Al Alvarez's recollections of Plath's last days, *The Savage God* (UK 1971/US 1972), and some years later by Anne Stevenson's controversial *Bitter Fame* – the latter ignited arguments about authority and ownership of truth which continue to smoulder to this day. A characteristic of such works – although we should note that this is not a problem unique to Plath studies – is a worrying conflation of poet and speaker, of lived experience and poetic text. Of late, more sophisticated treatments (Janet Malcolm's *The Silent Woman* (1994) and Jacqueline Rose's *The Haunting of Sylvia Plath* (1991), which she later supplemented with an essay entitled 'This is Not a Biography') take a step back and question the status, value and purpose of literary biography.

Another early approach to the study of Plath was through the lens of mythology. Judith Kroll, author of one of the first book-length studies of Plath's work, *Chapters in a Mythology* (1976), cites the profound influence on Plath (through Hughes) of Robert Graves's *The White Goddess*. Steven Gould Axelrod, however, demurs, arguing that 'Plath never actually cared much about *The White Goddess* except when she was feigning an interest in topics of interest to her husband' (*Sylvia Plath: The Wound and the Cure of Words* (Baltimore: Johns Hopkins University Press, 1990), p. 46).

A psychoanalytical approach to Plath's life and writing seems always to have proved tempting. David Holbrook's *Sylvia Plath: Poetry and Existence* (1976) examines the poetry in the light of what it diagnoses as the poet's schizoid personality – a condition which Holbrook wishes to ameliorate or neutralize in order to protect her vulnerable readers: 'these works may be offering falsifications or forms of moral inversion which are absurd, or even deranged, and may even do harm to the sensitive and responsive young person' ((London: Athlone Press, 1976), p. 2). In the same year, Edward Butscher's contentious *Sylvia Plath: Method and Madness* appeared. More recent psychoanalytical accounts, for example Jacqueline Rose's *The Haunting of Sylvia Plath*, Elisabeth Bronfen's *Sylvia Plath* (1998) and Christina Britzolakis's *Sylvia Plath and the Theatre of Mourning* (1999), have developed a rather different approach, one inflected by the insights of post-structuralism and feminism. Here, as in contemporary literary studies more generally, the shift has been away from analysing and pathologizing the author to an acknowledgement of the uncertainty of truth, the slipperiness of language and the indeterminacy of the subject.

Plath's writing coincided with the emergence of the second wave of feminism and thus her work has frequently been read in terms of its recognition and representation of the conditions of life for women of the 1960s onwards. Studies by Alicia Ostriker, Jan Montefiore, Suzanne Juhasz and many others established Plath's importance in a newly validated tradition of women's writing. More recent feminist approaches have challenged some of the assumptions of such criticism. Renée Curry's thought-provoking account of representations of whiteness in modern women poets, *White Women Writing White: H. D., Elizabeth Bishop, Sylvia Plath and Whiteness* (2000), critiques the essentialism and the colour blindness of Plath's poetry.

Plath's historical context and her engagement with issues of political, cultural and ideological concern have often been overlooked in the enthusiasm for reading her work as merely private and introspective – as 'mirror-looking' to use her own scornful term (*PS*, p. 170). Stan Smith's important book *Inviolable Voice: History and Twentieth-Century Poetry* (1982) redresses this, seeing the poetry as located very much in a particular place and time, and as engaging in affirmatory or contestatory ways with large questions of history, society, responsibility. Deborah Nelson's reading of Plath and her contemporaries in the context of Cold War cultures of privacy and surveillance (*Pursuing Privacy in Cold War America*, 2001) and Robin Peel's study of Plath's preoccupation with the political anxieties of the 1950s and early 1960s (*Writing Back: Sylvia Plath and Cold War Politics*, 2002) have also proved influential. In each of these cases, Plath is read as a politically engaged poet. Like T. S. Eliot, W. H. Auden and others (Denise Levertov and Thom Gunn of her own generation), Plath shifted cultures by moving across the Atlantic. Of late, Tracy Brain and Paul Giles have read Plath's language and themes in terms of this dislocation (Brain posits the notion of mid-Atlanticism and draws attention to the equivocal or liminal voices of Plath's writing).

To all these must be added the numerous studies of Plath's work which, while sometimes drawing on some of the broad approaches outlined above, develop their own perspectives and areas of interest. These include major studies by Marjorie Perloff, Helen Hennessy Vendler, Tim Kendall, Linda Wagner-Martin, Lynda K. Bundtzen, Susan R. Van Dyne and many, many others. What is striking in summarizing this heritage is its breadth and its diversity. *The Companion* treads a confident path through this rich and heterogeneous material.

Of particular importance to this *Companion* – and thus of real value to its readers – has been the recent publication of three key texts. *The Cambridge Companion to Sylvia Plath* is the first study of Plath to be able to make use of all these resources. The first of these is Ted Hughes's 1998 collection of poems *Birthday Letters*. This revisits the life and, more importantly, the work of Plath, in poems such as 'The Rabbit Catcher', which writes back to her well-known and fiercely contested poem of the same name, and 'The Beach', which offers a different perspective on the scene explored in her 1961 'Whitsun'. It is too simplistic to say that this is Hughes's version of the story of their marriage, or that this is Hughes in dialogue with Plath (if we think it important to register the nuances of Plath's poetic voices and to flag up the noncoherence of poet and speaker, surely we should adopt a similar approach in considering Hughes's work?) Nevertheless, what *Birthday Letters* does do, in what I regard as a profoundly self-conscious, troubled and troubling way, is remind us of the shared difficulties – for writer and reader alike – of engaging with this material, with these issues. Analysing the complexity of their creative partnership is the approach Diane Middlebrook takes in her book *Her Husband: Sylvia Plath and Ted Hughes – A Marriage* (2003).

The second key text to emerge of late, in 2000, is the more complete edition of Plath's extant journals (known as *The Journals of Sylvia*

*Plath: 1950–1962* in the UK and *The Unabridged Journals of Sylvia Plath* in the US). Edited by Karen Kukil, the Associate Curator at Smith College, the new *Journals* reproduce for the first time Smith College's extensive holdings of Plath's diaries. Running to almost 700 pages, the *Journals* are hugely valuable to our understanding of Plath's writing practices and sources, although as Bonnie Costello cautions of the work of Marianne Moore 'this multiplicity of sources is quite different from the multiplicity of references' (*Marianne Moore: Imaginary Possessions* (Cambridge, MA: Harvard University Press, 1981), p. 6).

Finally, what has been perceived by some as a troubling gap in Plath's oeuvre is closed by the publication of *Ariel: The Restored Edition – A Facsimile of Plath's Manuscript, Reinstating Her Original Selection and Arrangement* (2004) with a 'Foreword' by Frieda Hughes. As Ted Hughes disclosed in his 'Introduction' and 'Notes' to Plath's *Collected Poems*, the edition of *Ariel* which had been published posthumously in 1965 (UK/1966 US) did not follow the order, or even include all the poems, which Plath had planned (*CP*, pp. 14–15). The significance of Hughes's alterations to the trajectory of the volume are considered at length in Marjorie Perloff's 1990 article 'The Two *Ariels*: The (Re)making of the Sylvia Plath Canon' and Lynda K. Bundtzen's book *The Other Ariel* (2001).

In her 'Foreword' to the restored edition of *Ariel*, Frieda Hughes expresses concern about the repeated 'dissect[ion]' by readers of some of its key poems (her anxiety replicates Ted Hughes's own point, in defence of his editing of the 1965/66 version of *Ariel*, that he would have left more poems out had he suspected that they would ever be 'decoded' (*WP*, p. 167)). There is an anxiety in both of these cases about reading – about the power of other people's reading to yield unexpected, proliferating and uncontrollable meanings. Interpretation is experienced (or interpreted) as an attack on the hermetic body of the text, on the singular truth which is presumed to hide there. What I wish to argue here is that the text – Plath's poetry, any writing – cannot exist outside of such interpretative processes; it does not 'mean' alone. To suggest that it does is, arguably, to deny the complexity and richness of the writing, to reduce it to singularity. On this point I disagree with Frieda Hughes's suggestion that the *Ariel* poems 'speak for themselves' (*A Rest.*, p. xvi). What they 'speak', I would contend, depends on who is listening and when, how and why they are read.

As a counter to these arguments against interpretation, I propose a plea *for* interpretation. *The Cambridge Companion to Sylvia Plath* seeks to stimulate a plethora of ongoing readings – of primary and secondary sources alike (for biographies and critical studies, like poetry, reward careful and critical reading). Rather than positing a definitive truth about Plath's work, the essays collected below introduce relevant contexts and issues and offer diverse reading practices – all in the service of a multiplicity of interpretations. For it is only by interpretation, by reading, thinking, writing about and discussing these poems, that their richness, complexity and resonance will adequately be recognized.

Jo Gill

# ACKNOWLEDGEMENTS

Thanks, first, to Ray Ryan of Cambridge University Press who commissioned this *Companion*, to the anonymous reviewers who approved the idea and to the School of Humanities at Kingston University, London whose generous and timely offer of a Research Fellowship ensured that it could be completed. At Kingston I owe particular gratitude to Avril Horner, David Rogers, Sarah Sceats and Meg Jensen. Thanks, too, to friends and colleagues at the Universities of Gloucestershire and Exeter – in particular to Peter Widdowson, Shelley Saguaro and Mark Whalan. Others who have offered their interest and support include Stan Smith, Stacy Gillis, Alice Entwistle, Frances Hollingdale, Jeannette Gill and Sheena and Ray Hennessy. It has been a pleasure to work with all the contributors to this companion and I hope that the finished item does their scholarship justice. Final thanks, as always, to Neil Stevens and to Jacob, Freya and Keziah.

Unless otherwise indicated, poems discussed in this volume are from Sylvia Plath, *Collected Poems*, ed. Ted Hughes (London: Faber and Faber; New York: Harper & Row, 1981). Where there is a difference in pagination or contents between English and American editions (for example, in the case of *Johnny Panic and the Bible of Dreams*) the edition used is indicated in an endnote.

| | |
|---|---|
| *A* | Sylvia Plath, *Ariel* (London: Faber and Faber, 1965; New York: Harper & Row, 1966). |
| *A Rest.* | Sylvia Plath, *Ariel: The Restored Edition*, ed. Frieda Hughes (London: Faber and Faber, 2004). |
| *BJ* | Sylvia Plath, *The Bell Jar* (London: Heinemann, 1963 (under the pseudonym Victoria Lucas); London: Faber and Faber 1966; New York: Harper & Row, 1971 (as Sylvia Plath)). |
| *BL* | Ted Hughes, *Birthday Letters* (London: Faber and Faber; New York: Farrar, Straus & Giroux, 1998). |
| *C* | Sylvia Plath, *The Colossus and Other Poems* (London: Heinemann, 1960; New York: Knopf, 1962). |
| *CP* | Sylvia Plath, *Collected Poems*, ed. Ted Hughes (London: Faber and Faber; New York: Harper & Row, 1981). |
| *CW* | Sylvia Plath, *Crossing the Water* (London: Faber and Faber; New York: Harper & Row, 1971). |
| *J* | Sylvia Plath, *The Journals of Sylvia Plath: 1950–1962*, ed. Karen V. Kukil (London: Faber and Faber, 2000); *The Unabridged Journals of Sylvia Plath* (New York: Anchor, 2000). |
| *J Abr.* | Sylvia Plath, *The Journals of Sylvia Plath*, ed. Ted Hughes and Frances McCullough (New York: Dial, 1982) (abridged edition). |

JP      Sylvia Plath, *Johnny Panic and the Bible of Dreams and Other Prose Writings* (London: Faber and Faber, 1977; New York: Harper & Row, 1979).

LH      Sylvia Plath, *Letters Home: Correspondence 1950–1963*, ed. Aurelia Plath (New York: Harper & Row, 1975; London: Faber and Faber, 1976).

PS      Peter Orr (ed), *The Poet Speaks: Interviews with Contemporary Poets* (London: Routledge & Kegan Paul, 1966).

WP      Ted Hughes, *Winter Pollen: Occasional Prose*, ed. William Scammell (London: Faber and Faber, 1994).

WT      Sylvia Plath, *Winter Trees* (London: Faber and Faber, 1971; New York: Harper & Row, 1972).

1932    Sylvia Plath born 27 October in Boston, Massachusetts, the
        daughter of Aurelia Schober and Otto Emil Plath. Aurelia was
        first-generation American, Otto had emigrated to the US from the
        German-speaking Polish corridor as a young man. Aurelia Plath
        worked as a teacher and as a secretary. Otto Plath was Professor
        of Entomology at Boston University and an expert on bees.

1935    Birth of Sylvia's brother, Warren.

1939    Outbreak of World War II.

1940    Death of Otto Plath after complications arising from diabetes.

1941    Pearl Harbor; US enters World War II.

1942    Aurelia, Sylvia and Warren move to Wellesley, Massachusetts.

1945    Atomic bombs detonated at Hiroshima and Nagasaki. End of
        World War II.

1950-1  Plath attends Smith College, Northampton (majoring in English)
        on a scholarship granted by novelist Olive Higgins Prouty.

1950-3  Korean War.

1950-4  McCarthyism.

1953    Early January: Plath fractures her leg in a skiing accident.
        June: Execution of Ethel and Julius Rosenberg for espionage.
        Summer: Plath takes up a guest editorship at *Mademoiselle*
        magazine, New York. Returns home exhausted and close to
        breakdown, ECT administered, suicide attempt and hospitalization.

1954    Post-World War II food rationing in Britain ends.

1955    Graduates from Smith College *summa cum laude* and travels to
        England on a Fulbright Scholarship to study at Newnham
        College, Cambridge.

1956    25 February: meets Ted Hughes at the launch party for a student
        magazine.
        16 June: marries Ted Hughes in London. Honeymoon in
        Benidorm, Spain.

| | |
|---|---|
| 1957–9 | Plath and Hughes in the US. |
| | 1957: Plath teaches at Smith College. |
| | 1958: Plath attends Robert Lowell's writing workshop at Boston University alongside Anne Sexton, takes a secretarial post in a psychiatric clinic, enters therapy with Dr Ruth Beuscher. |
| | 1959: Travel through the US and period at Yaddo, the writers' colony. In December 1959 Plath and Hughes return to live in England. |
| 1960 | April: Plath's and Hughes's daughter, Frieda, born in London. |
| | 31 October: Plath's first collection of poetry, *The Colossus*, published in the UK. |
| 1961 | February: Miscarriage and appendectomy. |
| | March to May: Writing *The Bell Jar*. |
| | Late August/early September: Plath, Hughes and Frieda move to North Tawton, Devon. |
| | Antinuclear demonstrations take place in London. |
| 1962 | January: a son, Nicholas, born in Devon. |
| | *The Colossus* published for the first time in the US (14 May). |
| | 19 August: 'Three Women' broadcast on BBC radio. |
| | October: Plath and Hughes separate; Hughes leaves North Tawton. Cuban Missile Crisis. |
| | December: Plath and children move to London. |
| 1963 | January: *The Bell Jar* published in London under the pseudonym Victoria Lucas. |
| | 11 February: Plath dies by suicide. |
| 1965 | 11 March: *Ariel* published in the UK. |
| 1966 | June: *Ariel* published in the US. |
| | 1 September: *The Bell Jar* published in the UK under Plath's own name. |
| 1971 | 14 April: *The Bell Jar* published in the US under Plath's own name. *Crossing the Water* published (May UK/September US). |
| | *Winter Trees* published in the UK (September). |
| 1972 | September: *Winter Trees* published in the US. |
| 1975 | December: *Letters Home* published in the US. |
| 1976 | April: *Letters Home* published in the UK. |
| | *The Bed Book* (1959?) published. |
| 1977 | *Johnny Panic and the Bible of Dreams* published in the UK. |
| 1979 | *Johnny Panic and the Bible of Dreams* published in the US. |
| 1981 | *Collected Poems* published. |
| 1982 | *Collected Poems* awarded the Pulitzer Prize for Poetry. |

# PART I

# Contexts and issues

# I

SUSAN R. VAN DYNE

# The problem of biography

Because the poems and novel that have made Plath's name came to almost all her readers as posthumous events, her work has inevitably been read through the irrevocable, ineradicable and finally enigmatic fact of Plath's suicide. The challenge for her biographers has been to puzzle out the relationship not merely of her life to her art, but of her art to her death. Biographers promise to expose these relationships for scrutiny, and yet the genre itself is inexhaustible: there is never an end to what the biographer cannot know. If Plath's biographers differ sharply in their readiness to propose definitive and sometimes reductive explanations of her character, they also can be judged by their ability to register the quality of her achievement, to explain what Plath's work revealed so compellingly to readers, particularly women, of her own and the next generation, and why it will remain illuminating and important in the future.

Biographers of Plath demonstrate that the genre is always interested, although hers have been more noticeably partisan than most. In fact, each of the major biographies is in part motivated to counteract what is perceived as egregious bias in the one before. Reading them in sequence, we hear an edgy conversation that has lasted for three decades. Each biographer also takes up the story at a different moment in Plath's publication history and growing literary reputation, and not unimportantly, in Ted Hughes's oeuvre and reputation. In each decade biographers gained access to new published and archival resources that document in voluminous detail Plath's historical context, her professional and personal correspondence, her education and reading and her creative process in the drafts of her *Ariel* poems.[1]

When Edward Butscher published *Sylvia Plath: Method and Madness* in 1975, neither Plath's letters nor her journals had been published, nor had her fiction beyond *The Bell Jar* been collected.[2] By contrast, Linda Wagner-Martin began researching her 1987 biography when Plath's *Collected Poems* won the Pulitzer Prize in 1982.[3] She consulted the unedited letters from Plath to her mother acquired in 1977 by the Lilly Library at Indiana University, along with documentation of Plath's life from infancy through her year teaching at Smith in 1957–8. Wagner-Martin read Plath's poetry drafts and her censored and incomplete journals (a much larger selection of her journals than those published in 1982), which are among the most important materials Smith College bought from Hughes in 1981. Anne Stevenson's apparent mission in *Bitter Fame* was to counteract what by 1989 was represented by the Plath Estate as Plath's mistaken status as a feminist martyr.[4] In 'The Archive', a central chapter in *The Haunting of Sylvia Plath*, Jacqueline Rose takes the Hugheses (Ted and his sister Olwyn) to task for what she and others experienced as pressure from the Estate to adopt their view or lose permission to quote Plath's work.[5] Against these charges of coercion, Janet Malcolm's *The Silent Woman* (1995) struggled to recuperate Stevenson's efforts, as well as to forefront the unavoidable partiality of biography as a genre.[6] Diane Middlebrook's biography of the Plath–Hughes marriage, *Her Husband* (2003), attempts to take the measure of both poets after Hughes's bombshell publication of *Birthday Letters* in 1998, his unanticipated death from cancer months later, and the showering of England's most prestigious prizes on its poet laureate in the last years of the century.[7] She was the first to mine the Hughes archives at Emory University, a dauntingly rich and tangled repository of Ted Hughes's correspondence, drafts and workbooks, and of his editorial curatorship of Plath's work.

Finally, Ted Hughes is also Plath's biographer, despite his insistent refusal to be interviewed by biographers. Through his control of her archive and his own, through more than fourteen introductions to and annotations of Plath's work, and in a series of litigious public and private interventions to protest against invasions of privacy by biographers and critics, he has laid claim to irrefutable knowledge of Plath's inspiration, intentions and writing practices, and the chronology of her work. His late volume, *Birthday Letters* was read by many as an anguished memoir of their marriage and of her writing. Accompanying the rise in Sylvia Plath's stature as a major literary talent of the twentieth century is an apparently inexhaustible market for stories of her life (which seems emblematic of the gender norms that governed growing up talented, ambitious and female in the postwar US) and of this marriage between professional writers.[8]

## Reading the life

In thinking through these biographies, I want to highlight several bad habits of reading Sylvia Plath as woman and as writer that misunderstand the relation of biography to art. While some of these reading fallacies are more prominent in one biography than another, others are shared. First, beginning immediately after her suicide and continuing through Hughes's late poems about Plath, a powerfully influential narrative assumes that her suicide authenticates the truth of her poems. This reading assumes that the relation of creative writing to lived suffering is transparent and direct, and is predetermined rather than chosen by the poet. Further, her death is understood as a tragic but inevitable byproduct of her poetic method; her suicide is proof that the violent unresolved materials of her unconscious, once courted or confronted as subjects for poetry, couldn't finally be transmuted, ordered and contained by words. Al Alvarez launched this demonic teleology in his memoir of Plath, *The Savage God*, Robert Lowell promulgated it in his foreword to the American edition of *Ariel*, and Hughes reinscribes it in *Birthday Letters*.

Second, Anne Stevenson's is only the most egregious example of those who read the poet as pathological and her writing as symptomatic of her illness. Stevenson recycles Edward Butscher's binary logic of true and false selves, in which an unacknowledged, and essentially destructive true self is temporarily constrained through verbal technical polish only to break through in the searing denunciations of the *Ariel* poems. In this reading Plath's character is fixed from childhood by heredity, chemistry, trauma or family dynamics, and a compliant mask is held tenuously in place by middle-class propriety and ambition, until the mask breaks at the dissolution of her marriage.

A third misreading accepts the binary of true–false selves, but reverses their values. Plath is the product of rigid gender norms imposed by patriarchy, her mother's influence and a dominant husband until his defection causes the true, subversive, protofeminist self to erupt in fury. This reading oversimplifies the relation between individual subject and ideology by imagining that Plath's true self could be immune to repressive ideology. Rather, the subject is constituted through ideology; gender norms are not merely given and internalized, but are apprehended, resisted and negotiated constantly in conscious and unconscious ways.

What none of these reading habits can do justice to is Plath's agency as woman and artist. Perhaps because as a culture we subscribe so exclusively to paradigms in which personality is fixed by good or bad parenting, early trauma or brain chemistry, biography underestimates Plath's habits of conscious reinvention and the lucid artistic control of her poetry, even in her final days. Rather than assume that Plath is an unusually autobiographical writer, we need to understand that she experienced her life in unusually textual ways. In her letters and journals as much as in her fiction and poetry, Plath's habits of self-representation suggest that she regarded her life as if it were a text she could invent and rewrite. At the age of seventeen, her creation of a persona is self-conscious and potentially omnipotent: 'I think I would like to call myself "The girl who wanted to be God"' (*LH*, p. 40). At moments of crisis, throughout her life, she imagines that she can erase the inscription of lived experience and earlier textual selves and be reborn, unmarked as an infant, inviolate as a virgin. Each of the narratives she created, whether letters, journals, prose, poetry or interviews, served her as enabling fictions; these proliferating personae were self-consciously chosen and personally explanatory. The dissonance and contradictions among these self-representations are at once symptomatic, in that they demonstrate postwar American culture's powerful shaping influence on her imagination, and also strategic, in that they represent her efforts to imagine, dismantle and reconstruct her ongoing self-narrative into a script she could live with.

While Edward Butscher has been uniformly disparaged by the Estate and other biographers since the publication of *Sylvia Plath: Method and Madness* in 1976, this first full-length biography puts in circulation almost all the formulas that later biographers would adopt and reinforce. Butscher introduces the term 'bitch goddess' as shorthand for Plath's poetic persona and sometimes as a descriptor for the woman herself. In combination, his terms evoke 'a discontented, tense, frequently brilliant woman goaded into fury by her repressed or distorted status in male society' and 'a more creative one ... with fierce ambition and ruthless pursuit of success' (pp. xi–xii).[9] The bitch goddess is the profoundly angry subconscious force that Butscher claims underlies her overachieving adolescence, her contemptuous resentment of family and friends, and her urge to manipulate and control everything from boyfriends and mother figures to nature itself.

He sees Plath's character as deformed by mental illness. Although he claims to eschew a medical diagnosis, Butscher's account depends on frequent references to her split personalities, psychosis and narcissism (pp. 26–7 and 125, among others). Like Stevenson later, he faults Plath for the unjust attack in *The Bell Jar* on everyone who had supported her (p. 308). But unlike Stevenson's extension of the blanket of moral blame from Plath's character to her work, Butscher uniformly admires her craft. More than any later biographer, he praises the accomplishment of *The Bell Jar*, as 'a minor masterpiece of sardonic satire and sincere protest', comparing it to F. Scott Fitzgerald's *The Great Gatsby* and Nathanael West's *Miss Lonelyhearts* (p. 310). He recognizes in the *Ariel* poems not the mistaken fury of an unreasonable wife, but 'the fully conscious legend of the bitch self that she would assert with calculated genius' (p. 316).

Butscher also proposes the 'lost little girl' thesis of the poet arrested in her development by the childhood trauma of her father's death – a thesis most vividly deployed in Hughes's 1995 *Paris Review* interview 'The Art of Poetry LXXI' and in *Birthday Letters*. Butscher imagines in Plath's 'The Moon and the Yew Tree' an 'allegory of the lost little girl' which he claimed Hughes also recognized (p. 297). While he identifies the poem as a masterpiece, his reading emphasizes Plath's helpless passivity, even though the speaker nowhere identifies herself as little girl.

Butscher believes that their marriage benefited them mutually as poets. As Diane Middlebrook would argue more comprehensively three decades later, Butscher recognizes that 'their marriage vow above all was a mutual protection pact *against* the world and *for* poetry' (p. 188) and that their union 'provided two of the more original minds of their generation with an unprecedented and productive opportunity to feed and grow upon one another's stores of poetic insight' (p. 189). Most surprisingly, Butscher offers frequent insights that would coalesce in 1980s and 1990s feminist readings of Plath. He catalogues her justified resentment of male privilege in her culture, her domestic double day, even when Hughes shared childcare (p. 290), the submerged revenge plots of her poetry and magazine fiction (pp. 215–18, 270), and the appropriation of male powers by the *Ariel* heroines (p. 339). He recognizes that she mobilized weapons of self-defence and tools for survival in her late poetry (p. 342). Yet the latent misogyny of Butscher's representation is stronger than his nascent feminist sympathies. His version attributes to Plath a strong, innate distaste for sexuality (pp. 63, 77) and an attitude of condescension towards the men she used (pp. 95, 123). The greatest weakness of Butscher's argument is the internal contradiction suggested by his title. Is the repressed self articulated in the master works of the *Ariel* period (and foreshadowed in the novel and the revenge plots of the magazine stories) strategic method or symptom of madness? Is the bitch goddess manipulated guise, self-conscious persona or ungovernable eruption of the unconscious?

Among the valuable aspects of Butscher's biography for later readers is his persuasive critique of Alvarez's deterministic model of reading Plath's art as a fatal gamble with her own sanity. In his frequent, detailed analysis of the form of the poems, Butscher demonstrates that he takes all of Plath's poetry seriously, even the work that predates Hughes (labelled 'Juvenilia' in Hughes's edition of her *Collected Poems*). Butscher has unerring judgement about the important poems from each period, and reads many carefully. More than any later biographer, he identifies Plath's literary influences beyond Hughes and credits her with significant artistic growth before they met. He flags the bias in the interviews he draws upon, although he differs from later biographers in identifying the Comptons and Peter Davison as hostile and the Merwins as supportive after the separation. Finally, he unearths Plath's politics, important to critics three decades later, and emergent in her undergraduate days when she was part of the crowd who hissed Joseph McCarthy at Smith College (p. 69).

Although reviewers suggest that Plath has become a blameless martyr in the accounts of feminists, Linda Wagner-Martin's *Sylvia Plath* (1987) is a responsible, temperate account. Actually the sole biographer who takes an explicitly feminist stance, Wagner-Martin claims Plath is broadly feminist in her belief in her own talent, her professional devotion to her calling, the importance of female friends, mentors and artistic models, and her anger that her fame would be more difficult to achieve and her work judged by different standards because she was a woman (pp. 11–12).

Wagner-Martin's 'Preface' is quoted more often than any other part of her book (for example, in reviews by Alvarez, Helen Vendler and Butscher, and by Malcolm). This is perhaps because, taking her own experience as example, she candidly accuses the Estate of coercion and attempted censorship in withholding permission to quote at length from Plath's materials.[10] Calculating that together Olwyn's and Ted's suggested changes would have meant deleting 15,000 words from her manuscript, Wagner-Martin gave up her intended close-readings in favor of her argument – an argument which, in any case, is not markedly hostile to Hughes.

Wagner-Martin's revisions of the available narratives laid down by Butscher and Alvarez resist monocausal explanations. Wagner-Martin recognizes that even before Otto's death, staged performances of precociousness and femininity required by him in her early childhood would have disastrous developmental consequences for her relationships with men, and that her inevitable emotional dependency on her mother Aurelia, while at first sustaining, became deeply resented in adulthood. Her reprise of Plath's psychotherapy with Ruth Beuscher in 1958–9 reminds us that Plath reassessed all her primary relationships; she not only gained '"permission to hate"' her mother (*J*, p. 429) but also confronted the link between her suspicion of Hughes and her resentment of her father. Wagner-Martin also situates Plath's psychosexual struggles with her family and in her intimate relationship with Hughes in a larger cultural framework. Plath's overclose relationship with her mother emerged in part through the fragility of the family's ability to preserve the middle-class façade of their Wellesley address after Otto's death. Despite Aurelia's heroic efforts to provide, the house was overcrowded with her extended family, forcing the adolescent Sylvia to share her mother's room, in what she would describe in her journals as a 'stink of women' and a suffocating 'smarmy matriarchy of togetherness' (*J*, pp. 431, 429). Wagner-Martin does not privilege biology or childhood trauma as the exclusive source of her mental illness (though she documents a history of depression in Otto's female relatives), but usefully links these to historical and cultural pressures on Plath's self-construction.

Benefiting from the wealth of archival material available to her that Butscher lacked, Wagner-Martin finds more explicit trace evidence in the drafts for poems from spring 1962 that Plath was anxiously pondering violence and death in her relationship well before 'The Rabbit Catcher' articulated her anguish (pp. 202–4). She plausibly suggests an ominous yet unspoken exchange occurring that spring between the antifemale short stories and plays of Hughes that Plath typed and her own artistic production in which she anticipates her discovery of his infidelity. She finds in Plath's extensive correspondence in the Smith archives a circle of trusted women friends whom she reached out to in her final months and admiration for breakthroughs in subject matter and voice by fellow poets Anne Sexton and Stevie Smith. In retelling her final weeks, Wagner-Martin emphasizes Plath's plans with these female confidantes and professional approval for her work signaled by requests from several editors for submissions. This contrasts sharply with Hughes's widely repeated claim that her *Ariel* poems were largely rejected. She also departs from Hughes's contention (strenuously made to Aurelia in editing *Letters Home*) that far from intending to divorce him, Plath and he were on the verge of reconciliation.

Wagner-Martin's approach is never sensational; nor does she pretend to be exhaustive. Her account depends on the tremendous outpouring of feminist literary criticism that occurred in the fifteen years after Butscher's biography, some of which she had collected in her 1984 *Critical Essays on Sylvia Plath*.[11] In paraphrasing the archives that she was forbidden to quote, she also opens the way for much productive scholarship that followed in the 1990s. She offers an accessible, unargumentative introduction to Plath's work, with readings that are suggestive if somewhat embryonic.

Ted Hughes had multiple reasons for wanting an authorized biography of Plath by the mid-1980s, not least his need for control over what he emphatically insisted was his story as much as Plath's. Anne Stevenson began her research for *Bitter Fame* in 1985, the year after Hughes was named Britain's poet laureate. By 1982, with publication of Plath's *Collected Poems* and of the abridged edition of Plath's *Journals* (in the US only), everything Hughes intended to publish was out, and the Plath archives had been sold off. His decisions had made possible an avalanche of critical and popular attention to Plath's work and had amassed a sizeable personal fortune for Hughes. That income had been threatened during the 1970s by back taxes he owed on royalties from her books, reported in a letter to Lucas Myers as an oppressive debt.[12] During the 1980s Hughes's management of the Plath estate became the object of increasingly critical scrutiny and the source of financial anxieties that, in his letters, again reach monumental proportions. A libel suit was filed in 1982 against the film version of *The Bell Jar* (the book was by far the most lucrative of the Plath properties). This was not resolved until 1987. The mounting ironies were not lost on Hughes: fearing bankruptcy for the same reasons that he was wealthy beyond his imagination; Britain's poet laureate, but eclipsed in the US by Plath's rising fame, which he had helped to promote, Hughes shrank from further involvement in Plath affairs and at the same time longed for vindication in the ceaseless combat that had preoccupied him for the past decade.[13]

Stevenson's biography *Bitter Fame*, when it finally appeared in 1989, bore the wounds of another battle, the struggle between Olwyn Hughes's version of Ted's story and Stevenson's own. The equivocal author's note by Stevenson seemed to deny responsibility for the outcome under the guise of perhaps reluctant collaboration with Olwyn: 'In writing this biography, I have received a great deal of help from Olwyn Hughes ... Ms. Hughes's contributions to the text have made it almost a work of dual authorship' (p. x). In an interview a year later, Stevenson claims, 'She insisted on writing the author's note herself – on pain of withdrawing permission for the use of quotations.'[14] The equally unprecedented inclusion of three stand-alone memoirs by several of her sources as appendices prompted more widespread and sharply critical charges against the Estate's bias and editorial control than Wagner-Martin's direct accusations. Whether Stevenson was the helpless hostage of Olwyn Hughes or her willing collaborator, the informants she calls 'witnesses' were polarized camps that she felt forced to choose between, although Stevenson knew that each was unreliable.[15]

A quarter of a century separates Stevenson's interviews and the events she was researching. During this time memoirs by acquaintances had been sold and published and had become petrified in frequent rehearsals to other biographers, accumulating ever more historically distant annotation and elaboration. The new memoirs that Stevenson reproduces are from several peripheral witnesses who are uniformly unsympathetic to Plath. Dido Merwin, who was their London neighbour for a time, is unremitting in the pettiness, possessiveness and harridan hostilities she attributes to Plath. Lucas Myers, a Cambridge friend of Hughes, whose marriage, children and divorce paralleled Sylvia's and Ted's, seems to have known the Hugheses marriage almost exclusively through Ted's letters. Richard Murphy, an Irish poet, who was at most a casual acquaintance, accuses Plath of unwelcome sexual advances during a brief stay as his houseguest in September 1962.[16] For Stevenson to include these appendices as first-person accounts seems an odd choice because their perspectives have already been incorporated in the body of the biography. It is as if, in the contestatory battle that biographical accounts of the marriage had already become, Stevenson wants to buttress her own interpretation of Plath's bad behaviour with a final chorus of corroborating witnesses.

In a 1990 interview Stevenson claims that she willingly accepted Olwyn's aid, but eventually lost authorial control, as well as 45 per cent of the British royalties, to her. She ultimately agreed to a rewrite of the last four chapters as a 'mixture' of her and Olwyn's views ('Biographer's Dilemma', p. 2). Stevenson admits that Olwyn's interventions were shadowed by Hughes, who wrote a lengthy critical letter and reviewed two complete drafts: 'he was more responsible for the book than he lets on' ('Biographer's Dilemma', p. 3). Whatever the Hugheses' joint involvement, the biography's central flaw is its lack of sympathy for the poet, and, more importantly, for the poetry. Stevenson never presents Plath's point of view about the marriage, representing Hughes as saintly husband and generous tutor, while she is to blame for all their troubles. Her representation of Plath's character combines a litany of character flaws (narcissism, unreasonable jealousy, violent rages, perfectionism) and symptoms of mental illness (paranoia, violent mood swings of manic-depression, a split personality, hysteria) which, taken together, suggest a teleology that make her unsavable in the end and consequently everyone near her blameless.[17] *Bitter Fame* recycles Butscher's reductive evil twin paradigm: 'the "real" Sylvia – violent, subversive, moonstruck, terribly angry – fought for her existence against a nice, bright, gifted American girl' (*Bitter Fame*, p. 163). But unlike Butscher, Stevenson seems not to fathom the greatness of the poetry this alleged split produced. The language of moral blame affects her aesthetic judgements, especially of the late poems: 'What the poet seems to want is a remedy for her inability to accept a form of truth most adult human beings have to learn: that they are not unique or exempt from partaking in human processes' (p. 290).

To produce *Rough Magic* (1991), Paul Alexander claims that he read the entire archives at Smith and Indiana, as well as conducting 300 interviews.[18] Certainly this research enables him to present a much thicker description of key moments in Plath's life. We learn the harrowing details of Otto's illness and Aurelia's heroic homecare; we appreciate more fully the gross mismanagement of Plath's outpatient electroshock treatments, as well as Olive Higgins Prouty's interventions in her treatment after her suicide attempt. Alexander revisits the 1962 bonfire that apparently underlies Plath's poem 'Burning the Letters' to report three separate purges, the first two witnessed by Aurelia, in which Plath burnt her second novel and later all her mother's letters. The third, recalled by Clarissa Roche, includes a witchlike exorcism, with Plath dancing around a fire of Hughes's papers, his nail clippings and other 'scum' from his desk (*Rough Magic*, p. 286). Sometimes, though, the details he has amassed are merely numbing in their profusion.

Many of Plath's old boyfriends appear, mostly to testify against her. We are told that Eddie Cohen, her Chicago correspondent, advised Plath early on that she needed therapy and that Gordon Lameyer was deceived about Plath's virginity. To Alexander, Plath's sexuality has a desperate, manipulative cast to it, and is linked to a compensatory cycle, overfamiliar from other biographies: 'When she felt abandoned by a male romantic figure, she subconsciously experienced the sense of loss she harbored over the death of her father' (p. 183). A more serious flaw is Alexander's apparent readiness to present several far-fetched scenarios as fact. He does not document the source for the sexualized scene of Hughes's nearly strangling Plath on their honeymoon (p. 167), nor Assia's alleged seduction of Hughes at Court Green by dropping her nightgown over his head at the breakfast table (p. 277).[19] Although he identifies his source for Plath's alleged return to the US for an abortion in September 1961, and her return to England on a ship of Fulbright students, everything about the incident lacks credibility.

Alexander offers few new insights on the poetry, but he valuably charts the rhythms of composition and publication in Plath's and Hughes's shared work lives. For example, in August 1960 Hughes's *Lupercal* was published to excellent reviews and Plath's third manuscript was rejected for the Yale Younger Poets prize. Their joint BBC interview, 'Two of a Kind', a jolly report on marrying because they were good for each other's poetry, is broadcast in 1961 in the same month that Plath's story of submerged marital rage, 'The Fifty-Ninth Bear', is published. The Knopf acceptance of *The Colossus* probably buoyed her writing of *The Bell Jar*, her secret project in spring 1961. A densely textured record of Plath's daily life, Alexander's biography demonstrates the depth of the archives he has plumbed, but he fails too often to shape what he has retrieved into meaningful patterns.

Janet Malcolm's *The Silent Woman* might well serve as the definitive exposition and enactment of the problems of biography as a genre. Because each liability – the tingle of voyeurism, her partisan motivation, her self-doubt as a writer, the final unknowableness of her subject – is disarmingly revealed as her own, Malcolm gambles that the reader will come to trust her self-conscious fallibility as the most honest.

Like Middlebrook later, Malcolm seizes on Hughes's invented persona as 'her husband' to convey his split roles as protector of her children, destroyer of her journals and consummate editor. Malcolm's twin goals are to redeem Hughes as Plath's 'greatest critic, elucidator and impresario' (*Silent Woman*, p. 155), and to vindicate Stevenson's championing of the Hugheses' version. At the heart of Malcolm's sympathies – and the crux of her book as well as of earlier biographers' battles with the Estate – is Ted Hughes's struggle with Plath over ownership of his own life and his attempts to wrest it back from her representation in writing. If Plath's life has been dragged into the public domain, he vehemently resists the simultaneous infringement on his story: "'The main problem with S. P.'s biographers is that they fail ... to realize that the most interesting and dramatic part of S. P.'s life is only ½ S. P. – the other ½ is *me*'" (quoted p. 201).

Malcolm believes that she, Plath and Stevenson shared a common predicament as aspiring women writers in the 1950s. She claims that women's self-loathing, combined with their envy and resentment of male success, led them to believe it was "'the man's fault when the writing didn't go well'", a 'transferential misprision' that Malcolm identifies as '*the* central concern of contemporary feminism' (pp. 87–8). To exonerate both Hughes and Stevenson, Malcolm discredits Plath's earlier biographers with sharp, swift strokes. First and foremost she blames Alvarez's *The Savage God* for originating the narrative of 'Plath as an abandoned and mistreated woman and Hughes as a heartless betrayer' (*Silent Woman*, p. 23). To demonstrate the pitfalls of the mediated narratives collected through interviews, she revisits the pro-Plath witnesses whom Stevenson omitted and provides vivid portraits of their fallibility. Driven by ego, hostility or a simple need for cash, each finds the events they almost compulsively renarrate receding further from accessibility; Clarissa Roche, for example, is hypnotized to retrieve fresh information.

Malcolm trusts letters, over these discredited interviews, as her most reliable sources. To her, letters are 'fossils of feeling', the biographer's 'only conduit to unmediated experience. Everything else the biographer touches is stale, hashed over, told and retold, dubious, unauthentic, suspect' (p. 210). Malcolm's preference for letters powerfully argues for independent, detailed archival research. She structures her apparently desultory narrative by revelations from unpublished letters, in many of which the elusive Hughes comes forward as a passionately definitive biographer. He chides Stevenson for claiming that he could never forgive Plath for burning his papers: "'I never held that action against [Sylvia] – then or at any other time ... She never did anything that I held against her'" (quoted p. 143). Malcolm sees Hughes's interventions as motivated by redemptive affection for Plath that should preempt other accounts: 'when he writes about Plath, he renders all other writings crude and trivial. He writes with brilliant, exasperated intelligence and a kind of Chekhovian largeheartedness and melancholy' (p. 123).

Over another letter from Hughes, Malcolm does battle with Jacqueline Rose, whom she describes as the 'opposition's most powerful and plausible witness' (p. 177), 'the libber in whom the Hugheses finally met their match' (p. 176). Her struggle is in part staged through an unsent letter to Rose. Through a series of deconstructive moves intended to rival Rose's own critical practice, Malcolm exposes contradictions in Rose's avowed positions, most importantly that ethics are involved in interpretation and that

Rose's own fantasy may be to have sole possession of the unavailable Hughes. Satisfied that she has bested the critic at her own intellectual game, Malcolm can disavow the jealous triangle she constructed to shame Rose as perhaps more evidence of the biographer's unreliability: 'I no longer have the conviction I once had that Jacqueline Rose and I were fighting over Ted Hughes' (p. 183). Yet her layering of letters, sent and unsent, suggests otherwise.

Almost a decade later, when Middlebrook resuscitates 'her husband' as the image of Ted Hughes's lifelong partnership with Plath, Hughes again comes forward as Plath's most admiring consort. In her biography of a marriage, *Her Husband*, Middlebrook demonstrates that whatever damage their marriage ultimately produced in their lived experience, it was a mutually productive literary partnership of the first order. By moving discussion of their marriage into consideration of what was good for poetry – their creation of mythic personae – Middlebrook arranges a kind of no-fault divorce, the pain of which is transcended by a more lasting union through poetry. To Middlebrook, the couple's needs were diametrically opposed. Plath needs middle-class domesticity, with motherhood a core psychic requirement and Hughes as muse and mentor for her writing. Hughes's writing requires solitude and periodic escapes into wildness, usually through extramarital sex. *Her Husband* replaces blame for Hughes's behavior with sympathy for his artistic requirements. As far as poetry is concerned, there is no question of Hughes's infidelity; Plath remains his lifelong muse and most poignantly reappears to him in 'The Offers' to demand their reunion.[20]

Middlebrook underscores earlier biographers' and critics' judgement that Plath's investment in Hughes fostered her artistic growth. She differs most from her predecessors in the very persuasive evidence she offers of their stylistic habits of 'call and response' in which images, sound patterns and phrases are exchanged between poems, often to quite different ends. Middlebrook also advances an alternative understanding of Plath as mother and poet. Rather than the tension between the demands of poetry and the rigours of single-motherhood other critics find, she argues for continuity between Plath's prechildren idealization of motherhood, as measure of her domestic and poetic creativity, and the *Ariel* poems, which she sees as 'bursting from her motherhood' (p. 193.) It was the experience of maternity, Middlebrook claims, that rescued her from apprenticeship to Hughes (p. 153).

Middlebrook draws on new archival material, Hughes's letters at Emory University and the British Library, to give a fuller first-person account of Hughes's curatorship of the Estate than appears in any of his introductions to her work. Through these we see, even more vividly than in Malcolm, the emotional needs that produced the split persona, 'her husband', that she chooses as her title. In place of the familiar image of Hughes as destroyer of Plath's journals and despoiler of her finished *Ariel* volume, Middlebrook evokes a picture of Hughes as stunned participant in an ongoing conversation with Plath. Hughes's discovery of his poetry on her writing table after her death is evidence, she suggests, of Plath's 'continuing attachment to their creative partnership' (p. 219). Along with the carefully ordered and bound *Ariel* poems, Hughes found his poem 'Out', which contains poppy imagery echoed in her two poppy poems, and a typescript of his 'Full Moon and Little Frieda' next to reviews of *The Bell Jar* (p. 220). Middlebrook offers a romantic reading of *Birthday Letters* as their reunion (other Plath scholars might name it a rematch) in which Hughes rehearses old disputes on an 'intimate wavelength' (p. 279). Whatever the tone of the exchange, Middlebrook is entirely accurate in insisting on the text-based dynamics of the book: 'he has been prompted by her words to enter into dialogue with that self she made in language' (p. 279).

Given Middlebrook's impressively extensive new research, it seems curiously old-fashioned to appeal to Robert Graves's 'white goddess' paradigm to explain Plath's function in Hughes's artistic life. She is the awesome primal female required by Hughes's shamanistic journey: 'her destiny [is] to inflict devastation on Hughes as well as release his creative fluency' (p. 283). Certainly his accounts of Plath's development resort to similar formulas, as Middlebrook paraphrases: 'an old shattered self reduced by violence to its central core, had been repaired' (p. 114). Middlebrook sympathetically attempts to explicate the Gravesian worldview that she feels underlies his art, yet in granting the explanatory power for Hughes of this cosmology, she risks losing sight of how Plath's might have differed. Middlebrook's belief in the indissoluble nature of their union is likewise evident in her retelling of the final weeks of Plath's life. She underscores Hughes's later version of their potential reconciliation rather than Plath's letters about the finality of their separation.

Middlebrook makes a lucid and compelling argument from a wealth of new archival sources that is generous in its admiration of both poets, yet the portrait of the marriage that emerges is less marked by the contestation of gender norms that has made their story so emblematic for the end of one era and the dawn of our current age.

## The uncertainty of biography

Who is the Sylvia Plath that these biographies have produced? Taken one by one, these narrations purport to give us the real Sylvia, to penetrate the multiple guises and arrive at certain truth, verified by a chorus of eye-witnesses. Yet my purpose in emphasizing the contradictory stories these biographies tell is to demonstrate that what they communicate is uncertainty.

If we hope to piece together the definitive, documented facts that provide a causal link between Plath's experience and her art, we are bound to be disappointed. We need to recognize that biography produces and reproduces the stories circulating in our culture, particularly those that are used to make female experience legible. The credibility of the figure of Plath as psychotic, wounded, devious, narcissistic or death-driven does not lie with the objectivity of the witnesses the biographer draws upon, but comes from the multiple sites within culture that give shape and meaning to women's experience *as* story. These explanatory plotlines smooth over the contradictions, dissonances and unknowable motivations of the life in order to narrate a coherent identity unfolding developmentally in time that we as readers recognize as familiar and plausible.

More helpfully, feminist theorists have enriched our understanding of selfhood, not as an experiential certainty, but as a process. The female subject, like any other, does not preexist her awareness of culture but emerges through it, in language and representation. Further, as Joan Scott explains, 'it is not individuals who have experience, but subjects who are constituted by experience'.[21] Claiming experience as a property of selfhood is thus an act of interpretation and a process in need of interpretation. Culture itself is a site of competing solicitations and prohibitions that shape subjectivity, but unevenly and never completely. Plath's subjectivity, in her private and public acts of narration, can be read in Judith Butler's terms as a 'daily act of reconstitution'. She apprehends her gender, her sexuality, her embodiment in an 'impulsive yet mindful process of interpreting a cultural reality laden with sanctions, taboos, and prescriptions'. Her agency is not fully self-determining but is nonetheless present in the improvisations and reconsiderations through which this subjectivity is appropriated, not merely given: 'Not wholly conscious, yet available to consciousness, it is the kind of choice we make and only later realize we have made.'[22] The life-writing theorists Sidonie Smith and Julia Watson explain that the interaction between experience, subjectivity and story is constant:

> Every day, all day long, the material universe affects us, literally as well as discursively … But in making meaning of these events, we make that meaning, or the 'experience' of those events, discursively, in language, and as narrative. Thus, we retrospectively make experience and convey a sense of it to others through storytelling; and as we tell our stories discursive patterns guide, or compel, us to tell stories about ourselves in particular ways.[23]

What this reconceptualization of subjectivity as a process disturbs is the neat binary that an uncritical reading of biography rests upon; that before or behind the art is a coherent, unified self to be laid bare as the source or motor of the poetry. We need to resist the unexamined assumption (and often in biographies of women what amounts to the misogynist practice) that a woman can only write out of or about what she has actually lived. Such a premise disallows the transformative power of a woman's art as epistemology, as an alternative, equally self-constituting form of knowing and being.

Can we simply forgo biography? I think not. Every literary critic must inevitably confront what Jacqueline Rose describes as 'something untellable, but which has to be told, [which] enters the frame when the subject of biography dies by her own hand'.[24] We cannot simply dismiss biography; instead, we need to situate the story of a life differently, as part of more encompassing narratives. We need to take apart the ways that Plath's and Hughes's lives are forever conjoined in material ways, in the revenue Plath's texts generated for Hughes, as well as in texts they generated about each other. Their intertwined literary history suggests that Plath and Hughes were each moved to write (and to rewrite each other's work) because each believed that to be in possession of a story meant to be in possession of your life. Each uses poetry as an enabling fiction; having a story means creating a coherent narrative with an explanatory past and a plausible future. Telling a story is interpreting your life; it also makes that life possible. We could also use their cross-referential writing practice as a test case to examine the limits of genres; biography necessarily interpenetrates autobiography in the poems, as both poets tell the other's story as a way of telling their own. Nancy Miller, Leigh Gilmore and Paul John Eakin rightly contend that autobiography is always relational. Their subtle and provocative theories of life-writing scrutinize the malleability and permeability of established genres such as biography, autobiography, confessional poetry and literary criticism and identify new hybrid forms.[25]

Hughes's public and often litigious conflicts with biographers and literary critics demonstrate his aggrieved sense that Plath's autobiographical acts were in fact biography, imprisoning him in her misrepresentation. Any critical interpretation of her work, it seemed, also harmfully interfered with his own and his children's possession of the woman Sylvia Plath. In her 'Foreword' to *Ariel: The Restored Edition*, Frieda Hughes reveals what she experiences as the incursion of literary criticism and biography into life: 'The point of anguish at which my mother killed herself was taken over by strangers, possessed and reshaped by them. The collection of *Ariel* poems became symbolic to me of this possession of my mother ... and vilification of my father' (*A Rest.*, p. xiv). Dramatically, both Hughes and his daughter testify to the incredible power of texts to produce a figure with tremendous staying power, here a figure of Plath that they claim not to recognize.

That our sphere of enquiry is steadily expanding outwards from the hermetically sealed text, I am convinced, is a very good thing for literature. The critical practices that appear most promising to me are those that reveal how literary texts are illuminated by an enlarging network of other texts in which they are embedded; these methods require that we do not set aside biography, or history, or commercial 'packaging' but that we analyse their interrelation. I have suggested how the methods of feminist criticism, cultural criticism and life-writing theory enable us to see how artists are shaped by and reshape ideologies, how they engage cultural anxieties about gender roles, sexuality, happiness, materialism, politics, the environment and war – topics that recent critics have explored in Plath. Our questions now legitimately encompass the composition of literary texts, their publication and reception, and the cultural uses of poets as icons or caricatures. The meanings of Plath's poems, I am proposing, are not fixed but change depending on our tools and the contexts in which we have learnt, in the past four decades, to read them.

How will this change our practical reading practices, of Plath as artist and of her biographies? I recommend four strategies. First, approach biographies with a hermeneutics of suspicion about what we expect to find there. We need not only to interrogate the cultural scripts that structure the biography and produce the figure of Plath, but question as well our search for a final truth that we mistakenly imagine exists outside of culture or before mediation by its images and stories. Second, grant the artist her imaginative freedom to invent, misremember, substitute and play. Emily Dickinson's insistence on the difference between her existence and that of the 'supposed person' in her art is essential to reading Plath. Third, we need reading practices that honour the unconscious as an integral element of subjectivity and of narration. I offer my students Adrienne Rich's insight, 'Poems are like dreams in that you put in them what you didn't know you knew.' Last, we can develop habits of reading more reflexively, of including the historical moment of our own reception and consumption of these texts as part of what must be examined.

If, in our widening understanding of multiple sites and forms of mediation, Sylvia Plath seems to recede further and further from our comprehension, I am heartened that these strategies will actually make her more present to us textually – implicated, resisting, investing, improvising, revising the myriad texts around and about her, because each of these texts is, in turn, susceptible to interpretation.

# Notes

1. See my *Revising Life: Sylvia Plath's Ariel Poems* (Chapel Hill: University of North Carolina Press, 1993), and Lynda K. Bundtzen, *The Other Ariel* (Amherst: University of Massachusetts Press, 2001).

2. Edward Butscher, *Sylvia Plath: Method and Madness* (New York: Seabury Press, 1976).

3. Linda Wagner-Martin, *Sylvia Plath: A Biography* (New York: Simon & Schuster, 1987).

4. Anne Stevenson, *Bitter Fame: A Life of Sylvia Plath* (Boston: Houghton Mifflin, 1989).

5. Jacqueline Rose, *The Haunting of Sylvia Plath* (London: Virago, 1991).

6. Janet Malcolm, *The Silent Woman: Sylvia Plath and Ted Hughes* (New York: Vintage, 1995).

7. Diane Middlebrook, *Her Husband: Hughes and Plath – A Marriage* (New York: Viking, 2003).

8. See Dale Salwak, *Living with a Writer* (New York: Macmillan, 2004), and Frances Wilson, *Literary Seductions* (London: Faber and Faber, 1999).

9. See Rose's discussion of the origins of this term in *Haunting*, pp. 165–9.

10. See A. Alvarez, 'A Poet and Her Myths', *New York Review* (28 September 1989), p. 34; Helen Hennessy Vendler, 'Who Is Sylvia?', *New Republic* (6 November 1989), p. 100; Edward Butscher, 'Unfinished Lives of Sylvia Plath', *Georgia Review* (Spring/Summer 1990), p. 296; and Malcolm, *Silent Woman*, p. 25.

11. Linda Wagner (ed.), *Critical Essays on Sylvia Plath* (Boston: G. K. Hall, 1984).

12. Ted Hughes letter to Lucas Myers, 16 January 1977, Emory.

13. Ibid.

14. Anne Stevenson, 'A Biographer's Dilemma' (interview with Madeline Strong Diehl), *Michigan Today* 22.2 (April 1990), p. 2.

15. 'The animus of the pro-Sylvia side against Olwyn was so very great, and the misconception of what Sylvia was all about was so terrible, that I was thrown back in Olwyn's arms anyway', ibid.

16. Middlebrook mentions that he met the couple in London (*Her Husband*, p. 179). Plath knew him as prizewinner in a contest she judged; later, at Plath's initiative, the couple were his houseguests in Ireland (September 1962).

17. Among many other references, for split selves, see p. 23, 163–4; egotism, pp. 15, 21, 32, 164–5, 167; mood swings, pp. 15, 36, 59, 93, 298; paranoia, pp. 129–31; and hysteria, pp. 56, 60, 138, 187.

18. Paul Alexander, *Rough Magic: A Biography of Sylvia Plath* (New York: Viking, 1991), p. 1.

19. Assia Wevill and her husband David were acquaintances of Plath and Hughes. When the latter couple left London, the Wevills took over the lease of their flat. In May 1962 they spent a weekend with Plath and Hughes at their North Tawton home. Later that summer, Hughes and Assia Wevill began a relationship, which continued until 1969 when Assia died by suicide.

20. 'The Offers' was published in Hughes's limited edition *Howls & Whispers* (1998) and reprinted in Ted Hughes, *Collected Poems* (London: Faber and Faber, 2003).

21. Joan Scott, 'The Evidence of Experience', *Critical Inquiry* 17 (1991), p. 27.

22. Judith Butler, 'Sex and Gender in Simone de Beauvoir's *Second Sex*', *Yale French Studies* 72 (1986), p. 40.
23. Sidonie Smith and Julia Watson, *Reading Autobiography* (Minneapolis: University of Minnesota Press), p. 26.
24. Jacqueline Rose, 'Sylvia Plath – Again: This is Not a Biography', *London Review of Books* (22 August 2002), 2; reprinted in Jacqueline Rose, *On Not Being Able to Sleep: Psychoanalysis and the Modern World* (London: Chatto & Windus, 2003), pp. 49–71.
25. See Nancy K. Miller's hybrid genre 'personal criticism' in *Getting Personal* (London: Routledge, 1991); Leigh Gilmore's study of the markers of autobiographical acts in *Autobiographics: A Feminist Theory of Women's Self-Representation* (Ithaca: Cornell University Press, 1994) and *The Limits of Autobiography* (Ithaca: Cornell University Press, 2001); and Paul John Eakin's *How Our Lives Become Stories* (Ithaca: Cornell University Press, 1999).

# 2

DEBORAH NELSON

# Plath, history and politics

Sylvia Plath is arguably the best-known and most iconic poet of her generation. Try to imagine, for instance, a major Hollywood studio producing a film about any of her contemporaries, much less casting an A-list actor, Gwyneth Paltrow, in the feature role.[1] This reputation rests largely on one volume of poetry, *Ariel*, and a novel, *The Bell Jar*, that, while very good, would not be nearly as well known, nor so often taught, if not for the incandescence of the poetry. *Ariel* had this tremendous impact for three interlocking reasons. One, it is extraordinary, unmistakably original poetry. Two, its psychological intensity remains palpable four decades after its shocking debut. Three, its publication followed the suicide of the poet, who was young, beautiful and married to another major poet of the era. There is no way to separate these elements. As brilliant as the poetry is, there has been a good deal of excellent poetry written in the past forty years that has not earned international celebrity for its authors. Moreover, it is important *not* to separate aesthetic achievement, psychological extremity and biographical scandal. It is precisely this convergence that struck a nerve with postwar readers.

But we should also add a fourth element, one that is not part of the Plath legend, and that, in fact, spoils the myth of the tragic poet whose exploration of her own madness ultimately killed her. Plath was a remarkably astute cultural critic. Regarding Plath as a cultural critic obliges us to think historically about her career and about poetry itself, neither of which lend themselves easily to historical analysis. For instance, to think about Plath's career, we must begin with autobiography, not history. To think historically about lyric poetry, we have to violate some of our most cherished assumptions about the transcendence and autonomy of the genre. Nevertheless, historical analysis enriches Plath's work substantially, bringing out elements of critique and insight that are otherwise invisible. Plath's poetry, on the other hand, reveals aspects of the period in which she wrote that have been overlooked and misunderstood.

Let us begin with Plath's career and the problem of autobiography. Until the late 1980s, few critics understood Plath to be writing about anything but her own suffering, though how they interpreted this act varied considerably. Plath, however, saw her poetic material as representative, not merely personal. In a journal entry from 1956, Plath compiled a 'to do' list that ended with the following: 'Be stoic when necessary & *write* – you have seen a lot, felt deeply & your problems are universal enough to be made meaningful' (*J*, p. 569). Plath's severest critics simply did not (or could not) see her 'problems' as universal, in part because she was a woman, and women's experience is rarely deemed universal. Without universality, Plath's work appeared narcissistic and self-indulgent. Yet even Plath's ardent admirers hesitated to universalize her poetry, at least initially. They wanted to celebrate her exposure of her personal life as an act of rebellion, both literary and political. This polarized response to Plath's work attached to the label 'confessional poet' given to her by M. L. Rosenthal after her death.[2] We will return to this troublesome category shortly.

In her journal Plath did not assume that her problems were universally meaningful. Instead, she understood universality to be an effect of writing, that is, an aesthetic effect.[3] Her life could be 'made meaningful' but it was not *a priori* significant to her readers. Moreover, Plath linked the act of writing to 'stoicism', not the indulgence in feeling. 'Be stoic when necessary & *write*' appears as one entry on her list, not two. Evidently, poetry might be about feeling, but she did not imagine it to be an outpouring of feeling. These two distinctions are essential to rethinking Plath's oeuvre. To regard Plath's signature directness as a stoical mediation of feeling is, on the face of it, counterintuitive, and by the time she wrote the *Ariel* poems, somewhat misleading. She had learnt to risk greater candidness from Robert Lowell and Anne Sexton, two poets who were also designated confessional. Nevertheless, the presence of more intense feeling and more intimate suffering should not lead us to assume that Plath changed her mind about the craft involved in turning feeling and experience into poetry. If anything, Plath was a far better craftsperson in her late work. We might say instead that Plath was strategically intimate and deliberately intense because she understood the meaning and the effect of these choices on her readers.

Autobiography is significant for literary history and the history of American culture more generally. The broader turn towards autobiography in literature, of which confessional poetry is one part, constituted one of the most visible ways that post-World War II writing differed from modernist writing. Personal voice, which materialized not only in every literary form, but also in the fine arts, mass culture and politics, has been understood as an effect of new social forces like psychotherapy and mass celebrity as well as a lingering manifestation of American religious devotion. While these are certainly crucial factors, the decision to be personal in public was motivated more variously. It expressed the wish to represent a particular group; the desire to bring into public view previously hidden or ignored experience; the aim to see new experiences as universal; and the attempt to unmask universality as a fiction for a particular subject, white and male, that was not named as such. Speaking personally was, therefore, enmeshed in the politics of universality – who had it, who wanted it, and who wished to deprive it of its cultural power. The result was profound. The image of the American public would be dramatically pluralized in the latter half of the twentieth century. Writing autobiographically was, therefore, not simply an individual aesthetic choice; it was also a political decision.

Writing personally or writing about private life, which are not precisely the same thing, was also political in another sense. Private family life and the ability to withdraw from the scrutiny of others, most especially the state, were considered the bedrocks of American freedom in the Cold War. This respect for privacy was often used to draw a contrast between the US and its enemy, the Soviet Union, a totalitarian regime which by definition claimed all human activity for the state. The autobiographical and confessional trend in American culture erupted simultaneously with this ideological inflation of the value of privacy. Moreover, confessional poetry was not merely the personal in public. It was always the most secret, violent, damaging and disruptive elements of private life on display. Plath and her fellow confessional poets provided a counterdiscourse to the official ideology of privacy in the Cold War.

## Reading historically

Understanding Plath in history helps us to recognize how her poetry spoke of and to her generation and how the poetry she wrote reflected concerns of a particular historical moment. Nonetheless, thinking of Plath as a historical poet has been inordinately difficult. The most insightful reader of Plath's relationship to history, Jacqueline Rose, identified the problem as follows: 'history is either dearth or surplus, either something missing from Plath's writing or something which shouldn't be there'.[4] Rose's path-breaking book, *The Haunting of Sylvia Plath* (1991), initiated a major rethinking of Plath's work and 'the implication of psyche in history, and history in psyche' (p. 7). Exploring the Plath archive with a new set of assumptions taught readers to look at what Plath's writing and her public image – her iconicity – revealed about her culture. More specifically, the extent to which Plath wrote about American Cold War politics in her journals and annotated major works of political history and theory in her personal library suddenly appeared relevant to her poetry. After Rose's powerful revision, an increasing number of critical works began to read Plath's prose and poetry historically, exploring her engagement with mass media like advertising and women's magazines or her development of poetic technique in the newly professionalizing institutions of higher education. Directing analysis towards history revealed Plath's art as actively engaged in a critique of American Cold War culture and its gender ideology.[5]

*The Bell Jar* has been somewhat easier to read for its engagement with history than *Ariel*, which is attributable in part to the difference in genre – literary historians have traditionally considered the novel a social genre – and in part to Plath's journal-musings on the novel's composition. Plath wanted her own experiences growing up in the 1950s to provide the template for a 'generational' story. In her journal she wrote of the novel's narrator, Esther Greenwood, 'Make her a statement of the generation. Which is you' (*J*, p. 289). Like the journal passage quoted earlier, this one also shows Plath seeking wider significance for her story by positioning herself as a representative figure. And indeed, the first sentence of this generational novel locates the heroine in historical time by referring to the execution of Julius and Ethel Rosenberg, a Jewish couple from the Bronx who were tried, convicted and executed for espionage in 1953. The Rosenberg trial was one of the most spectacular and polarizing events of the early Cold War, a period marked by 'witch hunts' for communists, the most famous of which gave us the term 'McCarthyism'. Hysterical anticommunism was the defining event of her generation.

Nonetheless, the narrator does not allude to the crime for which they were convicted – passing nuclear secrets to the Soviet Union – nor describe the Cold War climate in which their trial took place. She concludes the opening paragraph of the novel by saying of the execution, 'It had nothing to do with me, but I couldn't help wondering what it would be like, being burned alive all along your nerves' (*BJ*, p. 1). The event seems noteworthy, it would appear, only in the gruesome manner of their dying, not in the larger meaning of their death for Cold War politics. Thus Esther narrates her story in psychological, not political terms, the event being irrelevant to her except insofar as it fuelled her attraction to extremity. Esther's comment seems to contradict Plath's stated goal. What does it mean to create a character representative of a generation who insists that its most significant events have 'nothing to do with [her]'?

If we forget that the novel is a comedy and a satire, and if we insist that Esther is Plath, we are likely to conclude that the author herself had no interest in politics or history, but simply a morbid fascination with death.

And this is certainly the way many have understood the *The Bell Jar* and the poems in *Ariel*. Plath does more than frame the novel with the execution, however. 'Esther Greenwood', which looks like a derivation of 'Esther Ethel Greenglass Rosenberg' – Ethel Rosenberg's full name – seems to name the heroine after a woman whom many Americans, Plath included, believed to have suffered a terrible injustice.[6] Plath clearly has more to suggest about this historical event than her character does. In naming her heroine after a victim of hysterical anticommunism, she casts Esther's rebellion against 1950s codes of femininity in Cold War terms. In Esther's response to the Rosenberg trial, Plath depicts her generation's inability to grasp the connection between public events and private life.

The framing of the novel with the Rosenberg trial was long overlooked because Plath was assumed to have little interest in history. In addition to the fascination with biographical readings, expectations of the genre and sub-genre in which Plath made her reputation (the lyric and the confessional poem respectively) reinforced the impression of her lack of interest. Understanding the privacy of the genre helps us to identify why historical reading is rarer with poetry than the novel. The notion that lyric poetry is a uniquely private genre has had a tenacious hold in the minds of readers and poets since the Romantic period.[7] From John Stuart Mill to T. S. Eliot to Northrop Frye, the lyric has been defined as a voice overheard speaking to itself. Withdrawing from the scrutiny of others to conduct a dialogue with oneself is one of the most powerful images of autonomy that we have, both aesthetically and politically. The speaker can express herself freely precisely because she is not in a social situation and is free from obligation, scrutiny and consequence. This freedom of expression translates into the freedom to self-create, which allows the speaker to transcend the constraints of place and time and the circumstances of social position. Moreover, that the poem itself was an autonomous form, complete unto itself, was the aggressive claim of modernist poets and of the New Criticism, the critical school in which Plath was trained. That is to say, the lyric is the form believed to imitate and express the human subject's autonomy from the social, historical world. To imagine the lyric springing not only from the mind of a solitary speaker but also from the muddy soil of history – the body, the economy, politics, family, social life – violated expectations of the genre.

## The public and the private

Labelling Plath a confessional poet intensified her remoteness from the events and struggles of her day. If lyric poetry was imagined as the private expression of a private individual, confessional poetry with its taboo subjects like mental illness, sex, alcoholism, infidelity, rage and domestic conflict was deemed altogether *too* private. Exposing the darkest aspects of private life, confessional poets were not exploring the autonomy that private space nurtured, but instead submerging themselves in the aspects of domestic life that curb autonomy and compromise self-expression. Confessional poetry, therefore, produced a double breach, violating poetic decorum by refusing to transcend the particulars of family and the body, and social decorum by flouting the tacit limits of public discourse. Whether celebrated as a rebellion against the reigning aesthetics of modernist impersonality or reviled as betrayal of taste and modesty, confessional poets were by definition interested only in their own domestic and psychic terrain, not in the public world around them.

In the rarer instances when history appeared in the foreground of her poetry, Plath's readers recoiled from it. It became, as Jacqueline Rose argued, a surplus, something that should not be there. Critics argued that when Plath did take an interest in history, she collected images of the gruesome, the violent, the damaged or the traumatic to express her own personal misery. A history that had 'nothing to do with [her]' seemed to have been used as if it did. Most controversially, Plath's use of the Holocaust in *Ariel* led to claims that she unethically appropriated the historical experience of others to figure her own pain. For example, in two of her most famous poems, Plath positions her speaker not only as a Jew, but also as a victim of the Holocaust. In 'Lady Lazarus' the speaker describes her skin as 'bright as a Nazi lampshade' and likens her face to 'featureless, fine / Jew linen'. In 'Daddy' she evokes an image of railway engines transporting Jews to the concentration camps, to 'Dachau, Auschwitz, Belsen', and explains, 'I began to talk like a Jew. / I think I may well be a Jew.' Determining who has the right to make imaginative use of the Holocaust has been enormously contentious, not only for Sylvia Plath. However, what most galled her critics was not just the use of this imagery, but the perceived incommensurability between Plath's experience and that of a Holocaust victim. As one commentator put it in an oft-quoted line, 'whatever her father did to her, it could not have been what the Germans did to the Jews'.[8]

The trouble came when Plath was suspected of making private use of public horror. Jacqueline Rose has argued that Plath's representation of the Holocaust brought into view a problem with metaphor and identification. She was trespassing in peculiarly dangerous historical terrain, a place where 'metaphor is *arrested*' and 'fixed', a space where fantasy identification is disabled (*Haunting*, p. 207). Susan Gubar suggests that we locate Plath in a tradition of postwar prosopopoeia, which summons the posthumous voice in order to give the dead a place in living memory.[9] Both Rose and Gubar want to keep open a space of identification and speaking for others. In other words, both see Plath making public use of public horror.

This suggestion helps us to interpret Plath's very self-conscious consideration of the relation of personal pain and historical violence in the *Ariel* poem 'Cut'. 'Cut' not only reverses the direction of analogy between personal and political, it undermines its very possibility. In the poem the speaker slices the top of her thumb while chopping an onion, a common domestic accident. The poem, however, quickly transforms a culinary mishap into a lesson in American history. The speaker addresses her thumb as 'Little pilgrim' and tells it that an Indian is responsible for its scalping (stanza three), observing that, from the cut, 'A million soldiers run, / Redcoats, every one'. Here we might imagine Plath to be inflating personal injury with historical analogy. Yet the irony of the poem makes this an unlikely reading. The opening line – 'What a thrill' – suggests that we are not meant to sympathize with the injured speaker, but to watch the horror and fascination evoked by the eruption of her own blood. With this irony in mind, we might more profitably consider how Plath uses self-mutilation to think through the history of violence in the nation-state.

The dominant rhetorical figure of the poem is apostrophe, an address by a speaker to an absent person, abstraction or nonhuman entity. The speaker addresses the thumb repeatedly, calling it not only 'Little pilgrim' but 'my / homunculus', 'Saboteur', 'Kamikaze man' and finally 'Trepanned veteran, / Dirty girl, / Thumb stump'. Amassing these apostrophes draws attention to the rhetorical figure, which accomplishes several important things in the poem. First, because apostrophe personifies or animates the nonliving, it displaces both violence and injury on to an other. It, not she, is both victim (the scalped pilgrim or trepanned veteran) and perpetrator of violence (the saboteur or kamikaze man). The address to the thumb also condenses a series of twentieth-century conflicts into one image. For instance, dressing the saboteur or kamikaze in a 'Ku Klux Klan / Babushka', Plath evokes the enemies of World War II, Germany and Japan; obliquely references the Cold War antagonism between the US and the Soviet Union; and recalls the nativist and anti-immigrant ideology of the Ku Klux Klan, best known for its persecution of African Americans. Scrambling the dichotomy between victim and perpetrator, insider and outsider, self and other, Plath makes it impossible to assign guilt to or claim innocence for the nation. Instead, by collapsing historical conflicts and positions of aggression and violation, Plath thwarts any comfortable moralizing about violence.

Second, because the apostrophe dissociates the speaker from the injury, the poem can explore the anaesthetizing effect of spectatorship. If a cut might be expected to induce pain, the apostrophe allows Plath to reverse the problem of feeling, creating a new dilemma: not too much pain, but too little. In stanza seven we find that she has attempted to kill the 'thin / Papery feeling' with a pill. Instead of deadening the pain, the speaker tries to release herself from the numbness that the spectacle of blood and violence has induced and which the rhyming ill/pill/kill hypnotically reinforces. The rhetorical figure of apostrophe creates a position – dissociation – that permits a distanced, depersonalized reaction to violence that lacks a moral compass. By reading American history as both a spectacle of blood and a domestic accident, Plath's poem explores the way war and violence become banal and morally ambiguous. In the climate of Cold War moral self-congratulation, 'Cut' offers a confrontation with American history where moral superiority is untenable. It also interweaves the personal and the political in a way that refuses the dichotomy between them.

## History-making

One way to read history out of (or into) poetry is to investigate specific references to events, persons or institutions, understanding that these references may be explicit or appear in metaphor, analogy or allegory. Another way looks at how poetry takes part in a wider cultural phenomenon. Seeing a poem not just through its attention to history but as a part of history – that is, as history-making – may seem to exaggerate poetry's impact in American culture. We ordinarily imagine this genre to lack a sufficiently large readership to have any widespread influence. While Plath might represent an exception to this rule, this is not precisely what I mean by history-making. Instead, poetry, like any other cultural or social form, absorbs and reflects the anxieties and pleasures of its times, often critically though not always. The difficulty of pursuing this kind of reading lies in the necessity to look outside the poetry to its context, which requires a body of knowledge most readers need to acquire. But how do we know where to begin? We do not simply import historical knowledge into a poem but first ask where the poem guides an investigation into history. If Plath's poetry is private, what exactly did privacy mean during this historical moment?

The historian who first discerned the link between Cold War international relations and patterns of marriage and childbearing in the 1950s, Elaine Tyler May, illustrated the paradox of Cold War domestic ideology by examining a photo spread from *Life Magazine*. In this 1959 issue a smiling newlywed couple honeymoons in a bomb shelter, in one photo surrounded by canned goods, in another descending into the steel and concrete bunker for two weeks of 'unbroken togetherness'.[10] While *Life* was clearly having fun with the image, slyly acknowledging the sexual element of the honeymoon in their 'togetherness', neither the photo spread nor the article accompanying it, was ironic. As May points out, these images inadvertently portrayed the contradiction of Cold War domestic life. As private, erotically charged and materially satisfying as it was meant to be, the home was also extremely isolating and vulnerable to external threats. Privacy and abundance were to compensate for insecurity, to provide the shelter from nuclear anxiety. May revisits the 'kitchen debates' between the American vice-president, Richard Nixon, and the Soviet leader, Nikita Khruschev, to show how important the ideology of privacy was to Cold War international relations. When Nixon and Khruschev squared off during Nixon's 1959 visit to Moscow over the relative quality of kitchen appliances, the success of either system, it was implied, depended not on the cultivation of a vibrant public sphere, but on the enrichment of private life.

Plath was no stranger to Cold War domestic ideology and, in particular, to its asymmetrical effects on women's lives. When she graduated from Smith College in 1955, the Democratic presidential candidate, Adlai Stevenson, gave a commencement address that featured the rhetoric of Cold War domestic ideology. Reprinted at the time in *Women's Home Companion* and cited some years later in *The Feminine Mystique* by fellow Smith graduate Betty Friedan, Stevenson's address championed the 'humble role of housewife':

> In short, far from the vocation of marriage and motherhood leading you away from the great issues of our day, it brings you back to their very center and places upon you an infinitely deeper and more intimate responsibility than that borne by the majority of those who hit the headlines and make the news and live in such a turmoil of great issues that they end by being totally unable to distinguish which issues are really great.[11]

In reassuring these newly minted college graduates that their place was in the home, Stevenson does not condemn female ambition. On the contrary. He grounds his appeal for housewifery in their ambition, urging them to take part in the 'great issues of our day' by devoting themselves to private matters of home, husband and childrearing. The Smith graduate can weigh in on the 'great issues', however, only by cutting off her aspiration for a role in the public world and for publicity itself. By staying out of the headlines and out of the news, remaining 'in the living room with a baby in your lap' or 'in the kitchen with a can opener in your hand', women could play a crucial role in navigating 'our crisis' (quoted in Friedan, *Mystique*, p. 60). Cultivating the private space of the home made the greatest possible contribution to the US's success in the sphere of Cold War international politics.

Stevenson's advice to exercise ambition in domestic duties helps us to understand the strangely ambivalent role that wives and mothers played in the Cold War 1950s. On the one hand, mass culture and public servants alike extolled the virtues of mothers and wives. They were idealized in magazines, political speeches, television programming and advertising and lauded by experts in psychology, medicine and child development. On the other hand, there was a creeping anxiety that wives and mothers enjoyed too much power in the home and could not be trusted with the care of future soldiers and statesmen. Philip Wylie's *Generation of Vipers*, one of the period's most widely cited screeds against mothers, rebuked women for exercising excessive power and thereby emasculating their sons. This drama of the suffocating and domineering mother, straight out of the Freudian family romance popularized in the 1950s, became a staple of American self-knowledge.

Plath engaged this ideological contradiction in the private sphere and women's place in it when she satirized the aggressive marketing of the institution of marriage in *Ariel*'s 'The Applicant'. The poem begins by disconnecting marriage from romance and placing it instead in a domain of work and social advancement. The opening line, which seeks to determine the applicant's acceptability, evokes the cosy exclusivity of the country club rather than the couple. The decision to wed is, therefore, not a fulfilment of personal desire but a social obligation. Plath then further evacuates personal intimacy by listing the qualifications of an applicant, accentuating the vocational aspect of marriage and taking Adlai Stevenson's admonition very literally. Drawing at times the language and at times the cadence of her lines from the realm of advertising, Plath reveals domestic ideology to be a con act on both women and men.

In 'The Applicant' Plath employs to savage effect one of the most characteristic moves of her late poetry: incorporating into her poems language drawn from nonpoetic or antipoetic sources, for instance, nursery rhymes, advertising slogans and bureaucratese. Here her poem stretches the euphemistic abstraction of bureaucratic or corporate rhetoric with the visceral specificity of the body. 'Our sort' is not blemish-free, but crippled, broken and wounded. As the list in stanzas one and two shows, the successful applicant will be someone with a 'glass eye, false teeth', with any one of a number of prostheses or surgical supports, with some obvious injury or disability, else 'how can we give you a thing?'. Marriage, it is implied, depends upon defect. 'You have a hole, it's a poultice,' the final stanza promises in lines that mock the declarative bombast of outrageous sales claims. The husband becomes a symbol of lack, a 'hole', while the wife supplements him prosthetically to make him whole.

Plath's poem speaks back to the ideological inflation of marriage ordinarily aimed at women by directing its sales pitch to the hapless groom, uncovering the assumption of male inadequacy that grounds appeals to women's ambitious domesticity. 'The Applicant' satirizes both Stevenson's appeal to female ambition and Wylie's angry repudiation of wives and mothers by taking their logic to the extreme. Women are meant to strive for perfection in menial domestic chores while men are told that they are inadequate for the tasks of ordinary life. 'The Applicant' interprets the ideological emphasis on marriage and family as a scare tactic disguised as the promise of fulfilment.

Plath's inversion of the appeal to marry also contains the Cold War paradox of domestic security. She derides the idea that the institution of marriage will protect the couple from nuclear conflict. It is important to remember that the speaker also encourages the applicant to marry the 'suit' as well as the 'living doll': 'Black and stiff, but not a bad fit. / Will you marry it?' (stanza five). The suit, which is to say the role of husband, might not be comfortable, but it promises security. The speaker pledges the suit's indestructibility; it is fire-, water-, shatter- and bomb-proof, and comes with a lifetime warranty that echoes the language of crisis that made marriage a refuge in a dangerous world. Like Elaine Tyler May's image of the newlyweds in the bomb shelter, Plath's poem sows anxiety into the promise of security. Stanza five ends with the ominous guarantee 'Believe me, they'll bury you in it.' Marriage becomes an institution built on fear and inadequacy, where the couple retreats from the insecurities of public life to heal the wounds to male ego and supply an outlet for female ambition. 'The Applicant' cannot properly be said to treat a private matter because the very logic of the poem reminds us how public and political contemporary marriage was.

## The personal is the political

Yet Plath does not always parody the discourses of Cold War ideology as explicitly as she does in 'The Applicant'. Confessional poetry takes part in the much larger debate about privacy that permeated nearly every area of American life. In the late 1950s and early 1960s, the period when Plath was writing her last and best work, alarms over the loss of privacy were being raised in relation to the suburbs, television, the computer, psychoanalysis, the FBI and the police, record keeping in institutions of higher learning, new technologies of surveillance, city planning, tabloid journalism, photojournalism and more. While, as I have argued, privacy and private life were being hailed as the core features of American democracy, American citizens began to recognize the loss of privacy as an increasingly familiar experience. We should therefore understand privacy in these debates as inherently paradoxical, which helps us to grasp why the US's confessional culture emerged simultaneously with deep anxiety about the loss of privacy. The more privacy was extolled, debated and measured, the less self-evident it became. If privacy was so valued, why was it constantly being violated? If it was so integral to a free and democratic society, why would artists and celebrities, politicians and ordinary citizens, choose to surrender it by offering private information about themselves to the public?

This debate suggests why confessional poetry's blurring of distinctions between public and private worlds was freighted with social meaning that extended beyond matters of aesthetic value. Postwar social transformations – like the growth of corporations and the expansion of the suburbs – seemed to corrupt Americans' desire for autonomy and freedom. Often linked, these trends created two of the most familiar targets of 1950s social censure: the 'organization man', who relinquished his individuality to the corporation,[12] and the suburban homeowner, who sought perfect conformity with the neighbours. In the reception of confessional poetry, Paul Breslin shows that the inwardness and emotional volatility of the poetry represented to its readers a revolt against this invasive, overly rational society. Madness and rage were reactions to the internalization of external social codes, that is, the colonization of the private self by society and the state. The willingness to violate these codes liberated the authentic self, which would necessarily be wounded since the organized society demanded the renunciation of individuality. Feminist critics, too, regarded Plath's rage and madness as a protest against inauthenticity, in this case the masks of femininity that stifled female creativity and self-expression. With the central insight of second-wave feminism – the personal is the political – Plath seemed to take on a more active, critical role, producing a damning critique of patriarchal institutions. In both these readings we can recognize a pattern of viewing authentic selfhood as something hidden from and damaged by an intrusive, oppressive society.[13] The authentic and free self remains associated with privacy, but achieves its liberation only by forsaking that privacy.

This heroic reading of Plath's confession should be balanced against her own complication of the familiar notions of privacy and confession. If we return to the image of the private home in *Ariel*, we see that Plath works in various poems to unsettle the idea of the home as a place in which to withdraw from scrutiny. For instance, 'Lesbos' presents us with a paradoxical image of the home in the image of the kitchen, 'all Hollywood' and 'windowless' with 'Stage curtains' and 'coy paper strips' instead of a door (stanza one). This description gives us a paradoxical theatricality, something like a closet drama, both performative and yet closed off from public viewing. Being 'windowless', no one can see inside the home, but neither can any one inside it see out. Moreover, the 'paper strips for doors' suggest that once in the home, it is impossible to withdraw from the other occupants. The home may be private – closed off from the world – but it is hardly a space of privacy. Moreover, its theatricality indicates that it is not a place of authentic selfhood either. The home is as much a place for masks as the theatre of public life.[14] The seething rage of the poem derives in part from the blending of claustrophobia and theatricality. The actors cannot get off the stage. Both women, rivals for the husband of the speaker, see through the performance of the other, know they are seen through themselves, and yet are compelled to act their parts.

As she does in 'Lesbos', Plath riffs on states of exposure everywhere in the poetry. The most famous example is 'Lady Lazarus', where we see multiple images of exposure, but we find it as well in the bee sequence, where the speaker encounters the danger of the sting with bare, unprotected skin. A great many of the poems written for *Ariel* (but not included in the version edited and published by Ted Hughes) feature surveillance, eavesdropping, spying and voyeurism. Not only is the space of the home devoid of privacy, but the body is frequently displayed, like the striptease in 'Lady Lazarus', or exposed, as in 'A Secret', like the watermark stamped on the body – 'wavery, indelible, true'. Messages seem to emerge from inside the body on to the surface of the skin, never by choice and sometimes by force. The surgeon in 'The Courage of Shutting-Up' forces internal secrets to light by tattooing 'blue grievances' on to the surface of the skin. One of the most common figures in confessional poetry, and Plath's in particular, the surgeon makes a living by breaching the surface of the body. This provides a figure of the forced trans-gression of bodily integrity. In so many of these poems – 'A Secret', 'Purdah', 'The Detective', 'Eavesdropper', 'The Other', 'The Jailer', 'Words heard, by accident, over the phone', 'The Courage of Shutting-Up' – there are irresistible pressures to reveal secrets.

This pressure to reveal and expose oneself casts 'confession' in a very different light from how we have ordinarily imagined it. Confession becomes an effect of coercion. Plath seems highly aware that the conditions of self-revelation militate against free and authentic self-expression. The perform-ance has an audience with its own agenda. Think of the last sections of 'Lady Lazarus', after the peanut-crunching crowds, when the speaker addresses 'Herr Doktor'. This figure of the psychoanalyst is waiting for the intimate details to be proffered by the analysand. While Plath was certainly a subject of analysis herself, the whole enterprise of psychoanalysis was very important in 1950s American culture, particularly for white middle-class women. Adjusting to the ambivalence of the role of woman, housewife and mother was aided by the (usually) male doctor. Plath need not be speaking just of her own experience, but more generally of an institution that demands secrets and hands them back in a new form, one which the patient has not given them. When the speaker tells 'Herr Doktor' that 'I am your opus, / I am your valuable', we can now understand the subsequent sneering line, 'do not think I underestimate your great concern'. The doctor has his own prestige and authority tied up in the patient, who has been turned into his opus, that is, his work of art. The shriek at the end of the poem resists confession by frustrating his appropriation of her words. The result is ambiguous. A howl of rage is not a triumph of self-expression, but neither is it a submission to coerced self-revelation.

Two years after Sylvia Plath's death, the US Supreme Court announced its decision in the case of *Griswold v. Connecticut* to affirm a constitutional 'right to privacy'. Surprisingly, for all the rhetoric about the value of privacy in a democracy, such a right did not exist until 1965. Echoing Cold War fears about the police state and pieties about the sanctity of marriage, Justice Douglas asked, 'Would we allow the police to search the sacred precincts of marital bedrooms for telltale signs of the use of contraceptives?' Since the answer could only be 'no', the new right to privacy in the 'zone of the home' was immediately welcomed as a major advance in American civil liberties. While new cases quickly showed that this zone would have to be expanded and revised, the right to privacy became one of the hallmarks of a modern democracy. While we can only wonder what Sylvia Plath would have made of this development, we do know that her work requires us to look back on this history more sceptically. *Ariel* invites us to reread a history we believed we knew, to question the logic of the court's affirmation of privacy and to ask whether the zone of the home is a suitable place for a woman to locate her autonomy.

## Notes

1. *Sylvia*, directed by Christine Jeffs, starring Gwyneth Paltrow and Daniel Craig. DVD (Icon, 2003).
2. M. L. Rosenthal, *The New Poets: American and British Poetry Since World War II* (New York: Oxford University Press, 1967).
3. Amy Hungerford, *The Holocaust of Texts* (Chicago: University of Chicago Press, 2003), p. 31.
4. Jacqueline Rose, *The Haunting of Sylvia Plath* (Cambridge, MA: Harvard University Press, 1991), p. 206.
5. For a fuller discussion of this period, see my *Pursuing Privacy in Cold War America* (New York: Columbia University Press, 2002).
6. Marie Ashe, '*The Bell Jar* and the Ghost of Ethel Rosenberg', in Marjorie Garber and Rebecca Walkowitz (eds.), *Secret Agents: The Rosenberg Case, McCarthyism, and Fifties America* (New York: Routledge, 1995), p. 216.
7. The most influential account of this modern history of the lyric is Theodor W. Adorno, 'On Lyric Poetry and Society', in Shierry Weber Nicholson (trans.), *Notes to Literature: Volume One* (New York: Columbia University Press, 1991).

8. Leon Wieseltier, 'In a Universe of Ghosts', *New York Review of Books* (25 November 1976), pp. 20–3 (p. 20).

9. Susan Gubar, 'Prosopopoeia and Holocaust Poetry in English: Sylvia Plath and Her Contemporaries', *The Yale Journal of Criticism* 14.1 (2001), p. 192.

10. Elaine Tyler May, *Homeward Bound: American Families in the Cold War Era* (New York: Basic Books, 1988), p. 3.

11. Betty Friedan, *The Feminine Mystique* (1963; New York: Dell, 1983), p. 60.

12. William Whyte, *The Organization Man* (New York: Simon & Schuster, 1956).

13. Paul Breslin, *The Psycho-Political Muse: American Poetry since the 1950s* (Chicago: University of Chicago, 1987).

14. See Christina Britzolakis, *Sylvia Plath and the Theatre of Mourning* (Oxford: Clarendon Press, 1999) for a brilliant reinterpretation of Plath's so-called authenticity.

# 3

LYNDA K. BUNDTZEN

# Plath and psychoanalysis: uncertain truths

Psychoanalysis is both a body of doctrine and a system of psychotherapy developed principally by Sigmund Freud. Concerned with the study and interpretation of mental states, the body of doctrine describes conflicts and processes originating in the unconscious. As a form of therapy, psychoanalysis seeks to alleviate neuroses and other mental disorders by the systematic technical analysis of unconscious factors as revealed, for example, in dreams and fantasies, slips of the tongue and free-association, neurotic symptoms or lapses in memory, and does so by revealing unconscious contents and motives in the patient's psyche and behaviour. Both as doctrine and therapy, psychoanalysis relies on the concept of the unconscious – mental processes, ideas and desires of which the conscious mind is unaware – and interpretively seeks to make what is unconscious, conscious. In the context of literary studies, psychoanalysis is particularly interested in the ways in which the language of the text may displace or conceal its subject. Psychoanalysis in this context should be understood not so much as a tool with which to diagnose the pathology of the individual author but as an interpretative and narrative practice which, as for example in the work of Jacqueline Rose, discussed below, is alert to the place of fantasy, desire and repression in our personal and collective lives.[1]

The sexual origin of almost everything Freud found in the unconscious and the often taboo nature of these ideas, wishes, desires and fantasies explain why the unconscious was, in Freud's view, undiscovered country. These contents are kept out of consciousness, claims Freud, precisely because of their illicit nature: it is socially and morally unacceptable, for example, to desire sex with one's mother and the death of the father as a sexual competitor for her affections, yet these are common themes in psychoanalytic doctrine and diagnosis. Freud explained the importance of repression and denial in keeping these oedipal desires and drives buried in the unconscious, but also the psychic cost of resistance in neurotic symptoms such as anxiety, depression, hysteria and paranoia.

36

By the time Plath came into contact with Freudian thought, psychoanalytic doctrine and therapy had been absorbed thoroughly into both popular and high American culture and might be understood, even when it was attacked, as a hegemonic ideology for defining both individual and family psychology. On the popular level, for example, Hollywood director Alfred Hitchcock could rely on the widespread currency of Freudian thought in his audiences when delineating his troubled, psychologically damaged characters in movies such as *Spellbound*, *Psycho* and *Marnie*. We also know that Plath, like many American intellectuals in the 1950s, was attracted by the non-commercial austerity and beauty of Swedish director Ingmar Bergman's films (see, for example, the entry in Plath's *Journals* for 1 November 1959 (*J*, pp. 521–2)). Bergman gained fame as a confessional artist, giving his own neurotic obsessions free expression in his films.[2] The psychological complexity of his characters, especially his women, inspired Plath's dramatic work 'Three Women: A Poem for Three Voices', which borrowed from Bergman's film *Brink of Life*. The 'marvelous new Ingmar Bergman movie' that Plath mentions seeing and enjoying in a 21 December 1962 letter to her mother was *Through a Glass Darkly* (*LH*, p. 491). The film is a harrowing study of the psychological breakdown of a young woman, Karin, who seduces her younger brother and then, in her final scene, has a hallucination in which a spider-god attempts to rape her. As the film unfolds, it becomes increasingly clear that this spider-god is a projection of Karin's familial ties with her husband, father and brother, who all have a predatory relationship to her. Karin's suffering may well have resonated with Plath's own psychological stress at the time.

If the 1950s was a historically contingent moment for the meeting of minds between Plath and Freud, she was certainly not alone. Plath's benefactor, Olive Higgins Prouty, had been a patient at Austen Riggs, a prestigious psychiatric hospital, and her popular novel, *Now, Voyager*, later a Bette Davis movie, is about the liberation through psychotherapy of its sexually repressed heroine. In addition to providing Plath with scholarship money at Smith College, Prouty was Plath's financial benefactor after her suicide attempt in 1953 and supported her expensive therapy at McLean Hospital. Like Plath, fellow poets Anne Sexton and Robert Lowell were both institutionalized mental patients there, and their experiences as patients provided inspiration and material for their poetry.[3]

Plath was encouraged by her therapist, Dr Ruth Beuscher, to explain herself to herself in Freudian terms and to fashion herself as a patient, an intellectual and artist by applying Freudian and other psychoanalytic doctrines and therapies. In her final months, for example, Plath was reading Erich Fromm's 1956 book *The Art of Loving*, apparently at Dr Beuscher's recommendation. Fromm is known as an ego psychologist, and this volume is more concerned with self-help than depth psychoanalysis.[4] For the critic who practises psychoanalysis on literary texts, their authors and their characters, Plath therefore poses a rather daunting problem: she is thoroughly conscious, and at times ruthlessly direct, in her appropriation of psychoanalytic ideas (Diane Middlebrook notes a similar tendency in her biography of Plath's contemporary, Anne Sexton). Plath often anticipates the psychoanalytic critic's strategies by making them her own, leaving the critic with little to do but expand upon ideas that are already planted in the text. The temptation is to read Plath as confessing to her own psychic conflicts projected into poetic personae and fictional characters that are transparent versions of Plath herself.

## 'Daddy'

Nowhere are the difficulties for the critic of this psychoanalytic self-interpretation more obvious than in 'Daddy', arguably Plath's most famous poem. Before its publication she read 'Daddy' for a BBC radio broadcast in October 1962, and later, in notes for the BBC on her new poems, described the poem as 'spoken by a girl with an Electra complex. Her father died while she thought he was God.' The girl's 'case', Plath proceeds to explain, is difficult because the father was a Nazi, and the mother may have been 'part Jewish'. These two inheritances meet in the daughter and 'paralyze each other – she has to act out the awful little allegory once over before she is free of it' (CP, p. 293, n. 183). Plath directs her reader to interpret the poem through the lens of a popular psychoanalytic narrative: a daughter with an Electra complex is one who desires her father sexually, her body incestuously devoted in this instance to a dead man's, as Electra's was to her father Agamemnon's. In a state of unfulfilled and impossible desire, the daughter's story might be one of static sexual frustration and father-worship; but Plath also insists on a paralysis of sexual roles historically derived from the Holocaust. Because the father is not just a dead God, but also a Nazi, and the mother 'very possibly part Jewish', Daddy is also a sadistic villain, and the daughter's feminine sexuality is marked by the mother's role as a victim, possibly in a masochistic relation to the father. As the speaker of 'Daddy' generalizes, 'Every woman adores a Fascist.'

The poem, Plath tells us, is also an 'allegory', suggesting that these sexual roles have been internalized by the daughter and are part of her psyche. They are symbolic figures enslaving her until the poem's utterance, which will be an acting out of the internal struggle, intended to free her from paralysis. Here, too, Plath embeds an analogy to psychoanalytic therapy – the famous 'talking cure'. In psychoanalysis the patient (the analysand) is encouraged by the analyst to speak, to free-associate, to thereby make what has been unconscious, conscious and available to control. 'Acting out' suggests the transference whereby the patient, unknowingly and unconscious of what she is doing, imposes on the analyst the role of father-oppressor. The daughter in Plath's poem has done just that, but with her husband, 'I made a model of you', she says, 'And I said I do, I do.' Catharsis or freedom is supposed to arrive with the conscious knowledge of what is being acted out, how it has wounded her, and an ensuing awareness of how to begin healing. Plath seems to be asking her reader to understand the poem psychoanalytically as both symptomatic of illness and curative.

Readers seldom feel, however, that 'Daddy' achieves resolution or closure. Passions are not spent or assuaged. Even without the knowledge that Plath committed suicide four months after the composition of 'Daddy', the rage expressed in the poem and its excessive accusations, that Daddy is a Nazi devil, a brutish torturer and a vampire, are evidence that the speaker's fury is ongoing and self-destructive. She has tried to kill herself once before, and when in the antepenultimate stanza she says the 'telephone's off' and she is 'finally through', it sounds ominously as though her own death is the only way to end the struggle with Daddy. Because the poem also stresses repetition, the confident 'once over' of acting out proposed by Plath in her introduction is suspect. The 'concept of repetition in Freudian thought', as critic Jacqueline Rose points out, can be liberating, but may also signify a deadly compulsion. The speaker might be understood as 'going back to the beginning in order to retrieve the mythic narrative of [her] individual history', and with retrieval, she achieves both understanding and release. Or this might be 'repetition as insistence without content' – a compulsion to repeat that is associated by Freud in *Beyond the Pleasure Principle* with the death-drive (*Haunting*, p. 50). One of Freud's best examples of this behaviour is Lady Macbeth's futile efforts to wash away the crime of regicide by repetitively rubbing her hands while sleepwalking, 'acting out' her tortured conscience even as she tries to exorcise its burden of guilt. This is, however, repetition for its own sake and does nothing for Lady Macbeth, who finally kills herself.[5]

The daughter in 'Daddy' may be interpreted in a similar way. After her first suicide attempt, she did not surrender the wish to 'get back' to him, but married a surrogate figure and significantly, a Daddy substitute who would punish her, repeating a masochistic relationship to a dominant male figure: the husband is pictured as 'A man in black with a Meinkampf look // And a love of the rack and the screw'. She must kill Daddy, she says, because he died before she had time, and if she has killed one man, she says, 'I've killed two'. This is crime *for* punishment, once again soliciting physical abuse. The poem's language is, in itself, highly redundant or repetitive in its rhymes and rhythms. The insistent 'you' in the opening line, as throughout the poem, is accusatory, as if the daughter is poking a finger in Daddy's chest. Finally, all these repetitions may suggest that the daughter's rage disguises unconscious guilt for wishing Daddy's death.[6]

The question of Plath's difference from her speaker also remains unsettled and unsettling for critics. Criticism has long favoured the proverb, 'Trust the tale, not the teller', encouraging a heavy demarcation between author and speaker in a lyric poem. In T. S. Eliot's famous formulation, 'the more perfect the artist, the more completely separate in him will be the man who suffers and the mind which creates', and 'the difference between art and the event is always absolute'.[7] With 'confessional' poetry, though, such distinctions are hard to honour. We know, for example, from the date appended to the text in Plath's *Collected Poems*, that 'Daddy' was composed on 12 October 1962, the anniversary of her father's leg amputation in 1940 (Otto Plath died of a cardiac embolism on 5 November 1940) (*LH*, p. 24). Is Plath attempting to 'amputate' Daddy from her own psyche? To put him to rest finally? Should we read 'Daddy' in Freudian terms as a symbolic castration of the father, an attempt to rob him of his sexual power over her? Evidence from the *Journals* supports just such an identification of the poem's speaker with Plath, who describes a typical moment in therapy with Dr Beuscher this way: 'If I really think I killed and castrated my father may all my dreams of deformed and tortured people be my guilty visions of him or fears of punishment for me? And how to lay them?' (*J*, p. 476). Suicide is, as Plath decided after reading Freud's 'Mourning and Melancholia', a 'transferred murderous impulse' from a loved one 'onto myself' (*J*, p. 447). I will return to this quotation later, but one explanation Plath seems to be formulating for her first suicide attempt is internalized guilt for wishing her father dead and having that wish fulfilled. He died before she had time to resolve and overcome these oedipal – not Electra – wishes, and the consequence is an overidealized paternal figure, a Daddy of divine proportions, godlike infallibility and abusive powers to match his omnipotence in Plath's psyche.

Before I explore the problematic nature of this Freudian psychoanalysis by Plath herself, let me recommend its explanatory power both locally, in several texts and textual moments, and theoretically, since it is an analysis that evolves in relation to later reconfigurations of Freudian ideas based on the daughter's preoedipal relationship to her mother. Other poems illuminated by the 'complex' that Plath discovers in her own psyche include 'Full Fathom Five' (1958), 'Electra on Azalea Path' (1959), 'The Beekeeper's Daughter' (1959), 'The Colossus' (1959), 'Little Fugue' (1962) and 'Sheep in Fog' (1962 and 1963). In 'Full Fathom Five' the father's domain is the sea, and the daughter both remembers and longs for an incestuous union with him in his 'shelled bed', even if she must drown, or 'breathe water', to join him. The 'dark water' of 'Sheep in Fog' is equally threatening, though here her immersion is in 'a heaven / Starless and fatherless', suggesting the daughter's fear of abandonment by a heavenly father. The identification of the speaker with Electra and the father with Agamemnon is reiterated in both 'Electra on Azalea Path' and 'The Colossus', as is the daughter's paralysis in an impossible desire, begging for pardon in 'Electra' for the love that 'did us both to death' and, in 'The Colossus', struggling as a solitary archaeologist under the 'blue sky' of the Greek *Oresteia* to mend the shattered statuary of his colossal form. In both 'The Colossus' and 'Little Fugue', the daughter longs to elicit the dead father's words, echoing the complaint in 'Daddy': 'I never could talk to you.'

The speaker of 'Little Fugue' is frustrated by the dead father's silence in her memories of him. She can see his voice, but not hear him, and what she sees is 'Gothic and barbarous, pure German', anticipating the Nazi father's 'obscene' 'gobbledygoo' in 'Daddy'. The 'fugue' of the poem's title refers to the speaker's amnesia; in stanza eleven she is 'lame in the memory' as her father is lamed by amputation. This version of paralysis, the compulsion to repeat without making any progress, is symptomatic of all these poems. In contrast to the daughter's fury in the later 'Daddy', the amnesiac of 'Little Fugue' suffers from affectlessness and an inability to piece together her memories of him into a coherence that might make her life whole.

Otto Plath was an entomologist and expert on bees, giving Plath (and later, Ted Hughes in *Birthday Letters*) yet another sexual and symbolic context for exploring her relationship to him. In 'The Beekeeper's Daughter' the garden setting is eroticized, 'a garden of mouthings', with its musky flowers, some of them trumpet-throated, 'open to the beaks of birds', or resembling 'little boudoirs'. The father, the master of the bees (stanza one), rules over 'many-breasted hives'. The potential for violence comes with the daughter's challenge and assertion of incestuous longing: 'Here is a queenship no mother can contest – // A fruit that's death to taste: dark flesh, dark parings.' The murderous wish that was to surface later in 'Daddy' is here translated into the mating (or pairing) of a daughter-queen bee with the father, who is also bridegroom-drone, and dies in the sexual consummation – a 'dark paring' (or cutting away).

In *The Bell Jar* as well, Plath shapes her heroine Esther Greenwood's fate in Freudian terms and retrospectively may be explaining the unconscious motivation for her own suicide attempt in 1953. The crucial moment of decision in the novel comes after Esther visits her father's neglected grave. She remembers that her mother neither took her to her father's funeral nor mourned her husband's death, and she resolves to enact her grief in recompense for these failures. In the following passage Esther is oblivious to her unconscious anger at both her parents: 'I had a great yearning, lately, to pay my father back for all the years of neglect ... I had always been my father's favorite, and it seemed fitting that I should take on a mourning my mother had never bothered with' (*BJ*, p. 165). With only a slight change in tone, from obsequious dutifulness to condemnation of both her parents, this passage can be read as vengeful – this is payback time for her father's neglect of her – and disdainful scorn for her mother, who obviously did not love the father as much as his 'favorite' daughter. Esther muses on what might have been if her father had lived, if he had been her intellectual mentor, and is appalled by the graveyard's impoverished appearance. To make up for her own lack of tears as a child, but also and especially for her mother's failure to cry, Esther begins to howl and weep. The episode ends abruptly here, but leaps forward immediately to the suicide: 'I knew just how to go about it', Esther says, suggesting that what she has learnt in the graveyard precipitates her action (*BJ*, p. 167). If we are fully persuaded by Plath's insistence on an Electra complex, then Esther, like the daughter in 'Daddy', desires 'to die / And get back, back, back to you' and unconsciously to 'get back *at* Daddy'.

## The mother

While Plath is everywhere confident of the baleful influence of this absent and overidealized father figure in her psyche and certain of the truth that, left as a child without the 'love of a steady blood-related man', she has been scarred for life (*J*, p. 431), she is more inclined to blame her mother both for his death and for her own self-destructive behaviour. The 'transferred murderous impulse' she describes (in the quotation I now return to about Freud's 'Mourning and Melancholia') is '*from my mother* onto myself: the "vampire" metaphor Freud uses, "draining the ego": that is exactly the feeling I have getting in the way of my writing: mother's clutch' (*J*, p. 447, my italics). Feminist critics and revisionists of Freudian thought such as Jessica Benjamin argue that 'the father and his phallus have the power they do because of their ability to stand for difference and separation from the mother ... As long as the traditional sexual division of labor persists, the child will turn to the father as the "knight in shining armor" who represents freedom, the outside world, will, agency, and desire.'[8] If we reformulate the daughter's, or Plath's, supposed Electra complex in these terms, what suddenly takes precedence over incestuous longing is the need for a dominant male figure to help the daughter to enter the world, become independent and, most important, loosen the ties to the mother. The preoedipal relationship between mother and daughter, as it is delineated in feminist readings of Freud by Nancy Chodorow and Dorothy Dinnerstein, forms an intense bond sustained by bodily likeness and is only reluctantly given up in the daughter's recognition that she can never take the father's place. The daughter, no less than the son, regards the father as a rival for the mother's affections.[9]

'Mother's clutch', it turns out, is a far more significant problem for Plath than that posed by the Electra complex. Immediately after her father's death, Plath asked her mother to sign a contract agreeing never to marry again (*LH*, p. 25). This might be construed as the little girl's protest against any man taking her beloved father's place, but equally important, perhaps, is gratification in having Otto Plath out of the way at last and Mother all to herself. Evidence suggests that Otto Plath's illness affected family life severely and the young Sylvia was often sent to stay with her grandparents while her mother tended both to Otto Plath's failing health and her younger brother's asthma attacks (*LH*, pp. 22–3).

Plath's notes on her psychotherapy with Dr Ruth Beuscher are preoccupied with establishing boundaries between herself and her mother, even if the only way she can do this is by aggressively attacking what she decides is Aurelia's 'defective' love (*J*, p. 448) and persistently dramatizing her mother as smothering, intrusive, disapproving and jealous of her marriage to Ted Hughes. She often sets up mother and husband as rivals for her allegiance, which may be interpreted as an 'acting out' of the original love triangle of Sylvia, Otto and Aurelia. This time Ted/Otto will be the victor. Dr Beuscher apparently gave her patient Plath 'permission' to hate her mother, validating for Plath her dramatization of Aurelia 'as an enemy: somebody who "killed" my father ... a murderess of maleness' (*J*, p. 433). Plath suggests that Aurelia's life had been reduced to 'a dry chittering stalk of fear' (*J*, p. 438). Her comments effectively sterilize and desexualize the mother, representing her as sacrificing her own life for her daughter's, but then exacting a debt of gratitude for her martyrdom.

When Plath records her 'ideas of maleness', they are associated with sexual and creative power (*J*, p. 437). The overvaluation of Otto Plath, and later Ted Hughes, as authoritative mentoring figures simultaneously strengthens her own masculine ambitions as a poet and helps her to define herself as an adventurous, desirable and sexually fecund woman, totally different from her mother. In one of her letters to Aurelia, written shortly after she falls in love with Hughes, this validation of her creativity as both a poet and a woman is recorded in soaring prose. She speaks of her own strengthening voice, of Ted's approval of her poems, poems which seem to him 'strong and full and rich', particularly in comparison with the work of other female poets (Sara Teasdale and Edna St Vincent Millay are mentioned). Her own poems, Plath says, are 'working, sweating, heaving poems born out of the way words should be said' (*LH*, p. 244). Giving birth to poems is intimately linked to the womanly power of giving birth to children, but Plath insists on her difference from other women poets, who are stereotypically feminine in their timidity; indeed, Plath embraces masculine virility and bravado for her creative powers, claiming to outdo Dylan Thomas, Gerard Manley Hopkins and W. B. Yeats in force and spirit (*LH*, p. 243).

Yet 'mother's clutch' continues to compete with Plath's sense of autonomy, even after her marriage to Hughes. At one point Plath writes that she wishes for her mother's death so that she 'could be sure of what I am: so I could know that what feelings I have, even though some resemble hers, are really my own' (*J*, p. 449). From a feminist psychoanalytic perspective, these fears of losing her independent selfhood to maternal domination would not be so exaggerated if the original closeness had not been so profound. The extensive correspondence between Plath as 'Sivvy' and her mother as 'Dearest Mummy' in *Letters Home* has been read by cynical critics as calculated self-posturing to placate Aurelia and to disguise Plath's true self, but may also be read as testimony to what Aurelia describes as the 'psychic osmosis' (*LH*, p. 32) she shared with her daughter. The letters are a gift to Aurelia of a vicarious 'golden girl' life in compensation for the mother's sacrifice of her own. Paula Bennett in her study of Emily Dickinson, Plath and Adrienne Rich, *My Life a Loaded Gun*, is especially eloquent on Plath's 'compulsion to present herself in the role of the good daughter'. She reads it as less about love than 'fear, fear of the loss of her mother's approval and, above all, fear of the sense of separation (of being rejected) that loss of approval would bring'. Bennett also contextualizes the mother-daughter bond shared by Plath and Aurelia in cultural terms, arguing from a feminist perspective that Plath was conforming to norms imposed by society in constructing her femininity. Hence Bennett describes the letters as written in 'the glossy, trivializing, "feminine" style that she [Plath] picked up from her reading in women's magazines during the 1950s ... It is a style appropriate to the girl her mother wanted ... a girl who could, like her mother before her, cope gallantly with any setback that came her way.'[10] The promise extorted from Aurelia never to marry again implies that her daughter would have to take her father's place, as she does, for example, in 'Electra on Azalea Path'. After her father's death, the speaker 'wormed' back with the mother's body in a bed where the only evidence of the father is 'the stain of divinity': 'As if you had never existed, as if I came / God-fathered into the world from my mother's belly'. The psychic cost of having the mother all to oneself is double, as we can see here: the apotheosis of the father, his elevation into the immutable and divine figure who will later exact punishment, and the survival into later years of a preoedipal dependency on the mother.

The companion poem to 'Daddy', written four days later on 16 October 1962, is 'Medusa'. The title ostensibly alludes to the Gorgon of classical mythology with her famous paralysing gaze, but also refers to the immature form of the jellyfish Aurelia, Plath's mother's name. Many of the poem's images suggest a symbiotic union like that of a foetus in a womb. The speaker is still tied to her mother by an 'old barnacled umbilicus'; the mother's body is 'fat and red, a placenta', or else a 'bottle in which I live'. The speaker refuses to sustain herself as a foetus in a womb, though, declaring in stanza seven that she will not 'bite' from it. The mother, in turn, threatens engulf-ment, 'touching and sucking' the speaker, sustaining her own life by figura-tively eating her daughter. Like 'Daddy', the poem ends with what looks like an emphatic dissolution of relationship: 'There is nothing between us', which ambiguously reads as 'nothing' existing to separate them.

Simultaneous with the composition of 'Medusa', on 16 October 1962, Plath writes two letters to Aurelia telling her that she 'must not go back to the womb', that she cannot return home to her mother in the US, but also expressing the need for help, the need for someone to 'protect' her, to nurse her back from the flu, and to defend her in her plight as a deserted wife to an unfaithful husband (*LH*, pp. 469, 470). The impossible position this puts Aurelia in – who better to satisfy these demands than a loving mother? – dramatizes the extraordinary defences that Plath erected to separate herself from her mother. Since Aurelia was present in July of 1962 when Plath's marriage began to crumble, there is shame associated with this distancing. In 'Medusa' the speaker claims that she feels 'overexposed, like an X-ray'; in a letter dated 9 October 1962, the day Hughes finished packing to leave the marriage, Plath had written to Aurelia of her reluctance to see her: 'The horror of what you saw and what I saw you see last summer is between us and I cannot face you again until I have a new life' (*LH*, p. 465). This excuse suggests that the mother has seen too much. In my earlier psychoanalytic account of this poem, I argued that this may have been a costly choice:

> In cutting herself off in this way from Aurelia and what Aurelia represents, Plath may well have felt herself cut off from all benevolent outside sources, and also from Sivvy, the ideal fiction created for her in the image of her culture – the old perfect self, free from blemish. As a result, only old yellow, the rival ingrate, was left to speak, and Plath was not yet strong enough to manage all the guilt in giving her voice. (Bundtzen, *Plath's Incarnations*, p. 108)

## Psychoanalysis and feminism

Many of the earliest books and essays on Plath were grounded in psycho-analytic thought, but as Jacqueline Rose has argued, they tend to reduce her life and work to a case study. Further, they tend to utilize this case study to advance arguments which, to Rose, illustrate 'the way critics read their unconscious into the text, repeating in their critical analysis the structures of meaning called up by the writing'. The famed transference I discussed earlier is one of 'mutual implication', with the analyst, no less than the patient-analysand, projecting his own unconscious struggles into a reading of Plath's texts. For Rose, this has created a '"psychotic" criticism' by predominantly male critics who have generated their own, often violent, 'sexual scenarios' to meet Plath textually (*Haunting*, pp. 12–14). As illustration, Rose juxtaposes David Holbrook's *Sylvia Plath: Poetry and Existence* with Al Alvarez's *The Savage God*. For Holbrook, the violence in Plath's poetry is a danger to culture and must be repudiated at all costs. She is '"sadly pseudo-male, like many of her cultists"', and her '"failed femininity"' explains her appeal to these '"women's liberators"' who threaten to overturn the sexual order (quoted in *Haunting*, p. 19). She must be stopped because, as Rose puts it, Holbrook's sexual fantasy is that she is 'a destroyer of men'. For Alvarez, who barely seems interested in the issue of her being a woman writer or in her feminine identity as such, Plath's '"extremism"' is worthy of admiration. Her violence, culminating in suicide, '"explains what the arts are about now"' (quoted in *Haunting*, p. 23). This may be, as Rose describes it, 'the romanticizing of art as pathology', but Alvarez argues that her assertion of poetic selfhood – even if it entails the risk of death – is a necessary antidote to a culture of mediocrity. The psychotic critical polarity represented by Holbrook and Alvarez and identified by Rose is in the choice between destruction and survival: 'Either the woman destroys the culture, or her self-immolation is the precondition for culture to survive' (*Haunting*, p. 23).

Rose's own application of psychoanalysis reflects a radical departure from the Freudian and feminist psychoanalytic practices I explore above, which depend on the certainty of an authorial presence in her writings. Michel Foucault's essay 'What Is an Author?' effectively argues that 'the author' is a cultural and critical construct.[11] This is a primary idea of postmodernist theory, which proposes 'the death of the author' as a necessary first step in perceiving Plath's, or any artist's, identity as a textual phenomenon, not a transhistorical category or universal truth in deriving meaning from her works. Rose, in a postmodernist move, similarly claims to have no interest in 'real people' like the artist or her parents, or in characters as reflections of these historically specific personages. Instead, she 'starts from the assumption that Plath is a fantasy' and asks 'what her writing, and responses to it, might reveal about fantasy as such' (*Haunting*, p. 5). She regards this as a way of evading the persistent effort to assign blame – to Hughes for leaving Plath, to Plath herself for her jealousy and paranoia, or to patriarchy for the way women, especially talented and ambitious women like Plath, internalize the antipathy and violence of the external world. For Rose, these tendencies in Plath criticism are testimony to the way Plath haunts our cultural unconscious, the way she mobilizes our own collective fantasy life in the task of deciding on guilt or innocence, what belongs to the inner world of the psyche vs. the outer world of culture and society, and the way we organize our sexual and political lives (*Haunting*, pp. 6–7).

Before leaving Rose, we should note that her efforts to rise above the critical fray she describes and deal with what she terms the historical and political 'residue' in Plath's texts (*Haunting*, p. 8) were misconstrued as a personal attack on both Plath's and Hughes's sexual identities. The publication of *The Haunting of Sylvia Plath* in 1992 was strenuously resisted by Ted Hughes and his sister Olwyn, who felt that Rose was fabricating her own fantasies about Plath's and Hughes's sex lives. In a rancorous exchange of letters to the editor of the *Times Literary Supplement*, Rose defended her reading of Plath's poem 'The Rabbit Catcher', arguing that 'to read sexual ambiguity into a poem is to say nothing about Plath's lived experience as a woman' (10 April 1992), and was answered by Ted Hughes that real people – a dead mother and her living children and husband – are indeed involved in her, Rose's, critical construction of a fantasized sexual identity. Very simply, he worried that fantasy would become fact when her critical speculations circulated in the real world (24 April 1992).[12]

## Telling stories

I have tried thus far to illustrate the explanatory power of psychoanalysis in relationship to Plath, first given her own familiarity with its concepts and her experience as a patient in therapy, and then in terms of critical revisions of psychoanalytic thought. What happens, though, if we decide that psychoanalysis as both doctrine and therapy has no greater purchase on truth than the myths it borrows from to name and delineate its concepts – Oedipus, Electra, Narcissus? Psychoanalysis is not a science, we are frequently reminded; it tells persuasive stories about people who are suffering mentally, who are confused and depressed, who do not know why or how to help themselves. For someone like Plath, these narratives may have seemed like discoveries of meaning and coherence and ready-made fictions to inspire and fashion her own myth. In her biography of Ted Hughes, Elaine Feinstein suggests that in psychoanalysis Plath came to focus on the then-popular idea of 'a key childhood trauma' (her father's death) as the reason for her 'violent mood swings and self-destructive impulses', and while her 'childhood loss' and the Oedipus complex may have inspired many of her greatest poems, Plath was also 'given an explanation of her inner distress that was to prove highly dangerous'.[13] Feinstein does not specify the dangers she sees, but one may also sense their presence in the 'stories' I have already outlined about Plath's relationship to her parents and her husband: a compulsive repetition of the original feelings of abandonment; a strong sense of guilt towards both parents and a need for sacrifice and reparation; and the impossibility of release or catharsis, even when, or especially when, her declarations and curses have a violent finality to them.

Ted Hughes's *Birthday Letters* may be read in this context as exploring the dangers of psychoanalysis both to Plath personally and as a poet. One of several ways Hughes fashions his persona in these poems is as the victim of the Freudian narrative Plath chose as a template to impose on both her life and her poetry. He implies that this choice was both fatal and unnecessary. Hence in his poem 'The Black Coat', the 'dead father' (or 'the body of the ghost') crawls out of the ocean and slides into or on to the first-person speaker (the two come 'into single focus') as if invoked by the power of Plath's projection of Otto's image on to her husband (*BL*, p. 103). As Hughes's speaker complains in 'A Picture of Otto', his wife 'could hardly tell us apart in the end', and he 'was a whole myth too late to replace' Otto in her affections (*BL*, p. 193). He blames his addressee, Plath, for sacrificing herself and wounding everyone she loved in homage to a story about her grief and longing for a dead father – a story opportunistically derived from her psychoanalytic therapy at a time when she felt artistically barren. In 'The God', especially, Hughes describes Plath's writer's block, or her 'panic of emptiness', and her urgent need for a story or 'tale' that would become her 'God, who calls / Out of sleep, inaudibly: "Write"' (*BL*, p. 188). This story, this ruling deity, is greedy for human sacrifice – for handfuls of her blood and 'blood gobbets' of him, for the 'myrrh' and 'frankincense' of the mother and father which she must feed to the flames (*BL*, pp. 189, 190). Hughes's poem ends with his bitter indictment of Plath's narrative of the supposedly grieving daughter. As Hughes portrays Plath's so-called 'Grief', it is born out of her fear that she has no story to tell but the one given to her by her psychiatrist whom Hughes portrays in another poem, 'Night-Ride on Ariel', as 'Twanging the puppet strings / That waltzed you in air' over a grave she would share with 'Daddy's bones' (*BL*, p. 174). In the closing line of 'The God' this 'Grief' is nothing but a euphemism for sacrificial violence (*BL*, p. 191).

As a reader of his wife's poetry and a husband-poet in dialogue with her work, Hughes also becomes implicated in the psychoanalytic process. For many reviewers, the poems in *Birthday Letters* are manipulative and self-exculpatory in their insistence that he 'was a whole myth too late to replace' Otto Plath in his daughter's heart (*BL*, p. 193). As Katha Pollitt describes the stance adopted in the volume, 'she was the sick one, I was the "nurse and protector". I didn't kill her – poetry, Fate, her obsession with her dead father killed her. The more Hughes insists on his own good intentions and the inevitability of Plath's suicide, the less convincing he becomes.'[14] Easily discerned in the reviewer's complaints is the psychoanalyst's classic enumeration of defences, projections and resistances to unconscious guilt. Alternatively, one might read these poems as moving towards catharsis and dissolution of grief in correspondence to what Freud described in 'Mourning and Melancholia' as the normal process of mourning. As each of Hughes's poems looks back at an incident from his marriage to Plath, there is a painful reliving of the moment and then release:

> The task is now carried through bit by bit … while all the time the existence of the lost object is continued in the mind. Each single one of the memories and hopes which bound the libido to the object is brought up … and the detachment of the libido from it is accomplished … [W]hen the work of mourning is completed the ego becomes free and uninhibited again.[15]

Melancholia is very different from mourning. Because the melancholiac cannot, but obviously must, give up the lost loved one, she narcissistically identifies with this person:

> hate is expended upon this new substitute-object, railing at it, depreciating it, making it suffer and deriving sadistic gratification from its suffering … It is this sadism … that solves the riddle of the tendency to suicide which makes melancholia so interesting – and so dangerous … [W]e have long known that no neurotic harbours thoughts of suicide which are not murderous impulses against others re-directed upon himself. (Freud, *Mourning*, pp. 172–3)

Here is the vengeful mix of motives that Hughes ascribes to Plath in her final poems and what he seeks to avoid in his own grieving verse. Suicidal depression, with its inevitable component of murderous aggression, is 'Catastrophic, arterial, doomed' (*BL*, p. 197) as Hughes describes Plath in her adoption of a muse that needed to be fed with bloody sacrifice in the final poem of *Birthday Letters*, 'Red'. In a gesture of homage to his dead wife, Hughes tells her that 'Blue was your kindly spirit – not a ghoul / But electrified, a guardian, thoughtful' (*BL*, p. 198). Hughes prefers to remember Plath's genial spirit as fertile and forgiving, a guardian who is a healer, not an 'open vein' and a 'stiffening wound'; a muse like Ariel to Prospero, inspiring the magician-artist to pity the enemies in his power.

As this brief survey of the impact of psychoanalysis on our understanding of Sylvia Plath and her work demonstrates, there is still much interpretative potential to examining both its ideas and therapeutic practices, but also multiple uncertainties about their explanatory power. Plath's suicide remains inexplicable and unacceptable to most readers, and psychoanalysis does not seem to provide answers. Nor does it explain her outburst of creativity in the final months of her life. How could someone be clinically and suicidally depressed and also accomplish so much of genius and in so brief a space of time? What were the final thoughts that led to the decision to take her life? When we take into consideration the effect of her suicide on those she loved, on those who knew her well or even, at times, on those who were briefly acquainted and on her critics and readers, psychoanalysis may be a useful tool in trying to understand their often extreme responses to her life and her art. We may not be ready, as Rose is, to yield our abiding interest in the 'real people' involved in Plath's story, but surely a strategic shift towards a psychoanalysis of the way Plath and her poetry continue to arouse our passions, or a contextualizing of Plath and psychoanalysis in terms of her cultural moment, is in order.

## Notes

1. Jacqueline Rose, *The Haunting of Sylvia Plath* (Cambridge, MA: Harvard University Press, 1991), p. xiv.
2. See Hubert I. Cohen, *Ingmar Bergman: The Art of Confession* (New York: Twayne, 1993).
3. See Alex Beam, 'The Mad Poets Society', *Atlantic Monthly* (July/August 2001), pp. 96–8.
4. Plath's copy of this volume is dated November 1962 and is held at Emory University as part of the Ted Hughes archive. It is heavily underlined and asterisked and seems to speak directly to her situation at the time.
5. Sigmund Freud, 'Some Character-Types met with in Psycho-Analytic Work', *On Creativity and the Unconscious* (New York: Harper & Row, 1958), p. 99.
6. In *A Closer Look at Ariel* (New York: Popular Library, 1973), Plath's roommate at Smith College, Nancy Hunter Steiner, quotes Plath as saying about her father, "'I adored and despised him, and I probably wished many times that he were dead. When he obliged me and died, I imagined that I had killed him'", pp. 62–3.
7. T. S. Eliot, 'Tradition and the Individual Talent', *Selected Essays* (New York: Harcourt, Brace and World, 1960), pp. 7–8, 9.
8. Jessica Benjamin, 'A Desire of One's Own: Psychoanalytic Feminism and Intersubjective Space', in Teresa de Lauretis (ed.), *Feminist Studies/Critical Studies* (Bloomington: Indiana University Press, 1986), p. 86.
9. For a more extended application of Nancy Chodorow's and Dorothy Dinnerstein's work, including discussion of Melanie Klein's importance to understanding the preoedipal phase, see Lynda Bundtzen, *Plath's Incarnations: Woman and the Creative Process* (Ann Arbor: University of Michigan Press, 1983), pp. 94–102.
10. Paula Bennett, *My Life a Loaded Gun: Dickinson, Plath, Rich and Female Creativity* (Urbana: University of Illinois Press, 1990), pp. 111, 110.

11. Michel Foucault, 'What Is an Author?', trans. Josué Harari, in Paul Rabinow (ed.), *The Foucault Reader: An Introduction to Foucault's Thought* (New York: Pantheon, 1979), pp. 101–20.

12. See Jacqueline Rose, 'Sylvia Plath – Again', *On Not Being Able to Sleep: Psychoanalysis and the Modern World* (London: Chatto & Windus, 2003), pp. 49–63.

13. Elaine Feinstein, *Ted Hughes: The Life of a Poet* (London: Weidenfeld and Nicolson, 2001), p. 54.

14. Katha Pollitt, 'Peering into the Bell Jar', review of *Birthday Letters* by Ted Hughes, *New York Times Book Review* (1 March 1998), pp. 4, 6.

15. Sigmund Freud, 'Mourning and Melancholia' (1917), trans. Joan Riviere, in Philip Rieff (ed.), *General Psychological Theory* (New York: Macmillan, 1963), p. 166.

# 4

LINDA WAGNER-MARTIN

# Plath and contemporary American poetry

To consider the effect of Sylvia Plath's writing on today's poetry scene is to marvel at the endurance of her poems. Nearly thirty years ago, Denise Levertov remarked that a poet need write only a few remarkable poems to be remembered.[1] It goes almost without saying that Plath wrote more than several such poems. More to the point is the fact that the poems of Plath's *Ariel* and, in retrospect, *The Colossus*, had the power to transform the direction of American – and to some extent, British – poetics. Here in the twenty-first century, the results of the impact of Plath's work are as pervasive as the influence of Ernest Hemingway's terse yet open prose. These effects are so commonplace that readers today no longer comment that contemporary fiction owes a great deal to Hemingway, the classic modernist. Nor do they align much of contemporary poetry with the influence of Plath's *Ariel* in 1965 and, even more dramatically, with her *Collected Poems* in 1981.

Changes in stylistic expression, in each case, marked more than shifts in the techniques of writing. Both Hemingway and Plath thrust deep into their inner lives to find what was worthy of their expression. Impolitic as it was for Hemingway to reveal the painful divergence of his Oak Park, Illinois, parents – which he did so sharply in such *In Our Time* stories as 'Indian Camp', 'The Doctor and the Doctor's Wife', and 'Cat in the Rain', even more dangerous to her family and her psyche was the insistent anger of Plath's 'Lady Lazarus', 'Daddy' and 'Medusa'. To voice these strident emotions was to unearth new ways of writing. Neither Hemingway nor Plath had earlier models to follow.

For Plath, gender complicated aesthetics. Much is made of the fact that her novel, *The Bell Jar*, published in England just weeks before her suicide on 11 February 1963, could be paired with Betty Friedan's 1963 *The Feminine Mystique*, the book about American women's 'Problem that has no name' and their frustration with their confining social roles.[2] The fact is that Plath never benefited from the language of the women's movement: there might well have been a century between Friedan and Plath. Living in England,

52

intentionally separating herself from what she saw as the stultifying suburban domesticity of the US, Sylvia Plath berated her mother for her conven-
tionality and her fear of living as she wanted – and for voting for Dwight D.
Eisenhower. In contrast, Plath enjoyed playing the role of the shocking
daughter who slept with many men, married the penniless British poet, and
supported Adlai Stevenson.[3] If Friedan's *The Feminine Mystique* had been
published before Plath's death, it would surely have been as influential for
her as Anne Sexton's early books of poems, *To Bedlam and Part Way Back*
(1960) and *All My Pretty Ones* (1962) had been. Unfortunately, it was not.
With the exception of Sexton, Plath felt as isolated – as both woman and
writer – as if she were living in Antarctica.

The irony that Sylvia Plath and her poems were to become icons of the
women's movement – the poems viewed as expressions of a previously stifled
but brilliant woman's voice – accrued from the terrible isolation of her
last months. The last years of her life, too, Plath had spent breaking free
from her excellent education, the training that was thoroughly male-centred
and focused – as was most American education – on such Anglo-identified
poets as W. H. Auden, W. B. Yeats and T. S. Eliot. But breaking free had
destructive results, too, and the shaky filaments of Plath's newly-born aesthetics were not yet strong. For all the admiration women readers had for the
Plath poems and for *The Bell Jar*, published in the US in 1971, the chorus of
women's acclaim may have separated her further from the established great
writers of English tradition.

During the later 1970s, even before Ted Hughes finished the collating and
editing of Plath's *Collected Poems*, Plath was consistently seen as one member of a group of American women poets who spoke primarily for feminist
ideology. Among those women writers were Marge Piercy and the Canadian
Margaret Atwood (both better known for their fiction), Anne Sexton, Lyn
Lifshin, Robin Morgan and Alta. Kim Whitehead, in *The Feminist Poetry
Movement*, assesses these writers' legacy as giving all poets permission 'to
write in freer, more personal modes and to challenge the tradition'. She sees
their probing the 'depths of self-exploration' as a tactic that influenced
'virtually all the poetry of the 1960s'.[4]

For poet Alicia Ostriker, this group of women writers changed the
pervasive use of myth in the making of poetry. Their work was, accordingly, 'revisionist': 'In them [their poems] the old stories are changed,
changed utterly, by female knowledge of female experience' and they consequently 'involve reevaluations of social, political, and philosophical
values'.[5] One of Ostriker's key contributions in this essay, 'The Thieves
of Language', was to emphasize the stylistic means of this achievement;
what she termed 'the gaudy and abrasive colloquialism' which

'simultaneously modernizes what is ancient and reduces the verbal glow
that we are trained to associate with mythic material'.[6] Again, to break
with traditional subject matter through the use of innovative technique was
stunning. In the recent assessment of Diane Middlebrook, the impact of
Plath's *Ariel* has never diminished: while the book sold well in the UK,
in the US 'Sylvia Plath became a public figure overnight'. As a result,
Middlebrook continues, 'Within two decades *Ariel* was standing alongside
*The Waste Land* as one of the masterpieces of twentieth-century poetry in
English, in having found a poetic mode that is the perfect medium of its
culturally significant content, and that conveys an instantly recognizable
subjectivity, one that matters to readers'.[7]

Despite such praise, few critics in the late 1970s had the means to see the
Plath oeuvre entire; critical stances changed rapidly once her *Collected
Poems* appeared in 1981.

## The *Collected Poems* of Sylvia Plath

Most of the poems included in Ted Hughes's edited collection of Plath's
poetry had been published earlier. Besides the poems in her books *The
Colossus* (UK 1960/US 1962) and *Ariel* (1965/1966), a number of her later
poems had been published in, first, limited edition chapbooks, then, two
commercially published books, *Crossing the Water* (1971) and *Winter Trees*
(1971/1972). Seeing the 274 poems as a whole, however, prompted recon-
sideration: even previously sceptical readers were brought to praise. The
book is a panorama of excellence, moving from the recognizably steady
mid-century crafted poems to the 1960s poetry that voiced brilliant new
directions for Plath, from the eloquent *Three Women* to the macabre 'Cut'
and 'Fever 103°' to the unforgettable, searing 'Lady Lazarus' and 'Daddy'. In
1982 the book won the Pulitzer Prize for Poetry, a prize almost never given
posthumously.

Reviewers from George Steiner to Katha Pollitt, Louis Simpson to
Laurence Lerner and Dave Smith, expressed their disbelief at Plath's accomplishment. In Dave Smith's words:

> During those six years Plath had learned to write what would be her poem, the
> poem which was unlike any other, the poem Ted Hughes and others call the
> *Ariel* poem ... Evanescence wasn't enough for her; she had to be the flame and
> the radiance, the electrical horse ... The *Collected Poems* is a record of how
> she learned to ride that electric horse sitting, then trotting, then galloping,
> finally becoming the current, the motion itself. The *Collected Poems* is that
> shimmering change, a gothic fairy tale with the properties of dry ice: it keeps, it
> burns, it lives.

Smith also spoke to the unquestionable influence that Plath's work had already had, by 1981, on contemporary poetry:

> If they [other writers] breathe poetry, they breathe that which has Plath in it . . . Plath's presence abides in the ways any contemporary poem gets written: in what is possible, what is assumed, and most especially in the conviction that the self and its myths – their constructions and sources, evidences, spoors – are the only true and inevitable subject for the poet.

He closes, 'We know her because the shape of her words contains the shape of our lives.'[8]

Despite the consistently high praise for Plath's poems, however, there were quibbles with Hughes's editing of them for the collection. His labelling many of her already published poems 'Juvenilia' seemed to condescend to such American magazines as *Harper's Magazine* and *Mademoiselle* where her early writing had often appeared. Similarly, 'Initiation' and 'Sunday at the Mintons', two stories which Plath had published in *Seventeen* and *Mademoiselle* respectively, appear in a separate section from the 'more successful short stories and prose pieces' in Hughes's edition of *Johnny Panic and the Bible of Dreams*. Most importantly as far as Hughes's editing of the *Collected Poems* was concerned, there was consternation at the revelation that the selection and ordering of the poems in the published edition of *Ariel* was not the same as that which Plath had left in manuscript.[9]

Nevertheless, from that time forward, Dave Smith's premise proved true. American poetry, in particular, surged into new experiments, new challenges – what was earlier assumed had given way to what was, or what might be, possible. With the Pulitzer Prize, Plath's influence was no longer limited to women writers. All poets felt the need to try for the impossible.

### Influence

Influence is slippery to determine. There is, in Smith's words, the amorphous sense that the writer in question has known Plath's work, has been in some manner personally freed by her daring effects. During the first decade of Plath's influence – which was dependent largely on *Ariel* – she was often read alongside Anne Sexton, and sometimes John Berryman, W. D. Snodgrass and Robert Lowell. As confessional poets, these loosely linked writers were thought to be drawing on real life and, often, on intimate experience. As critics managed to discredit that quasi-autobiographical impulse as inappropriate for the best of lyric poetry, the concept of Plath as one member of a group faded. She remained the most important of the five poets, casting her shadow over both Sexton and Lowell; and she retains that prominence into the twenty-first century.

Readers isolated the elements of the most successful confessional poems as personal, voiced in the sometimes harsh colloquial rhythms of the twentieth century; for poets, however, the way the poet achieved effects was of more interest. For other practising poets, Plath's poems became try pieces: rapid rhythms, curt rhymes, the poem as a whole spun around metaphor, sometimes one, sometimes several. Young poets and those new to the publishing process did not care if their work seemed imitative. In the 1970s the world of little magazines was awash with Plath effects, just as the modernist world of earlier decades had been inundated with the typographical tricks of young e. e. cummings-wannabes.

Separate from the thousands of imitative poems was the more recognizable kind of patterning – the echo, a mode in which the writer consciously draws on lines, phrases, imagery from the Plath oeuvre, expecting the material to be recognized. In the dialogue between the later poet and the originating one (here, Plath), the reader is forced to become a participant. Part of the success of the poet who aims for echoes is that the reader is privy to the source of the material.

One of the best examples of this kind of influence is the accomplished American poet Susan Fromberg Schaeffer, now better known as a novelist. Her 1972 collection, *The Witch and the Weather Report*, from the small New York press Seven Woods, replayed a number of Plath themes – mother-daughter conflicts, the stability of knowing one's ancestors, metaphoric refigurations of the common and the domestic ('Housewife', 'The Hills', 'Meditations'). In a matter-of-fact voice, the Schaeffer persona delivers surprising lines: 'Some day, I shall walk out of this, as out of a house. / The door will slam, and the house will fall over / Like a prop . . .'[10] Or, from 'Housewife', the macabre tooth image, 'I did not feel this pain, not then, / Almost in my mouth, I wiggle this life / And find it loose' (p. 16).

A clearer echo of Plath powers the tercets of Schaeffer's 'The Child Proves She Is Immortal' where the subject faces a firing squad, her skin perforated: 'She didn't mind the wind whistling through // And besides, no one looked twice' (p. 25). The repetition in the poem builds to an eventual death (at the insistence of the protagonist's mother) but the tone remains comic: 'She slashed her wrists; they didn't even bleed. / She swallowed sleeping pills like popcorn / And watched the Late Late Show twice' (p. 26). Besides Schaeffer's use of quick-moving tercets so reminiscent of Plath, she also probes the unexpectedly bleak image, as in 'Famine Days' ('Oh God, in this disrepair / It is myself I eat') or in 'The Witch and the Weather Report', filled with grim old bones that are 'cold stainless steel' (pp. 38, 46). In 'Elegy for Sylvia Plath' the poet mourns the imaginative recreation of Plath's death; she watches as the earth 'spins, spins you away' (p. 52).

By 1980, in *The Bible of the Beasts of the Little Field*, Schaeffer's voice has grown more consistent. Still reflecting some of the cadences of Plath's late poems, the poet persona is stoically calm, as in 'Rest': 'the bones / Sleep inside the body // Like sleek white lemurs'[11] or elegiac, as in the chantlike 'The Book of Hours', 'The Book of Fear', 'The Living' and 'The Windows'.

Amid poems about moons and enigmatic women characters, Schaeffer's poem 'Love' has other somewhat comic echoes as she deals with the brutality of marriage, a woman's death, the poultice of housekeeping. The images of bald eyes recall Plath's 'The Colossus' and 'The Disquieting Muses', among others: 'I will bandage the walls with drapes, / And wig the bald windows with ruffledom. / The eyes of the house shall not stare'. Much about the characteristics of Schaeffer's poetry can be transferred to the feminist poems of the 1970s and the 1980s, work by such contemporary poets as Sharon Olds, Marge Piercy, Margaret Atwood and Ellen Bass available in Florence Howe's classic collection *No More Masks, An Anthology of Twentieth Century American Women Poets*.[12] I except Adrienne Rich from this discussion because she had won the Yale Series of Younger Poets prize and was a well-published poet some years before Plath. Her own development to what has become a magisterial maturity owed less to the confessional influence than it did to such earlier poets as Muriel Rukeyser and Louise Bogan, and to the interplay between her own – and others' – compelling prose. For Jahan Ramazani, however, Rich, too, has been influenced by Plath's *Ariel* poems – beginning soon after that book's publication.[13]

The wryly-voiced persona in Marge Piercy's poetry, frequently caught in run-on sentence constructions, brought home the angry and sometimes comic statement with an emphatic close, for example, in 'The Woman in the Ordinary': 'It is time to bust out of girlscout camp' (Howe, *Masks*, p. 274). Ellen Bass's unabashedly sexual poems recast the weird catalogues Plath loved to play with, as in 'In Celebration', where emergent love is like 'the head of a turtle, like / an accordion, like / an expandable drinking glass' (Howe, *Masks*, p. 402). A later poet, the accomplished Rita Dove, uses the same technique, along with the acerbic flatness of a distant persona, in the Beulah poems from her 1986 collection *Thomas and Beulah*.

Dove's 'After Reading *Mickey in the Night Kitchen* for the Third Time Before Bed' begins 'My daughter spreads her legs / to find her vagina: hairless' (Howe, *Masks*, p. 443). Such lines call our attention to the fact that it is not only the appropriation of myth – as Alicia Ostriker saw – but the writers' choices of language that mark much contemporary women's poetry. What is 'polite'? What is 'literary'? What is suitably 'ladylike'? Plath's innovative poems from the early 1960s had pointed the way to this kind of innovative and surprising diction. Sharon Olds in 'First Sex' describes a woman's male partner's ejaculation (Howe, *Masks*, p. 348). Through their choices of language as well as subjects, such poets may be said to be not just appropriating myth, but creating it as well.

During the later 1980s and the 1990s, a number of women poets in the US abandoned some of the more strident themes of feminist-inspired work (after all, what writer could compete with Margaret Atwood's 'Power Politics' or Adrienne Rich's 'Diving into the Wreck'?). The modulations of Carolyn Forche's art, as she moved from the image-centred poems of her Yale Younger Poets award-winning *Gathering the Tribes* to her 1994 *The Angel of History*, are in some ways reflective of the turn to pervasively darker themes as the century ended.[14] Yet even as Forche began writing in webbed, elongated lines – almost meditative – for both her 1994 book and her 2003 collection, *Blue Hour*, many of the tactics she had earlier borrowed from Plath's poems reasserted themselves. Forche's 'Prayer' opens with a catalogue of strangely unique elements: 'Tin spoon, teacup, tremble of tray, carpet hanging from sorrow's balcony'.[15] In the title poem Forche extends her merging of concrete and abstract, as if emphasizing the fluidity of image and memory: 'A viola, night-voiced, calls into its past but nothing comes. // A woman alone rows across the lake' (*Blue Hour*, p. 2). The image recalls Plath's 'Crossing the Water'. In her surreal montage the poet draws out the sharp imagery of both sound and sight, centred in the more human visibility of the woman persona – her whole life encapsulated in these lines.

In 'On Earth', Forche's monumental long poem from *Blue Hour*, which is written in the Gnostic abecedarian hymn format, she presents 'the silence of a new language / the soft houses of heaven / the soldiers' moonlit helmets' alongside 'the story of empty rice sacks / the street's memory of abandoned shoes' (pp. 58–9). Filled with fragmentary lines from some of the world's great writers, this poem answers Eliot's *The Waste Land* in providing a heart of human awareness, fed by cultural memory as well as personal, whorled around scenes of spiritual triumph. In the work of Forche and such other poets of her generation as Michael Palmer, Robert Haas and Joy Harjo, the use of personal myth has become aesthetically complicated by a consciousness of the world's anguish. Half a century ago, William Carlos Williams demanded that poets use techniques to express the real ('No ideas but in things'). Today's poets have expanded a definition of 'things' to include memory, evanescence, joy, pain and the spiritual; Plath would surely have made such a transition easily.[16]

This merging, and emerging, aesthetic appears to govern the work of the younger poet Adrian Oktenberg, as she writes her tersely metaphoric untitled poems in *The Bosnia Elegies*: 'Away we fled houses past suburbs outside the town / Outside Do you understand?' (*sic*). If the poet used titles, this one might well be her title poem, for it ends with the stunning metaphor of 'All Bosnia // is a towering mountain standing in its own blood.'[17]

Neither Oktenberg nor Forche will be remembered for their creation of comedy, but perhaps the time lapse – and world conditions – between their later generation of poets and that of Sylvia Plath is partly responsible for the tonal difference. Several of the more interesting critical studies of Plath – Jahan Ramazani's *Poetry of Mourning* and Christina Britzolakis's *Sylvia Plath and the Theatre of Mourning* – emphasize that much of her work is elegiac, evoking the poignant image, its loss and the speaker's reaction to the loss. Ramazani's critique reads Plath in an historical line from Thomas Hardy and Wilfred Owen through Wallace Stevens, Langston Hughes and W. H. Auden to her and some of her contemporaries (creators of what he calls 'the American family elegy') and past these writers to Seamus Heaney. Ramazani points out that much modern elegiac poetry is 'anti-elegiac (in generic terms) and melancholic (in psychological terms)' and sees some of the poets he treats as more influential than others (*Poetry of Mourning*, p. xi). Plath is influential, Ramazani contends, because she shatters earlier traditions of female elegies as submissive, consolatory. Rather 'she attacks the dead, herself, and elegiac tradition more vehemently and persistently than any other major poet. Plath's patricidal mourning is inextricable from a melancholic violence toward herself' (p. xiii).

Ramazani sees her ability to express 'the mourner's aggression toward the dead, summoning a violent anger that earlier elegists had channeled into homosocial bonding, professional competition, and wars of patrilineal succession' as one reason why her poems were so quickly adopted by feminists: 'The daughter's elegy for the father was among the subgenres that enabled Plath's generation of women writers to voice anti-patriarchal anger in poetry' (pp. 262–3). In tandem, he sees Plath's 'self-elegies' ('Tulips', 'Ariel', 'Fever 103°', 'Getting There' and 'Lady Lazarus') as even more significant because they are both death poems in content and 'commentary on death poems', creating a technique that allows Plath to emphasize the constructedness of the poetry: 'dying too is theatrical – we perform death for others' (p. 285).

Less concerned with the characteristics of the elegy, Britzolakis treats many of Plath's poems from the perspective of performative art, an approach which confirms the importance of the aesthetic over the autobiographical. Contradicting the too-ready premise that Plath's poems changed as she matured – what this critic calls 'the psychobiographical', Britzolakis sees her late aesthetics as 'the product of a reflexive engagement with the modernist and surrealist legacy of twentieth-century art'. This reading creates a self-reflexive Plath, 'a highly rhetorical poet whose work is shaped by an awareness of audience, of the complex legacies of literary tradition, and of the cultural authority wielded by poetic discourse'.[18]

## Tradition

Several recent critical studies have argued that Plath was at her best when she worked within recognizable formal strictures – as if to place her back into a critical line of descent that extends directly from T. S. Eliot's essays and the poems that reflect those. For Helen Vendler, writing in *Coming of Age as a Poet: Milton, Keats, Eliot, Plath*, Plath's strongest poems – with some exceptions – occur in *The Colossus*.[19] For Deborah Forbes, Plath's abandonment of ostensible formal control poses great problems (she calls 'Edge' and 'Daddy' 'very imperfect poems, from a formal standpoint').[20] Forbes assumes a kind of perfect integration in earlier Plath poems, and thus can find no reason for her breaking away from that control: 'Her later poetry, rather than consolidating this unification in an integrated act of self-expression, actually fractures what was previously united, in particular the unification of poet and speaker. It is this fracture, the opening of the gap between form and content, rather than its suturing, that releases a new kind of voice.' The problem with the new voice, according to Forbes, is that the poet has lost both 'formal self-control and moral self-control' (*Sincerity's Shadow*, p. 75).

That these two studies take, at best, a less sympathetic stance towards Plath's breaking away from traditional form may be a signal that the reputation of Sylvia Plath may be about to take on new layers of critique. Known as the brilliant innovator, the writer who brooked no inheritance that she did not tamper with as she created her own uses for an effect, a theme or a structure, Plath may become a kind of phoenix of the myriad styles of modernism and incipient postmodernism that she had studied and experienced: Mina Loy, Stevie Smith, Wallace Stevens, Gregory Corso, Thom Gunn, Anne Sexton, William Carlos Williams and all the rest. But for now, early on in the twenty-first century, Jacqueline Rose may have given us the most telling lens for considering Plath and her work.

Firmly set within the daily popular culture of her times – mostly American but increasingly British – Plath worked into her poems elements that readers could both understand and relate to. It is these disturbing parts of the poetry – an art itself of the highest and most elite reputation – which give readers and critics pause. Rose points out that none of us should fence Plath into an elite space where the real force of her voice is limited. Her writing reflects the contemporary confusion about both meaning and the forms of culture:

> As divided as Plath's writing is in relation to identity or subjectivity, so it is in relation to the multiple destinations of the culture for which she writes. She participates in them, she provides her own commentary on them ... *inside* the writing itself. The problem and divisions of culture are a reiterated theme of her prose writing ... Plath is a hybrid, crossing over the boundaries of cultural difference with an extraordinary and almost transgressive ease.[21]

And because she is so omnipresent, she 'haunts' our culture. Both 'execrated and idolized, Plath hovers between the furthest poles of positive and negative appraisal ... she lays bare the forms of psychic investment which lie, barely concealed, behind the processes through which a culture – Western literary culture – evaluates and perpetuates itself' (Rose, *Haunting*, p. 1).

Neither negative nor positive: above all, as Jacqueline Rose and Dave Smith both emphasize, the art of Sylvia Plath brings readers into the aesthetic process as great writing seldom does. There will be only scant attention to the details of the ways in which her followers mimic her work, attempting to incorporate those sometimes unimaginable lines, insights, metaphors into their own processes, until the cumulative effect of a 'Plath poem' in the oeuvre of many other poets cannot be ignored.

## Notes

1. Conversation with the author (spring 1976).
2. See, among others, Catharine R. Stimpson's 'Literature as Radical Statement', in Emory Elliott (ed.), *Columbia Literary History of the United States* (New York: Columbia University Press, 1988), pp. 1060–76.
3. See my *Sylvia Plath: A Biography* (New York: Simon & Schuster, 1987), p. 90.
4. Kim Whitehead, *The Feminist Poetry Movement* (Jackson: University Press of Mississippi, 1996), pp. 12, 5.
5. Alicia Ostriker, 'The Thieves of Language: Women Poets and Revisionary Myth-making', in Diane Wood Middlebrook and Marilyn Yalom (eds.), *Coming to Light: American Women Poets in the Twentieth Century* (Ann Arbor: University of Michigan Press, 1985), pp. 14, 27.
6. Ibid, p. 28.
7. Diane Middlebrook, *Her Husband: Hughes and Plath – A Marriage* (New York: Viking, 2003), p. 227.
8. Dave Smith, 'Sylvia Plath, the Electric Horse', in Linda Wagner (ed.), *Sylvia Plath: The Critical Heritage* (London and New York: Routledge, 1988), pp. 273–4, 269, 276.
9. For an overview of these issues, see Lynda K. Bundtzen, *The Other Ariel* (Amherst: University of Massachusetts Press, 2001).

10. Susan Fromberg Schaeffer, 'Exit', in *The Witch and the Weather Report* (New York: Seven Woods, 1972), p. 21.

11. Susan Fromberg Schaeffer, 'Rest', in *The Bible of the Beasts of the Little Field* (New York: E. P. Dutton, 1980), p. 2.

12. Florence Howe (ed.), *No More Masks: An Anthology of Twentieth-Century American Women Poets* (New York: Harper Collins, 1993).

13. Jahan Ramazani, *Poetry of Mourning: The Modern Elegy from Hardy to Heaney* (Chicago: University of Chicago Press, 1994), p. 293.

14. Elizabeth Dewberry Vaughn's 1990 novel *Many Things Have Happened Since He Died*, like Beth Henley's play (and film) *Crimes of the Heart* a decade before, recast Plath's quasi-comic treatment of suicide in *The Bell Jar* into a more contemporary mode.

15. Carolyn Forche, *Blue Hour: Poems* (New York: Harper Collins, 2003), p. 21.

16. See my *Sylvia Plath: A Literary Life*, 2nd edition (Basingstoke: Palgrave Macmillan, 2003), p. 92.

17. Adrian Oktenberg, *The Bosnia Elegies* (Ashfield: Paris Press, 1997), p. 57.

18. Christina Britzolakis, *Sylvia Plath and the Theatre of Mourning* (Oxford: Clarendon Press, 1999), p. 5.

19. Helen Hennessy Vendler, *Coming of Age as a Poet: Milton, Keats, Eliot, Plath* (Cambridge, MA: Harvard University Press, 2003).

20. Deborah Forbes, *Sincerity's Shadow: Self-Consciousness in British Romantic and Mid-Twentieth-Century American Poetry* (Cambridge, MA: Harvard University Press, 2004), pp. 112–15.

21. Jacqueline Rose, *The Haunting of Sylvia Plath* (London: Virago, 1991), p. 167.

# 5

ALICE ENTWISTLE

# Plath and contemporary British poetry

## Tradition

Sylvia Plath has been lionized by a host of scholars and critics, by successive generations of poets and by an enormous readership. Her voice resonates insistently through postwar twentieth-century British poetics. As Ruth Padel observes, crisply, 'Plath . . . is a permanent influence'.[1]

Sylvia Plath and Ted Hughes were married in June 1956. Arguably, the ceremony set in train the sequence of events which would propel Plath into the critical limelight on both sides of the Atlantic. It now seems ironic that 1956, treated by Hughes as a 'watershed' in Plath's development (*CP*, pp. 13–17),[2] also saw the publication of *New Lines*, the anthology edited by Robert Conquest which explained and enshrined the poetic practice of the so-called 'Movement'.[3] This loose grouping of writers, Philip Larkin at its centre, has shadowed postwar British poetry ever since. It was their under-stated, self-consciously disciplined, 'academic-administrative verse, polite, knowledgeable, efficient, polished, and, in its quiet way, even intelligent' which Al Alvarez's anthology *The New Poetry* was openly intended to counter.[4] Alvarez's decision to include Plath in the 1966 second edition did much to underwrite her existing reputation. Further, in ranging her – along-side names like John Berryman and Thom Gunn, Geoffrey Hill and of course Hughes – against what Alvarez dismissively calls the 'gentility' of postwar British poetry, the anthology constructed Plath's distinctive poetics as influentially radical. It still seems so nowadays. As Padel reminds us, 'Plath is deep inside most British poets today, both women and men. Not because she is a feminist icon, but because of her poetic brilliance: extraordinary linguistic control, wit, imagery and risk; how her poems move, laughter in the face of despair' (*52 Ways*, p. 44).

Padel's reluctance to gender Plath's influence confirms the reach of a presence which Edna Longley boldly parallels with that of T. S. Eliot: 'Their combined influence on British and Irish poetry is incalculable.'[5] Yet

63

while Plath is one of the few women poets to have consistently attracted critical interest and respect from men, there has been little scholarly discussion of the wider effects of her poetic influence. Peter Childs, for example, presents her as a 'cardinal example of the engaged, committed poets of the new poetry'. Contending that Plath's 'direct experience of suffering is inextricably tied up in her poetry with fundamental postwar issues of anonymity, torture and pain, the relationship between the individual and the mass-produced, the ownership of bodies and the production of identities', Childs implies that Plath's poetics resonated with and beyond her own historical moment, in part because he contrives to skirt the issue of gender altogether.[6] Martin Booth takes a broader view of the impact of what he calls 'a newness in the poetic firmament'. Isolating 'the unique use of language that opened up the floodgates on conservatism in poetry', Booth claims that 'Plath made it possible for one to speak of the most basic pains and truths without self-consciousness or equivocation'. Although I, and others, relish Plath's self-consciousness and equivocation, Booth's preparedness to justify his sense of her influence is refreshing, as is his assertion that 'since many males also took wholeheartedly to her poetry ... for the first time in a long time ... Plath showed that a woman could be a prime force in poetry'.[7] Since the focus of this discussion rests on Plath's impact on British women poets, I will only flag some of the men who might be argued to have absorbed her example in different ways and for different reasons. These would include, among her contemporaries, Seamus Heaney, Thom Gunn and Ted Hughes (although, as Tracy Brain resignedly notes, it is habitually presumed that the ideas flowed from husband to wife, not vice versa).[8] There is much work to be done on the ways in which later generations of male poets (like Douglas Dunn, Peter Redgrove, Tony Harrison, Hugo Williams, Matthew Sweeney and Duncan Bush) draw on Plath's example.[9]

As one of the best-known women poets of the twentieth century, Plath has helped to ensure that successive generations of women writers are not left, as Elizabeth Barrett Browning famously felt, bereft of literary 'grandmothers'. She was not alone, of course, but it has taken several decades to make many of the names now beginning to cohere into a loose-limbed female canon generally available. On the other hand, Plath makes a problematic exemplar, too easily cast as unstable and self-destructive: the morbid emphases of her work, the argument goes, are confirmed and compounded by her suicide. Vital, visible, innovative as her example has always seemed, Plath's poetry, like her name, can appear relentlessly and unhelpfully to model nothing but its own self-silencing.

Critical discourse is beginning (at last) to work her poetry free of its biographical burden, but it is harder to disentangle Plath's biography from the influence of her poetry, not least because of the way in which her writing helped to foreground female experience, played out amid the tensions of the domestic – or at least private – context. The effects of this have been controversial. As I have argued elsewhere, the early postwar period, in which women are being tugged simultaneously towards and away from the workplace by state and society alike, frames an ambivalent concern with domesticity among many women poets.[10] For these, like Plath, the home becomes a paradoxical source of inspiration, savoured as stable haven in which a woman's changing identity (from daughter to wife to mother) is secured and nurtured in loving, generative relationships, but resented as inescapable burden, its routines and conventions frustrating any attempt to make imaginative use of the very creativity it nourishes. Such tensions can be detected in poetic elders like Denise Levertov, Ruth Fainlight and Anne Stevenson, as well as successors like Eavan Boland, Medbh McGuckian, Carol Rumens, Gillian Clarke and Elaine Feinstein.[11]

Their shared sociohistorical and cultural context suggests why such writers gravitate towards such a subject at such a time; they can be under-stood as reflecting and contributing to a collective reclaiming and revaluing of female experience and identity in postwar Western culture. As Cora Kaplan explains:

> If it was slightly more feasible for a woman to choose poetry as a profession in the postwar world, it was definitely not easier to practice it in the cultural and political climate of the 1950s. Sylvia Plath wrote almost all of her published poetry in that decade and it rings with an angry alienation which is both personal and political.[12]

Having just compared herself with Plath, Stevenson says of her own collection, *Correspondences* (1974), 'All the anger, the confusion, the misery and the doubt I experienced during the fifties and sixties went into it, and because they were a woman's angers and miseries, they exposed part of the general consciousness of the age – a part that in the past had been suppressed.'[13] Stevenson's comments confirm and are confirmed by Padel's:

> When feminism got going in Britain in the seventies it affected poetry instantly, but two elements tended to ghettoize women's poetry as a specialist sub-category. One was subject matter. Seventies feminism claimed domesticity – domestic space, childcare, women's work, lives, fabrics, memories – as a valid subject for poetry along with the earth mother, earth goddess role for the poet ... The other was emotion. (*52 Ways*, p. 43)

Perhaps inevitably, Plath's influence has been detected in both the changing subject matter and the emotional freight of postwar women's poetry. For

Childs, critical debates over the relationship between women, poetry and politics may be said to develop from Plath's 'attempts to write a poetry beyond the male literary tradition ... though she had no established political voice to use in her poetry, she engendered one for others' (*Twentieth Century*, pp. 161–2). Kaplan is blunter: 'Plath has made it possible for women to "curse and write"' (*Salt*, p. 290). Certainly (as critics are in the habit of pointing out) many of the poets who emerged in the 1970s, including those from the writing collectives of the Women's Liberation Movement, cite Plath as inspiration if not influence.[14] Yet while the survival of respected names like Judith Kazantzis, Michèle Roberts, Gillian Allnutt and Jeni Couzyn now testify to the power of her legacy, Plath is also damned by association with 'feminist' poetry. A contemporaneous review of one anthology complains about 'the general maelstrom of feminist angst. The ghost of Sylvia Plath haunts page after page.' It concludes, 'Miss Plath's influence on young ... poets seems to have been wholly disastrous.'[15]

Fleur Adcock defuses the problems of 'feminist angst' by acclaiming Plath's 'technical ability to transform her emotions and experiences into literature and not just self-expression'.[16] The implication that self-expression is not literary has been hotly contested, especially in relation to feminist poetry. Claire Buck, for example, argues that Plath's feminist followers reformulate 'the confessional model inherited from Plath and Anne Sexton ... as a poetics of consciousness-raising in which women's personal experience becomes central to the poetry, but only insofar as its status as private and individual experience is challenged by means of a feminist political perspective'.[17] That debate notwithstanding, Adcock's emphasis on transformation suggestively licenses the nature of Plath's poetic legacy in ways beyond choice of subject matter and/or emotional stance. Her argument is endorsed by practitioners and commentators alike.

## Influence

Eavan Boland and Carol Rumens both encountered Plath in their twenties. The former, deep in her literary studies, was initially disturbed:

> She'd been dead about a year then ... I was a student at Trinity ... being taught the canon, which seemed both nourishing and remote. Then suddenly, here was this young dead woman whose story made me shudder ... I was listening in a kind of fog of male poets dismissing her work as 'therapy', or else male critics discussing her suicide as extremism. In both cases I flinched from this voyeurism ... I was struggling to work out ... some very preliminary connections between women and poetry. Her image was almost too new and too raw.[18]

By contrast, Rumens was unaware of Plath's suicide. Her response was less complex, more emphatic:

> When, in my early twenties, I first read Sylvia Plath's late poems, I knew almost nothing of her biography ... I managed to divine that the writer probably had two small children, as I did. A great poet who was a mother and had two children! This was biography enough to set the seal on my ... apprenticeship.[19]

Sean O'Brien has noted that for Rumens 'the task of poetry is that it should imagine the possibility of *becoming*'.[20] Whether one understands this requirement in terms of the process of her personal and professional development, or aesthetically – or both – it is tempting to retrace Rumens's conviction, at least in part, to the lessons of that early apprenticeship:

> Reading Plath was totally interlinked with my adult experiences – sex, childbirth, marriage. I had felt these things were beyond the reach of poetry. So ... she was very important in enabling me to go on ... [I]n an odd way I felt I had met some version of myself ... The imagery, the voice – I connected at once ... I liked the way she could make personal subjects resonate and feel big.[21]

Such an 'enabling' was to have a lasting effect; the international recognition which Rumens would subsequently earn for herself was always anchored in that same ability to 'make personal subjects resonate'. Rumens is a much more explicitly political writer than Plath could ever be argued to be, yet poems like 'Two Women', 'A Meeting of Innocents: A Birthday Sequence', 'Walking Out' and 'To the Spirit of My House', among numerous other examples, confirm that the cultural reach of her poetics of becoming, as O'Brien has it, is habitually secured in and defined by the immediate and personal experience (never, of course, necessarily the poet's own).[22]

Rumens's latest book, the compendious *Poems 1968–2004*, contextualizes the emergence and subsequent toning down of what she has called her 'Plathy voice', not least in some of the poems in 'Uncollected Poems' (1968–81), and in early collections like *A Strange Girl in Bright Colours* (1973), *A Necklace of Mirrors* (1978) and *Unplayed Music* (1981). One explicit tribute is 'Sylvia Plath' (Rumens, *Poems*, pp. 82–3); a much later reference in 'Against Posterity' – addressed to a 'marvellous sisterhood' of 'older poets' and first collected in *Hex* – seems to reproach more than commend Plath's 'hard rage'.[23]

For her part, Eavan Boland learnt how to mobilize Plath's difficult example only when she began to reunderstand how it worked. She retraces this to the experience of reading *Winter Trees*: 'the book and the world outside the room and the children inside it and the language of those poems began to establish some rich, shifting and shared boundary. That's when I began to see the superb nature poet she was ... and to dismiss forever the views of her work as hysterical or theatrical.' Her ambivalence sharpened into respect, Boland was prompted to reappraise her own poetics in an unexpected way:

> When I reread ['Night Dances' and 'Nick and the Candlestick'], it fascinates and moves me how this young woman ... did something radical to the perspective of the nature poem: she stopped addressing nature and she became it ... I felt as if I was caught, or even captured, in some new and powerful world where nature began and the poem ended ... That part of her work helped me think that the poems of *Night Feed* were actually nature poems. And that gave a dignity to the way I thought about what I was doing. (Randolph, 'Backwards', p. 45)

In both cases Plath nudges another (female) poet into a transformed awareness of herself, and urges her into a reconstructed sense of her own creative possibilities. To some extent this reinforces Cath Stowers's claim that Plath's self-conscious literary repossession of her own body not only constitutes 'the starting point for her imaginative autonomy', but extends into 'an assertion of the female poet's activity and an exercise of the artist's power to reshape the nature given to her in free forms of energy and desire'.[24] It is in this territory that poets as diverse as Adcock, Feinstein, McGuckian, Elizabeth Bartlett, Penelope Shuttle and Grace Nichols can be argued to find company with Plath.[25] In her conclusion Stowers avers that Plath's depiction of a 'woman's body in and for herself, in assertions of independent creative powers ... give[s] body to a new body of women's writing' ('Revolutionary', p. 164). The claim is validated in the work of accomplished and powerful poets like Padel, Vicki Feaver and Linda France, to name just three. While a younger generation (including Anne Rouse, Deryn Rees Jones, Sarah Maguire, Tessa Rose Chester, Julia Copus and Jane Duran) is only too eager, meanwhile, to acknowledge Plath's significance, it seems just as important, somehow, that a poet like Selima Hill should seek to assert her distance from Plath.[26]

Adcock claims that 'Sylvia Plath has been innocently responsible for a mob of more or less feeble imitators: powerfully individual poets usually make bad models' (*Women's Poetry*, p. 13). Surely, to make any kind of mark on posterity, a poet can only be 'powerfully individual', which almost by definition will attract 'a mob of more or less feeble imitators'? But this does not mean that important poets must make bad models. Arguably, their influence is better judged by the ways in which any example can be shown to anchor, and/or resonate in the work of the 'powerfully individual poets' who emerge in his or her wake. There seems little doubt that without Plath, late twentieth-century British poetics would look rather different.

# Notes

1. Ruth Padel, *52 Ways of Looking at a Poem: A Poem for Every Week of the Year* (London: Vintage, 2004), p. 34.

2. In his 'Introduction' to Plath's *Collected Poems*, Hughes nominates 'early 1956' as a decisive moment in her development as a poet: 'because from later this year come the earliest poems of her first collection, *The Colossus*. And from this time I worked closely with her and watched the poems being written' (*CP*, p. 16). Poems written before 1956 he controversially labels 'Juvenilia' and prints as an appendix at the end of the book. Diane Middlebrook argues that Hughes's 'Introduction' 'establishes 1956 as the year Plath became the poet we want to collect. It is the year they met. By placing himself inside the story from its beginnings, Hughes suggests that neither could be written about, as poets, without reference to the other' (*Her Husband: Hughes and Plath – A Marriage* (New York: Viking, 2003), p. 263).

3. Robert Conquest, *New Lines: An Anthology* (London: Macmillan, 1956).

4. A. Alvarez (ed.), *The New Poetry* (Harmondsworth: Penguin, 1962), p. 19.

5. Edna Longley (ed.), *The Bloodaxe Book of Twentieth Century Poetry* (Tarset: Bloodaxe Books, 2000), p. 21.

6. Peter Childs, *The Twentieth Century in Poetry: A Critical Survey* (London: Routledge, 1999), p. 138.

7. Martin Booth, *British Poetry 1964–1984: Driving Through the Barricades* (London: Routledge & Kegan Paul, 1985), pp. 188–90.

8. See Tracy Brain, *The Other Sylvia Plath* (London: Longman, 2001), pp. 191–4. Remarks made by Hughes bear her out; see Ted Hughes, 'The Art of Poetry LXXI', in *Paris Review* 134 (1995), pp. 54–94 (p. 77).

9. See, for example, Hugo Williams, 'Leaping Versus Blabbing', in W. N. Herbert and Matthew Hollis (eds.), *Strong Words: Modern Poets on Modern Poetry* (Newcastle upon Tyne: Bloodaxe Books, 2000), p. 231, and Matthew Sweeney, 'Matthew Sweeney', in Clare Brown and Don Paterson (eds.), *Don't Ask What I Mean: Poets in their Own Words* (London: Picador, 2003), p. 279.

10. Jane Dowson and Alice Entwistle, *A History of Twentieth Century British Women's Poetry* (Cambridge: Cambridge University Press, 2005). See especially chapter 6: 'The postwar generation and the paradox of home'.

11. The parallels between Plath, Fainlight (her fellow American and friend), Stevenson (another American and also her biographer) and Levertov (who emigrated to the US in the mid-1950s) would repay detailed scrutiny.

12. Cora Kaplan (ed.), *Salt and Bitter and Good: Three Centuries of English and American Women Poets* (New York and London: Paddington Press, 1975), p. 289.

13. Anne Stevenson, 'Writing As a Woman', in Mary Jacobus (ed.), *Women Writing and Writing about Women* (London: Croom Helm, 1979), p. 175.

14. See Janet Montefiore, *Arguments of Heart and Mind: Selected Essays 1977–2000* (London: Macmillan, 2002), p. 35.

15. 'All whimsy were the anthologists', review of Eva Figes, Abigail Mozley and Dinah Livingstone (eds.), *Women Their World* (1980), in *PN Review* 7.5 (1980), p. 56.

16. Fleur Adcock (ed.), *The Faber Book of Twentieth Century Women's Poetry* (London: Faber and Faber, 1987), p. 5.

17. Claire Buck, 'Poetry and the Women's movement in postwar Britain', in James Acheson and Romana Huk (eds.), *Contemporary British Poetry: Essays in Theory and Criticism* (Albany, NY: State University of New York, 1996), p. 91. See also Sally Minogue, 'Prescriptions and Proscriptions: Feminist Criticism and Contemporary Poetry', in Sally Minogue (ed.), *Some Problems for Feminist Criticism* (London: Routledge, 1990), pp. 179–236, and Clair Wills, 'Contemporary Women's Poetry: Experimentalism and the Expressive Voice', in *Critical Quarterly* 36.3 (1994), pp. 34–52.

18. Jody Allen Randolph, 'A Backwards Look: An Interview with Eavan Boland', in *PN Review* 26.5 (2000), pp. 44–5.

19. Carol Rumens, 'Sense and sensibility', review of Tim Kendall, *Sylvia Plath: A Critical Study*, in *Poetry Review* 92.1 (2002), p. 53.

20. Sean O'Brien, *The Deregulated Muse* (Newcastle upon Tyne: Bloodaxe Books, 1998), p. 155.

21. Rumens, interview with Alice Entwistle, conducted July 2004 (unpublished).

22. Carol Rumens, *Poems 1968–2004* (Tarset: Bloodaxe Books, 2004), pp. 197, 285–90, 299, 341.

23. Carol Rumens, *Hex* (Newcastle upon Tyne: Bloodaxe Books, 2002).

24. Cath Stowers, 'Sylvia Plath's Revolutionary Wieldings of the Female Body', in Vicki Bertram (ed.), *Kicking Daffodils: Twentieth Century Women Poets* (Edinburgh: Edinburgh University Press, 1997), p. 160.

25. See, for example, Carol Rumens, 'Strange Territory: Elizabeth Bartlett interviewed', *Poetry Review* 85.1 (1995) p. 20; Grace Nichols, 'The poetry I feel closest to', in Herbert and Hollis, *Strong Words*, p. 212.

26. See Anne Rouse, 'Anne Rouse', in Brown and Patterson, *Don't Ask*, p. 251; the profiles contained in *Poetry Review* 84.1, 86.4 (1996/7); and Selima Hill, 'God's Velvet Cushions', in Alison Mark and Deryn Rees-Jones (eds.), *Contemporary Women's Poetry: Reading/Writing/Practice* (London: Macmillan, 2000), pp. 28–9.

# PART II

# Works

# 6

STEVEN GOULD AXELROD

# The poetry of Sylvia Plath

Sylvia Plath produced one of the most riveting poetic oeuvres in English. Her poems reveal a perspective and a language use that are utterly unique. Yet they are also related to the Renaissance, Romantic, modernist and Cold War rhetorics she inherited and to the postmodernism that her work helped to generate through both positive and negative example. Plath's poems seethe with anger, hope, desire and disappointment. They glow with brilliant turns of phrase: 'What is so real as the cry of a child? / A rabbit's cry may be wilder / But it has no soul' ('Kindness'). They construct breathtaking images of the injured body and psyche – the 'trepanned veteran, / Dirty girl' of 'Cut', for example. And they evoke their social and political milieu in a telling way, expressing the dilemmas of a woman enmeshed in a sexist, racist and classist social structure, yearning for affirmation, 'waist-deep in history'. Plath's poems plunge into the contradictions of mid-twentieth-century Anglo-American selfhood and culture. Written within a remarkably brief timespan, they emanate a heat and light that can still combust a reader today.

Although much has been written about Plath's rapid alteration from a sedate early style to the abandon of her final year, a close examination reveals some common threads binding all of her poetry. One of those threads is an exposure of material meant to be taken as personal. Whereas these revelations often appear to be peripheral elements in Plath's early poems, they take centre stage in the poems Plath wrote in October 1962, the month she turned thirty. Such poems as 'Daddy' and 'Lady Lazarus' reflect what Plath called 'an intense breakthrough into very serious, very personal, emotional experience' (*PS*, p. 167–8), revealing interiority not as a realm of spiritual privilege but as what Deborah Nelson calls a space of 'isolation, loneliness, domination, and routine'.[1] At the same time, the poems are structured, as Christina Britzolakis has said, 'by an unstable and theatricalized irony' that turns them into a genre of hyperbolic performance.[2] Plath's poems thus enact a paradoxical project of staged self-exposure. Her theatre of subjectivity marks

Cold War culture's difference from the impersonalism of both modernism (its precursor) and postmodernism (its successor).

Another common thread is a critical exploration of public issues. Often presented as subtext or ironic implication rather than as a poem's central motif, Plath's critique emanates from a position on the political left and the social margins, and it reflects a feminist awareness that was ahead of its time. Nevertheless, this critique is ideologically complex and uncertain. Complicit as well as resistant, it often assumes the very racial and class privileges it would seem to contest.[3] Nevertheless, Plath's metaphors in such poems as 'Three Women' and 'The Jailer' unmistakably indict patriarchy, totalitarianism and militarism. As Plath explained her method:

> The issues of our time which preoccupy me at the moment are the incalcul-able genetic effects of fallout and ... the terrifying, mad, omnipotent marriage of big business and the military in America ... Does this influence the kind of poetry I write? Yes, but in a sidelong fashion. My poems do not turn out to be about Hiroshima, but about a child forming itself finger by finger in the dark.[4] (*JP*, p. 64)

Plath considered herself 'a political person' (*PS*, p. 169). Her poems, both early and late, represent an osmotic exchange between the political and the personal, a seepage between the two categories until they blend into each other.

A complementary thread in Plath's early and late poetry is its self-referentiality. Plath focused her life on her creative quest, averring, 'I am a writer and that is all I want to do' (*LH*, p. 472). The poems highlight their intertextual swerves and echoes, their will to make a place for themselves in the already overpopulated landscape of English-language poetry. They glory in their figures and tropes, their formal innovations, their rhetorical flourishes. Such poems as 'Poems, Potatoes' and 'Words' provide a meta-commentary on their own language and procedures. For all their personal and public dimensions, Plath's poems are centred in a sense of literariness. Never pretending to be acts of transparent communication, they always insist on being situated within the institution of poetry. Yet they are rebellious inhabitants of that structure, intent on ripping holes in conventional boundaries, in their own coherence, in the fabric of poetry itself. In a larger sense, Plath's poems compose a single imaginative enterprise. They provide an image of a woman's immense creative drive at war with forces that would impede, paralyse and silence her voice. Paradoxically, those negative forces become integral to her project. Plath's ferocious attempt to inscribe her texts against the odds, to complete her signature, becomes one of the great stories in the history of English-language poetry.

## Juvenilia

One might posit that Plath's poetry evolved through four stages. The first is the period of her juvenilia, culminating in the poetry she wrote at Smith College in 1950–55. These early poems already display her characteristic concerns. The villanelle 'To Eva Descending the Stair', for example, addresses a woman who may bear some resemblance to Plath herself or, more likely, an aspect of self that Plath was consciously rejecting. Goddesslike Eva denies time, change (the 'circling zodiac'), and her own sexual passion, thereby remaining a frozen, fabricated image of perfection: 'Intolerant beauty never will be learning. / Clocks cry: stillness is a lie, my dear. / (Proud you halt upon the spiral stair).' Already Plath was confronting the contradictory notions of femininity that circulated though American culture in the 1950s: sexual decorum in conflict with desire; vocational achievement at odds with heteronormative romance. Eva stands outside the heterosexual romance narrative, and is critiqued for doing so. But in a companion poem, 'Cinderella', the outsider protagonist liberates herself from feminine stereotype, gaining more in autonomy than she loses in social standing and sensual gratification.

These early poems explore the dilemmas of female subjectivity, just as the later texts do. They also reflect on the classical politics of war and peace. The free-verse narrative 'Bitter Strawberries', as Camille Roman has shown, critiques the militarism and xenophobia of the Cold War era.[5] All morning in the strawberry field, the workers 'talked about the Russians', with the head woman saying, '"Bomb them off the map".' When a young woman and then a girl protest, the female boss silences them abruptly. All return to 'snapping' off the strawberry stems, an image of the deaths then occurring in the Korean War, sanctioned by the discourse of the dominant ideology. This poem is less metaphorical than Plath's political poems would ultimately become, but it shows her characteristic concern with the language and consequences of organized violence.

Finally, Plath's early poems demonstrate a subtle awareness of the limits and possibilities of figuration. In ostensibly seeking to escape textuality, the sonnet 'A Sorcerer Bids Farewell to Seem' paradoxically alludes to a host of prior texts, including Shakespeare's *Hamlet*, Lewis Carroll's *Alice in Wonderland* and Wallace Stevens's 'The Emperor of Ice Cream' (with its resonant if impossible imperative 'Let be be finale of seem').[6] Attempting to leave the 'looking-glass hotel' of self-referential language, the speaker seeks a place where things *are* rather than *seem*, a place beyond metaphor, a poetry of reality: 'that authentic island where / cabbages are cabbages; kings: kings'. Yet cabbages and kings are not simply 'authentic' entities but, especially when yoked together, another literary allusion, inevitably evoking Carroll's 'The Walrus and the Carpenter' (in *Through the Looking Glass*). Plath's poem moves from a 'looking-glass' hotel to an 'island' inhabited by tropes – a tropical island where figures of the imagination cavort. Thus the terms of Plath's project are clear at the outset of her career: a poetry that explores the odd and dark corners in our psychology, our politics and our art.

## Growth and experiment

Plath's second stage, a period of growth and experiment, lasted from when she married Ted Hughes in 1956 to their permanent settlement in England in 1959. In this period she extended her psychological and political explorations while honing her remarkable verbal skills. This poetry, much of it collected in *The Colossus and Other Poems* (UK 1960/US 1962), has not received the attention it deserves. Robert Lowell, her teacher and mentor, initiated the prevailing attitude when Plath presented some poems to him in a seminar in 1959, and he found that 'none of it sank very deep into my awareness'.[7] Although *The Colossus* received positive reviews, it was soon supplanted in the public imagination by the posthumously published *Ariel* (1965/1966), which included much, though not all, of Plath's later poetry. Coinciding with the publication of this book, Ted Hughes published an essay in which he depicted Plath writing the poems of *The Colossus* 'very slowly, with her Thesaurus open on her knee ... as if she were working out a mathematical problem'.[8] This portrait had an enormous influence, implying as it did that the early poems were mere intellectual exercises whereas the later poems came from the heart, written 'without her usual studies over the Thesaurus, and at top speed, as one might write an urgent letter' (Hughes, 'Notes', p. 193). Even Plath seemed to share her ex-husband's judgement, telling an interviewer shortly before her death: 'My first book, *The Colossus*, I can't read any of the poems aloud now. I didn't write them to be read aloud. They, in fact, quite privately bore me' (*PS*, p. 170). But one of Plath's biographers, Linda Wagner-Martin, has convincingly debunked the thesaurus theory:

> Ted Hughes and others ... have given us the familiar image of Sylvia writing poems, sitting with the heavy, red-covered thesaurus that was her father's open on her lap, consulting it frequently. But as early as 1956, even before she had met Hughes, Sylvia had begun trying to write poems that spoke more colloquially. She had come to think of the poet as song-maker, not as scholar with her head buried in books.[9]

In truth, Plath's poems of this period display her typical strengths of psychological intensity, social awareness and imaginative richness. The difference between her early and late texts is subtle. As Langdon Hammer has observed, 'there is something real in the artificial selves of Plath's early work, and something artificial in the real self of the *Ariel* poems'.[10]

The seemingly distanced poems of Plath's second stage actually provide astonishing access to an uncanny and contradictory interior world. Freud argued that literary creation is intimately connected to dreaming and that dreams, in turn, are influenced by the childhood exposure to fairy tales.[11] In Plath's early adult poems, which evoke 'sulfurous dreamscapes' ('The Ghost's Leavetaking'), we frequently discover figures of immense, pervasive and frightening power who seem to belong in a dream or fairy tale. The male figures appear variously as a stalker ('Conversation Among the Ruins'), a 'panther' ('Pursuit'), an erotic master ('Ode for Ted'), a bellowing 'black bull' ('The Bull of Bendylaw') or a 'maestro' whose foot presses on a young woman's heart ('The Beekeeper's Daughter'). Peering out from behind Plath's father's thesaurus, the figure of the dominating patriarch haunts her poetry of this period. Parallel to this dangerous yet sexually charged masculine figure is an almost equally frightening maternal figure. This repellant and controlling presence appears in the guise of a 'grisly-bristled / Boar' ('Sow'), an 'antique hag-head' ('The Lady and the Earthenware Head'), a museum-cased skeleton clutching at her ('All the Dead Dears') or sirens luring a young woman to her death ('Lorelei'). Such poems of gendered and generational conflict recurrently tell the story of a young female subject in search of identity, autonomy and standing. She must fight for her life against spectral figures with whom she feels inextricably enmeshed yet from whom she feels alienated – figures who resemble familial ghosts ('The Ghost's Leavetaking').

The complex of angry, yearning and avoidant feelings towards the other receives a particularly memorable dramatization in 'The Snowman on the Moor'. Plath once said that in her early poems the 'darker emotions may well put on the masks of quite unworldly things – such as ghosts, or trolls or antique gods'.[12] So it is in the Dantesque tercets of 'The Snowman on the Moor'. The protagonist responds to her husband's 'insults' by escaping into a white, cold dreamscape. Although warned by 'winter-beheaded daisies' to remain indoors, she hurls herself like 'a driven ghost' across moor snows in order to regain a modicum of power over her glowering male antagonist. Instead, the moor discloses to her an even more frightening figure: 'a grisly-thewed', 'corpse-white' giant who carries on his belt the gathered skulls of offending women. The terrified protagonist – no longer a woman at all but a disempowered 'girl' – retreats homeward, resigned to obedience. Although she had left her husband with the insubordinate taunt, '"come find me"', she returns submissive, having discovered that the price of defiance is decapitation. In making her journey on to the moor, the woman may have thought she was seeking independence, but she was also determined to arouse the sleeping patriarchal force that oppressed her unconscious and haunted her daily life. When she reached the world's white edge, she 'called hell to subdue an unruly man', thereby summoning a ghost of awful proportions – a combination of father-demon and father-corpse. In effect, the husband's disapproval has evoked a primordial vision of the all-powerful, malevolent father. The woman has a clear choice: to stay indoors or to proceed to a fatal confrontation. Because both options require her to sacrifice power and selfhood, the choice is a futile one. As she returns home, she closes the circle that has led her away from the husband/father only to return her inexorably to him once more.

Other poems posit a psychologically momentous struggle with older female figures who threaten to smother or swallow up the female subject. In 'The Disquieting Muses', for example, this figure of absorption is the 'mother', a repressive, normalizing figure in whose stories 'witches always, always / Got baked into gingerbread' and heroines floated amid 'flowers and bluebirds'. The poem's protagonist rejects this imago of regulation, conformity and illusion in favour of mentors who are more realistic, if equally unnerving: three silent, sightless spirits. These companions eerily stand guard over the young woman and her world. Although the protagonist cannot escape maternal power entirely, she can discover a darker, truth-telling version of that power in the guise of these muses who facilitate (or personify) poetic vision. Yet even vision carries risks. In 'Crystal Gazer' the fortune-teller Gerd wishes 'to govern more sight than given to a woman / By wits alone', but she ends up seeing more than she bargained for: 'Earth's ever-green death's head'. At the culmination of a creative urge precipitated by fear of and aggression towards the phallic mother, the Plathian subject glimpses death. We see here the development of an excruciating counterpoint between aesthetic desire and personal oblivion that would haunt Plath's entire career.

In these years Plath continued to write poems informed by history, now inserting images from the public sphere into what appear to be subjective dramas. The texts suggest that the zone of domesticity is no longer sheltered from the concerns of the polis, as Hannah Arendt thought they were in classical times.[13] Horrific external events leak through the household walls, permeating the human subject and the poem of privacy. Such public-private poems also reflect Plath's need to evoke but not manage the psychic flow, her wish to acknowledge the interchange of incommensurable and contradictory materials, her interest in her own ambivalence. After World War II, Theodor Adorno famously commented, 'No poetry after Auschwitz.'[14] Because language had served at the death camps, there was a pervasive sense that words had failed in the encounter with genocide, that they were now tainted with genocide's guilt. On the other hand, there was also a sense that poetry must keep the memory of the victims safe within language that endures. One might wish that there were *only* poetry after Auschwitz. To deal with this dilemma as well as to satisfy her own artistic desires, Plath translated genocide into a personal nightmare. Her task, as Susan Gubar has written, was to remember what she never knew.[15]

Plath, the daughter of a German immigrant to the US, never got over the shock of seeing the postwar photographs and news footage of emaciated survivors and dead bodies found in the Nazi concentration camps. In 'The Thin People' the speaker laments the way that newsreel images of war victims have come to possess her imagination. Here she inserts those memories into a poem that resembles a particularly bad dream. The speaker evokes the horror of those visual documents – and the unspeakably worse reality behind them – by exposing her contradictory feelings towards the images. She resents the 'thin people' for making her feel guilty and sad, for exposing her own problems as trivial by comparison, and for reminding her nevertheless of herself. Plath would later draw an analogy with 'the person out of Belsen – physical or psychological' as a way to explain and justify her poetic practice of conflating death camps with her own interior life (*LH*, p. 473). In one sense the 'thin people' are an incommensurate fantasy of her own suffering, but in another sense her suffering is a metaphor for theirs. She uses her experience to keep their lives, their pain, their significance alive and before us. In 'The Thin People' Plath innovates a new kind of historical poem – shocking, unfiltered and immersed in its topic rather than standing aside or above it.

Plath's brilliant language practice in all the poems we have been discussing suggests how intense and self-conscious her poetic pursuit was. Her titles often have a self-referential air: 'Street Song', 'Rhyme', 'On the Difficulty of Conjuring Up a Dryad', 'Metaphors'. The psychological and social intensity of her texts always connects to the drive towards significant form. In 'Poems, Potatoes', for example, Plath eloquently reflects on the limits of poetry. Just as the written word instigates meaning, so it creates a cognitive prison, for the chosen word supplants and 'muzzles' the even more suggestive 'mistier' meanings lying just beyond its reach. The barrier between what Jacques Lacan called the symbolic and the imaginary orders,[16] between what Plath herself called the 'worded world' and the 'inner wordless Sargasso' (*J*, pp. 338, 401), stuns and frustrates the speaker of this poem. Words, she says, 'shortchange me continuously'. And yet the words are haunted by 'imagined lines' – an allusion to both the definitions that rein in a signifier and the verses that string such signifiers together. Plath's 'I' here acknowledges that language treads a path between precision and undecidability. Therein lay the magic for Plath, because she wanted both to find boundaries and to transcend them. Her imagination would thus be compelled to engage in an exhausting struggle for both limits and freedom, for both form and what was beyond form, for language that was self-aware and vision that was heedless.

## Passion and self-discovery

The poetry of Plath's third stage, a dynamic period of passion and self-discovery, lasted from 1960 through the dissolution of her marriage in 1962. This period produced the texts that made her name and by which she is known today. These poems continue to explore Plath's three main *topoi* of introspection, history and self-reflexivity but often with a heightened theatricality that seems new and indeed unprecedented. Plath attributed her poems of this period to the precursory 'breakthrough' of her teacher, Robert Lowell, in *Life Studies* (*PS*, pp. 167–8). But in fact, Plath's poems have little in common with his ironic, distanced, highly visual depictions of loved ones and self. If Lowell produced a gallery of photographs or painted portraits of figures from his past, Plath produced a melodrama of her feelings, a collage of discourses, a cauldron of mourning.

In this great period of her poetic production, Plath typically combined psychic retrievals with intense domestic dramas. But she sometimes posited psychological material in a different genre, one she had worked in from her earliest years as a child poet: the nature poem. Beginning with the Romantics, nature poetry has often involved a close inspection of the physical scene, a meditation on what has been observed, and an enhanced sense of the unity between self and environment. More recently, a 'postpastoral' poetry has expressed a keen ecological awareness of the dynamism, contingency and vulnerability of both self and green world.[17] Plath's nature poems break from both these traditions. In her poems nature is an empty vessel, a landscape of alienation, an inimical force. In such poems as 'The Moon and the Yew Tree' and 'Elm', nature reflects back to the observing subject no feeling of shelter or sensation of delight, but only the subject's own hostility, vacuity and aloneness. Moon, sky, tree and bird function as exterior threats and simulacra of the self.

In 'Blackberrying', for example, a walk in the country becomes an occasion for the speaker's numbed encounter with the void: 'nothing but blackberries', 'nothing but a great space'. The speaker's interior pain becomes evident through her paranoid relations with a natural scene that is aggressive and ugly in almost every detail. As she walks, she confronts the 'hooks' of blackberry bushes, the cries of 'cacophonous' birds, the 'slapping' of the wind. The sea towards which she wanders is not beautiful, comforting or transcendent but 'heaving', making an incomprehensible noise. This uncanny world of hurtful sights and sounds becomes a specular image of the subject's own loneliness ('nobody in the lane'), anger ('protesting, protesting'), and despair ('beating and beating at an intractable metal'). Composed in apparently conversational free-verse, the monologue is artfully formed into nine-line stanzas suffused with a music of repeated end words (blackberries, sea, me), widely separated rhymes (eyes/flies, sea/me, face/space), slant rhymes (mainly/love me, eyes/sky, within/screen / heaven/end), internal rhymes (thumb/dumb, face/space), and consonance (fingers/flocks/flies, black cacophonous flocks). The music comes to an abrupt halt in the poem's final, dystonic couplet (silversmiths/metal). The poem itself ends in a metallic din, its sonic structure suddenly becoming as inorganic as the birds resembling 'bits of burnt paper' and the sea made of 'pewter'.

Plath's motif during this period of an eerie, unconsoling nature that mirrors and heightens subjective terror reaches its climax in 'Ariel'. Here the lyric 'I' depicts herself riding a horse at dawn. She merges first into the horse, then into the 'dew that flies' and finally 'into the red / Eye, the cauldron of morning'. In this strange complex of images, the self is simultaneously an arrow speeding towards the target and the mist evaporating into the sun's dry heat. More than an alienating setting, nature here has become synonymous with the death-drive, suffused with a supernatural aura of excitement and grief, as suggested by the irregular slant rhymes of flies/drive/ eye (all suggesting but not naming the near-homophone *die*) and the overdetermined, multiplicitous images of 'eye', 'cauldron' and 'morning'.

Other poems explore psychological extremity within the borders of what I have elsewhere called the 'domestic poem'.[18] In such poems the speaker seems to have one layer too little of skin; her interior being becomes alarmingly visible. She becomes a voyeuristic spectacle for our gratification but also a means to our self-recognition, just as do King Lear, Cleopatra and other Shakespearean characters. Like other great tragedies, Plath's domestic narratives may evoke mixed feelings of pity and fear. They have the power to shake up one's world, to produce catharsis, and even to enhance awareness of alterity within as well as outside the self. 'In Plaster', for example, charts the speaker's growing sense of conflict between alternative identities or body senses – pure and dirty – that vie to possess her. 'Tulips' discovers a malevolent alter ego in the object world outside of her: in the form of cut tulips that talk to her 'wound', that 'eat' her oxygen, that understand her unspoken desire to 'efface' herself. After 'Words heard, by accident, over the phone', which was written in June 1962 to commemorate her husband's adultery, the self-splintering, angry feelings and desperation intensify. In 'Fever 103°', for example, the speaker disintegrates under the pressure of a temperature rise that seems to her a nuclear blast, perhaps because it gives materiality to her psychic fever. In 'Cut' the speaker initially depicts her injury in a distanced fashion as a 'thrill' (in the newer sense of pleasurable feeling as well as the older sense of throbbing sensation), but she ultimately regards it as yet another imago of her injured subjectivity: a 'trepanned veteran', a 'dirty girl'.

The personal and interpersonal angst culminates for many readers in a trio of family poems, 'Daddy', 'Medusa' and 'The Jailer', followed by a coda, 'Lady Lazarus'. Written in October 1962, each of these poems expresses rage at a dominating male or female figure, as if Plath is returning to the scene of 'The Snowman on the Moor' and 'The Disquieting Muses'. This time her gloves are off, her nerves are splayed, and her willingness to accommodate has vanished. The precise tone of these poems is hard to pin down. Although she called 'Daddy' a 'gruesome' poem (LH, p. 472), she also characterized it as 'allegory' or 'light verse'.[19] The mixed elements of nursery rhyme, vampire story and Holocaust narrative in 'Daddy', the overtones of classical and Christian myth in 'Medusa', the hints of prison melodrama in 'The Jailer', and the hyperbolic metaphors of performance, dance and striptease in 'Lady Lazarus' all produce an alienation effect that at once ironizes the poems' emotional resonances and, paradoxically, heightens them. If this is the fully processed version, what must the immediate experience have felt like? In these poems, as in all Plath's best poems, the words, powerful as they are, are nothing in comparison with the silences they imply.

'Daddy' suggests the speaker's grief and anger first of all in its repetitive form. The poem begins (and it is one of the most gripping beginnings in poetic history): 'You do not do, you do not do / Any more, black shoe.' The first line uses just three different words, and the first two a total of seven, all of them belonging to a four-year-old's vocabulary. The effect is propulsive, compulsive, redundant, wild. The first line seems less an articulation than a presymbolic scream; the second line alludes, only slightly more sensibly, to the Mother Goose rhyme about 'an old woman who lived in a shoe'. The sense of being caught in feelings that fall short of, or exceed, rational language is deepened by the *aaba* internal rhyme scheme of the first two lines (do/do/more/shoe), supplemented by even more rhyme words (you/do/you/do). This sonic pattern then extends as the poem rolls on. Forty-one of the eighty lines end in the *oo* sound, forty-six if one includes the slant rhyme of *oot*. The repeated sounds produce a keening effect, as if the bereft speaker is howling her loss to the void. The effect is heightened by other repetitions in the poem: 'wars, wars, wars', 'ich, ich, ich, ich', 'brute / Brute heart of a brute like you', and so on.

The poem starts in the language of the child ('Achoo' in stanza one), but it soon adopts a distinctly adult vocabulary: 'the waters off beautiful Nauset' and 'the snows of the Tyrol' (which sound like phrases from tourist brochures); 'Dachau, Auschwitz, Belsen', 'Luftwaffe', 'Aryan' and 'Meinkampf' (names from the history of World War II); and 'Taroc pack', 'black man', and 'vampire' (allusions to the gypsy clairvoyant in Eliot's *The Waste Land*, Satan in Hawthorne's *The Scarlet Letter*, and the title character of Bram Stoker's *Dracula*). This collision of discourse types reflects the poem's journey back in time to uncover a repression and reexperience a deidealized past. This is a personal past, to be sure, but an historical one as well. In this poem of conflicts between daughter and father, and wife and husband, the speaker dredges up the guilty and complicated knowledges she has wished or needed to keep secret from herself, evoking them in the most powerful vocabularies, narratives and sonic structures at her disposal. Plath implied that the speaker ultimately exorcises her feelings (*CP*, p. 293), but the evidence of the poem suggests something different and more ominous, that the speaker's released emotions have absorbed her identity. If the poem's first line is convention-shattering, its last line is legendary. Does the assertion 'Daddy ... I'm through' mean that the 'I' is through with the poem, through with her father, or through with life? She attempts to ward the patriarch off, to get him out of her soul, but the violence of her fantasy (villagers 'stamping' on Daddy) suggests that just the opposite has happened, that she has fused with him. This poem represents object relations in a whole new way – obsessive, heedless and unresolved.

The next poem of the domestic trilogy, 'Medusa', suggests the enormous psychic energy flowing between daughter and mother. The Medusa in classical myth is one of the Gorgon monsters. Her head covered with serpents rather than hair, adorned with wings, claws and enormous teeth, she turns everyone who looks at her to stone. In the natural world, though, a medusa is a small jellyfish, translucent, shape-shifting and able to sting. (Another name for the medusa is the aurelia, and as a biographical sidelight we note that Plath's mother was called Aurelia.) In this poem, written in five-line stanzas similar to those in 'Daddy', the mother is 'always there', an 'old barnacled umbilicus'. Whereas the figure of Daddy is associated with violence, fear, loss and abandonment, the figure of Medusa is associated with ever-present surveillance and control. Both figures have a deific hold over the daughter's psychic life; Daddy is a 'bag full of God' whereas Medusa's paralysing head is a 'God-ball'. The effort to escape from Medusa, like the effort to defeat Daddy, ends in ambiguity. The daughter proclaims, 'There is nothing between us.' Does this mean that she no longer has anything in common with the matriarch or that they are so close, so enmeshed with each other, that nothing can come between them?

Similar issues of avoidance, co-dependency, loss and mourning appear in the final poem of the trilogy. 'The Jailer' also employs the five-line stanzas characteristic of the trilogy, though the lines are distinctly shorter than those used in 'Daddy', as if the speaker has less to say as she sinks from anger to numbed despair. The 'I' asserts that to be herself is 'not enough' for her husband. He has 'drugged and raped' her, harmed her in psychological and perhaps physical ways. Yet she takes back her wish to be rid of him, asking herself, in a reversal of the first line of 'Daddy', 'what would he / Do, do, do without me?' Perhaps she really means to ask what she would do without him. Like George Lowndes in H. D.'s autobiographical novel *Hermione*, and like Leo Stein in Gertrude Stein's self-portrait 'Two', the male associate dominates and inhibits the female subject, yet he also facilitates her voice. She lives and writes under his 'shadow', just as the speaker of 'The Colossus' feels 'married to shadow'. Her ambivalent wish that her husband were 'dead or away' occupies her consciousness and generates her language, and she therefore cannot complete her severance from him because such freedom would put her consciousness and language in doubt. She obtains her identity, her abject existence, from her anguished symbiosis with him. Yet despite his constant company and surveillance, she feels overwhelmed with loss. She thus registers the multiple disappearances from her life: of their love, his care for her, and her potential for both autonomy and intimacy. And from these absent presences, she makes her poetry.

'Lady Lazarus' acts as a coda to the trio of domestic poems, though it is written in a different form, that of irregularly rhyming tercets. After the increasing paralysis of 'Medusa' and 'The Jailer', 'Lady Lazarus' returns to the *topos* of 'Daddy', which seems to provide the possibility of a rebellious agency, however compromised. More consistently than in 'Daddy', the speaker figures herself as the Jewish victim of Nazi atrocity – and again the dominating male (no longer necessarily the father or even any specific biological entity) is a Nazi functionary. The trope of the striptease emerges in the poem as a metapoetic element, a self-reflexive comment on the poetics of exhibitionism that are so fundamental to these poems, grounded as they are in Cold War concerns about privacy and exposure, in the interplay of body, gender, celebrity and power. The 'peanut-crunching crowd' pretty straightforwardly refers to the readers of the kind of poem 'Lady Lazarus' is. The speaker asserts that dying is 'an art', reflecting back, perhaps, on the many poems that Plath wrote about death. Both dying and art become, in this telling, a spectacle, a 'theatrical' performance that involves a charge (both a fee and a jolt).[20] Unlike the preceding three poems, which all devolve to stasis, this poem ends in a violent rebirth, with the speaker rising from the ashes to 'eat men like air'. This conclusion suggests a rage of retribution, but how much of this assertion is real and how much bravado? And how nourishing to the self is it to 'eat men like air'? This poem, like so many of Plath's other psychological poems of this period, uncovers repressed desire and aggression in an unprecedented way. It fuses feelings of anger, grief and yearning to an eclectic set of popular culture motifs: the Holocaust, the New Testament story of Lazarus, burlesque, saints' relics, mourning customs, the Phoenix bird. Written mere months before the publication of Betty Friedan's *The Feminine Mystique* (1963), it expresses contemporary women's sense of victimization and need for power and gratification. Stunning in the audacity of its images, the complexity of its imagination, the originality of its humour, and the extent of its outrage, 'Lady Lazarus' brings Plath's psychological writing to an unrepeatable and unforgettable climax.

Beyond their psychological power, these four texts also stake out new territory as political poems. Plath's references to minority groups and historical atrocities have often been considered methods of thickening the social texture of her poems, as ways to dignify what are essentially very personal revelations. But, as I have previously suggested, Plath's implications of her personal story might conversely be seen as ways to vitalize the social aims of the poems. Plath raises what Jacqueline Rose calls 'the question of fantasy ... in its fullest historical and political dimension'.[21] 'Daddy' and 'Lady Lazarus', like the earlier 'The Thin People', might therefore be said to commemorate the Holocaust in a new and powerful way. As Susan Gubar has written, they are 'a private confession of grave public harm' (*Poetry After Auschwitz*, p. 206). These poems, in which the speaker impersonates a Holocaust victim, bear close resemblance to some of the best poems written by actual Holocaust survivors, for example Paul Celan's 'Todesfugue'. How is a poet with no firsthand experience of the Holocaust to write of it, to explore its emotional significance, to preserve its memory? How is she to allude to it without seeming overly intellectual or didactic? Plath discovered that she might juxtapose its imagery with her personal immanence. She in effect merges her own 'living name' (to use Robert Lowell's phrase)[22] with remembered images of the death camps, the kind of places where human bodies were notoriously stripped of 'wedding ring' and 'gold filling', turned into 'lampshade' or 'cake of soap'. Plath thereby keeps cultural memory alive, blessing the victims through a fantasy of identification.

She does the same with the nuclear blasts in Hiroshima and Nagasaki. Plath once commented that if a poem dwells on personal experience it should 'be *relevant*, and relevant to the larger things, the bigger things such as Hiroshima and Dachau and so on' (*PS*, p. 170). In 'Fever 103°', for example, she conflates a bout of fever with both the Holocaust ('yellow sullen smokes') and the atomic bomb blasts ('Hiroshima ash', 'radiation'). Similarly, in a stanza of 'Lady Lazarus' recited on the BBC but unfortunately altered in the published version by the omission of the third line, she wrote, 'These are my hands, my knees. / I may be skin and bone, / I may be Japanese.'[23] Some readers have praised these references to historical tragedy for their empathy, while others have disparaged them as appropriation. I think they may be better viewed as commemoration. They resist the aesthetic drift to moral anaesthesia and political amnesia.

Another of Plath's important social poems is one written some months before the celebrated October poems we have just been discussing. *Three Women*, written in March 1962 as a radio drama for voices, reflects on the dilemmas of women's bodies and choices in a masculinist society. It meditates on ways that female subjects may resist the effects of centralized authority and bureaucratic will. Plath's longest poem and her most sustained effort to approximate the voice of the other, the poem permits three women in a maternity ward to speak their thoughts. The first, by implication a wife and homemaker, has a baby boy and is contented; the second, a wife and secretary, miscarries and mourns; and the third, an unmarried student, gives her baby girl up for adoption. Each of their alternating monologues expresses some form of opposition to contemporary social structures.

The first voice – frightened, powerless and marginalized – aligns herself with historical victims: 'I am the center of an atrocity', 'I am breaking apart like the world.' And this is the positive character, the one who contrasts with the luckless others. The third woman, who must give up her child, feels lost and alone. She blames the male doctors for her plight, perhaps because of their reluctance to research and distribute birth control materials, or perhaps because of male sexual aggression. Like all three of the characters, she identifies the maternity ward with torture and medical experiments. This character, ultimately the most tragic, faces a dark future: 'I am solitary as grass. What is it I miss?' The second woman, who is particularly articulate, is the one with whom most readers (and, possibly, the author) identify. This speaker utters the poem's most sustained critique of sexist and hierarchical social arrangements. She associates masculinist regimes with 'that flat, flat, flatness from which ideas, destructions, / Bulldozers, guillotines, white chambers of shrieks proceed'. Having experienced death in the distant past (represented by an image of moss-covered tombstones) as well as a miscarriage in the present moment, the second voice has been cast to the social margins, a 'heroine of the peripheral'. Her abjection permits her to diagnose and resist the culture of destruction and the 'love of death' that reigns in the world. She believes that 'important men', as abstract in their thinking as Blake's Urizen, feel 'jealous' of the roundness they associate with the female body. Unlike the devastated third woman, the second woman finds a way to survive and heal.

A secretary and seamstress, the character with the most to say, this voice may be the voice of the artist – prophetic, oppositional and enduring.

As the last sentence implies, many of the poems of 1960–62 reflect on their own verbal processes. Such poems as 'Daddy' portray the struggle of the lyric 'I' for creativity amid the burdens of 'daddy-poetry' (Axelrod, *The Wound*, pp. 52, 59) – that long, overbearing and unavoidable tradition of masculinist utterance. In such a reading the lines 'the tongue stuck in my jaw' and 'I could hardly speak' take on a very particular valence concerning the poet's inhibition when confronted with her poetic predecessors. In a similar vein, 'Three Women', with its characters described only as 'voices', may be to do with a female poet's painful effort to achieve poetic utterance, to give birth to poems. The first voice, despite its complexities, may represent a traditional literary voice, while the second and third voices evoke more pained and resistant discourses.

## The final stage

Plath's final stage, a brief time of depression and withdrawal, occurred in the last weeks of her life in early 1963. Her metapoetic code becomes strikingly evident in these poems. Just weeks before her suicide on February 11 – a death that may be interpreted as willed, inadvertent, or both – Plath was writing (as one might expect) elliptical poems of resignation and despair, but she was also writing, almost compulsively, about poetry in general and her own poetry in particular. These poems reveal that even in her final days poetry was her most profound concern, her most enduring obsession. As her life wore down and her will to live wore out, she realized that (as she put it in 'Kindness'), 'The blood jet is poetry, / There is no stopping it.' The organicity of her texts, the suture of her creativity and life processes, meant that her crisis poems would reflect intensively on themselves. 'Words', for example, meditates on the fate of poetry after the excitement of composition has terminated. If creation may be metaphorized as axe strokes into a tree trunk, the resultant poem resembles the ringing echoes of those strokes, an ever fainter trace. When the poet later rereads her poem, it seems 'dry', faded, foreign. Ironically, though, it is the 'indefatigable' poem that lives, not the welling life that produced it. The struggle of 'Words' to sustain its verbal energy against entropic forces generates lines of irregular length (ranging from 'Axes' and 'While' to 'From the bottom of the pool, fixed stars') and a lively interplay of monosyllabic, Anglo-Saxonate words ('wood', 'rings', 'sap', 'tears', 'skull', 'fixed', 'stars', 'life') with multisyllabic, Latinate diction ('re-establish', 'encounter', 'indefatigable'). Nevertheless, Plath's echoing wood must finally yield to the stillness of a pool.

Metaphors of waning and cessation dominate 'Contusion' and 'Balloons' as well. Self-objects become 'washed out', 'hollow', 'the size of a fly', 'globes of thin air', merely a 'shred'. In the aptly named 'Edge', which may be the last poem Plath wrote, the woman and her poems pass over a final precipice to silence. The depiction of the dead protagonist brims with references to now-terminated inscription ('Greek necessity', 'scrolls', 'folded') and utterance ('smile', 'throats', 'crackle'). Her children (perhaps metaphorically her poetic productions) are dead, and her breasts (her creative powers) are empty. Plath's poetic quest, which began with such passion and promise, ends in exhaustion. Yet the linguistic brilliance lives on, as do the stunning self-awareness, fantastic historicity, emotional intensity and acrid humour. Sylvia Plath's poems are as vital and unsettling today as ever.

## Notes

Many thanks, as always, to Rise B. Axelrod for her support and advice.

1. Deborah Nelson, *Pursuing Privacy in Cold War America* (New York: Columbia University Press, 2002), p. xiii.
2. Christina Britzolakis, *Sylvia Plath and the Theatre of Mourning* (Oxford: Clarendon Press, 1999), p. 121.
3. See Renée R. Curry, *White Women Writing White: H. D., Elizabeth Bishop, Sylvia Plath and Whiteness* (Westport, CT: Greenwood, 2000), pp. 123–4, 167–8.
4. References throughout are to the US edition of *Johnny Panic and the Bible of Dreams* (New York: Harper & Row, 1979).
5. Camille Roman, 'Cold War 1950: Elizabeth Bishop and Sylvia Plath', in Laura Jehn Menides and Angela Dorenkamp (eds.), *'In Worcester Massachusetts': Essays on Elizabeth Bishop* (New York: Peter Lang, 1999), pp. 247–58.
6. Wallace Stevens, *Collected Poems* (New York: Alfred Knopf, 1969), p. 64.
7. Robert Lowell, 'Sylvia Plath's Ariel' (1966), reprinted in Robert Giroux (ed.), *Collected Prose* (New York: Farrar, Straus & Giroux, 1987), p. 125.
8. Ted Hughes, 'Notes on the Chronological Order of Sylvia Plath's Poems' (1966), reprinted in Charles Newman (ed.), *The Art of Sylvia Plath: A Symposium* (Bloomington: Indiana University Press, 1970), p. 188.
9. Linda Wagner-Martin, *Sylvia Plath: A Biography* (New York: Simon & Schuster, 1987), p. 166.
10. Langdon Hammer, 'Plath's Lives', *Representations* 75 (2001), p. 83.
11. Sigmund Freud, 'Creative Writers and Day-Dreaming' (1908), reprinted in James Strachey (ed.), *Standard Edition of the Complete Works of Sigmund Freud*, 24 vols. (London: Hogarth Press, 1959), IX, pp. 141–54; Freud, 'The Occurrence in Dreams of Material from Fairy Tales' (1913), reprinted in James Strachey (ed.), *Standard Edition of the Complete Works of Sigmund Freud*, 24 vols. (London: Hogarth Press, 1958), XII, pp. 279–88.
12. Quoted in Linda Wagner-Martin, *Sylvia Plath: A Literary Life*, 2nd edition (New York: Palgrave Macmillan, 2003), p. 92.

13. Hannah Arendt, *The Human Condition* (Chicago: University of Chicago Press, 1958), pp. 28–37.
14. George Steiner, *Language and Silence* (New York: Atheneum, 1970), p. 51.
15. Susan Gubar, *Poetry After Auschwitz* (Bloomington: Indiana University Press, 2003), pp. 177–206. Whereas literary criticism initially focused primarily on Plath's depiction of the self (variously conceived of as isolated, evolving, transforming, reincarnated, victimized, narcissistic, performative, or transcendent), it has more recently emphasized Plath's involvement in history. For other examples of the historical turn in Plath criticism, see Stan Smith, *Inviolable Voice: History and Twentieth-Century Poetry* (Dublin: Gill and Macmillan, 1982), pp. 200–25; James E. Young, *Writing and Rewriting the Holocaust* (Bloomington: Indiana University Press, 1988), pp. 117–33; Al Strangeways: *Sylvia Plath: The Shaping of Shadows* (Cranbury, NJ, and London: Associated University Presses, 1998), pp. 77–131; Harriet Parmet, *The Terror of Our Days: Four American Poets Respond to the Holocaust* (London: Associated University Presses, 2001), pp. 53–109; and Robin Peel, *Writing Back: Sylvia Plath and Cold War Politics* (Madison: Fairleigh Dickinson University Press; London: Associated University Presses, 2002).
16. Jacques Lacan, *Ecrits*, trans. Alan Sheridan (New York: W. W. Norton, 1977).
17. See Terry Gifford, 'Pastoral, Anti-Pastoral, Post-Pastoral', in Laurence Coupe (ed.), *The Green Studies Reader* (London: Routledge, 2000), pp. 219–22.
18. Steven Gould Axelrod, *Sylvia Plath: The Wound and the Cure of Words* (Baltimore: Johns Hopkins University Press, 1990), pp. 59–70.
19. A. Alvarez, *Beyond All This Fiddle: Essays 1955–1967* (London: Allen Lane, 1968), p. 56.
20. For complementary analyses of the music-hall motif in 'Lady Lazarus', see Britzolakis, *Theatre of Mourning*, pp. 151–6, and Kathleen Margaret Lant, 'The Big Strip Tease: Female Bodies and Male Power in the Poetry of Sylvia Plath', *Contemporary Literature* 34.4 (1993), pp. 620–69.
21. Jacqueline Rose, *The Haunting of Sylvia Plath* (Cambridge, MA: Harvard University Press, 1992), p. 207.
22. Robert Lowell, 'Epilogue', *Day by Day* (New York: Farrar, Straus & Giroux, 1977), p. 127.
23. A. Alvarez, *The Savage God: A Study of Suicide* (New York: Bantam, 1973), p. 16.

# 7

JO GILL

# *The Colossus* and *Crossing the Water*

Sylvia Plath's first collection, *The Colossus and Other Poems*, was published in England in October 1960 and in the US in 1962. *Crossing the Water*, the third of Plath's collections, was published posthumously, after *Ariel*, in 1971. It contains some poems written around the same time as those in *The Colossus* ('Private Ground' (CW) and 'The Manor Garden' (C) were both written in 1959) and others which predate, or in some cases coincide with, the poems of *Ariel*; 'In Plaster' (CW), for example, was written on the same day as *Ariel*'s 'Tulips'.

The poems in these two collections, then, span some five or six years. They include a range of voices, themes and styles and have their roots in diverse locations; the American coast and desert, the Yorkshire moors, Cambridge, Devon and numerous indeterminate and imaginary places. Influenced by Yeats, Eliot, Auden and Marianne Moore, among others, they look back to classical mythology, to Shakespeare and to folk stories. Ted Hughes describes these poems as mathematical in design and as a form of science or alchemy (*WP*, pp. 174, 180–82, *J Abr.*, p. xiii). One might equally think of them as visual and painterly, as influenced by art and sculpture (Brueghel, de Chirico, Baskin, Gaugin, Klee (*J*, p. 359)). And one might also note their struggle to represent the unconscious and unknown.

*The Colossus* had been several years in the making and the rearranging. Plath's *Journals* record, from the outset, her determination to have her work published, to gain an audience for her writing and recognition as a poet (*J*, pp. 36–7, 131). From 1956 she had been seeking a market for this constantly changing collection of poems, submitting it fruitlessly to seven American publishers and for the prestigious Yale Series of Younger Poets prize (*J*, p. 294). She had seen successive peers and competitors (Adrienne Rich, George Starbuck, Anne Sexton) acquire publishing success before finally deciding to 'forget America' and try her luck in England (*J*, p. 523). On receiving positive signs from her English publisher Heinemann (an editor there had written to her after seeing her poems in the *London Magazine*), she commented, '[H]ope springs. England offers new comforts ... My tempo is British' (*J*, p. 521). Several critics, as we will see below, have remarked on the self-conscious transatlanticism of Plath's poetics.

It is helpful to consider this publishing history. First, because it offers a reminder of the sheer persistence of Plath's endeavours and thus a counter-argument to the common misapprehension that her poetry emerges spontaneously and inevitably, as though in spite of herself.[1] Second, it gives a valuable insight into changing perceptions of poetry in the 1950s and early 1960s and, relatedly, of changing expectations of the role and responsibility of the woman writer. Plath, in this early stage of her career, is constructing or negotiating her personal and her poetic identity and it is the difficult processes of recognition, resistance, assimilation and change that the poems of *The Colossus* and *Crossing the Water* record.

Plath's struggle to be a poet coincides with a shift in the US and in England from a modernist, academic school of poetry – a school which values allusiveness, reticence and clarity – to a new approach. This 'new poetry' (the name is appropriated by Al Alvarez as the title of his influential anthology) seems to emphasize authenticity and subjectivity, personal confession, intimacy of voice and the possibility of cathartic gain, though as Anne Sexton (one of the leading figures in the confessional movement) explains, authenticity may be an aesthetic – and a deceptive – effect: 'I've heard psychiatrists say "See, you've forgiven your father. There it is in your poem." But I haven't forgiven my father. I just wrote that I did.'[2] There is a separation in such poetry between the 'I' as subject and the 'I' as object of the text akin to the split between subject and persona which John Berryman famously announces at the beginning of his *Dream Songs*.[3] It is important to bear these qualifications in mind as we consider Plath's writing, particularly if we choose to think of it in a 'confessional' framework.

Persuasive though it is to argue that *The Colossus* shows its allegiance to the earlier formalist heritage, while *Crossing the Water* exemplifies a move away from this inheritance and towards new subjects and more personal voices, this is probably too schematic a distinction to make. It is more helpful to think of these poems as embodying in their own vacillations of voice and theme, in their multiplicity of styles and perspectives and certainly in their self-consciousness or self-reflexivity – a theme I shall examine later – something of the changing currents and tendencies of their time.

The tension between competing literary and gender models is embodied in many of these poems. Specifically, it can be seen in the work's contradictory influences or roots. These range from popular and domestic idioms used in the service of deeply personal experience (a strategy learnt, perhaps, from Sexton) – for example, in the opening lines of 'Suicide off Egg Rock' (*C*) – to more impersonal and cerebral notes inherited from T. S. Eliot. The opening line of 'Whitsun' (*CW*), for example, mimics his 'The Love Song of J. Alfred Prufrock', while the rats which unexpectedly close 'Watercolor of Grantchester Meadows' (*C*) bring to mind his 'The Hollow Men'. Plath's 'Magi' (*CW*) implicitly addresses the question Eliot raises in his 'Journey of the Magi': 'were we led all that way for / Birth or death?'. What, Plath's poem asks, is to separate 'Good' from 'Evil'? The image in stanza four of the child rocking like a hammock hovers between these two poles. 'The Stones', the closing poem of *The Colossus*, draws on a line from Eliot's 'Little Gidding' – 'the fire and the rose are one'.[4] Plath's subject endures trial by fire in the hope of finding 'the elusive rose' which here, as in two later poems ('Edge' (*A*) and 'Kindness' (*A*)), represents the fruits of creativity.

Equally, there are poems which draw on the quiet introspection of Roethke (most famously 'Poem for a Birthday', parts of which were omitted from the American edition of *The Colossus* because of the too-obvious influence) alongside Audenesque poems of social and moral responsibility: Plath's 'Two Views of a Cadaver Room' (*C*) owes something to Auden's 'Musée des Beaux Arts' as well as to 'September 1, 1939'.[5] There are poems of observation and epiphany akin to the work of Elizabeth Bishop ('Mussel Hunter at Rock Harbor' (*C*)) and apparently confessional and self-revelatory poems such as 'Point Shirley' (*C*) which recall Robert Lowell's 1959 *Life Studies*.

It has become a commonplace of Plath criticism to describe the poems of *The Colossus* as evidence of a necessary apprenticeship, to see *Crossing the Water* as a 'transitional' book which marks a certain stage in the development of Plath's poetic career (*A Rest.*, p. x) and to regard *Ariel* as the true achievement. Jacqueline Rose summarizes this orthodoxy as 'presenting all Plath's work in terms of a constant teleological reference to *Ariel* with the result that everything else she produced is more or less offered as *waste*'.[6] The present essay, while acknowledging these arguments, does not seek to resolve them, nor does it seek definitively to establish the place of these pre-*Ariel* poems in Plath's oeuvre. Its aim, rather, is to recuperate this 'waste' and to illuminate what is interesting and valuable about these poems both individually and as a group.

### The Colossus

Early critical responses to the English edition of *The Colossus* are summed up thus: 'Critics recognized a sure new voice, speaking in tightly wrought patterns and conveying a definite sense of control . . . Plath was obviously a well-educated, disciplined writer.'[7] Reviews of the first American edition of

1962 were less positive. As Linda Wagner points out, in the two years since the English edition, the confessional mode of poetry with which Plath was later to be associated had gained considerable currency. In the context of, say, Sexton's *To Bedlam and Part Way Back* (1960), the formal structure and careful allusiveness of *The Colossus* may have seemed rather passé (*Critical Heritage*, pp. 2–4).

Given this background, what are we to make of *The Colossus*? Is it, as Peter Davison writing in 1966 argued, that these poems 'have no absolute necessity for being: they read like advanced exercises' (Wagner, *Critical Heritage*, p. 81) or, as Tim Kendall has more recently put it, that '*The Colossus* and other early poems are most important because without them, *Ariel* would not have been possible'?[8] Or should we agree with the anonymous reviewer for *The Times* that it contains some of 'the best things she ever wrote' (Wagner, *Critical Heritage*, p. 92)?

I begin by discussing the book's title poem. 'The Colossus' was written in October 1959, though its roots lie considerably earlier. Days after writing it, Plath referred to it with a weary familiarity as a poem on 'the old father-worship subject' (*J*, p. 518). As Ted Hughes notes, it replaced another poem on a similar theme – 'Full Fathom Five' – in providing the title for the collection (*WP*, p. 170). Other poems, too, draw on this subject ('Electra on Azalea Path' (*CP*) for instance). Helen Vendler provides a list of some nineteen earlier poems on these themes all of which, arguably, prefigure the subject's full and final treatment in 'Daddy' (*A*).[9]

'The Colossus' is spoken in the first person and depicts a dreamscape (*WP*, p. 182) or, more properly, a nightmare scene in which the lone female subject struggles with the overwhelming task of restoring the shattered features of a colossal statue. This is variously referred to as 'an oracle', 'some god or other' and 'father'. The poem is elegiac in tone, bleak in outlook and evokes the sheer futility of the speaker's task; a persistent sense of foreboding is generated in part by the allusion to the 'oracle', in part by images of destruction ('anarchy', 'lightning-stroke' and 'ruin' in stanza five) and in part, as Vendler has shown, by the falling rhythms and weak endings of the lines (*Coming of Age*, p. 126). The palette is monochrome, with brief flashes of colour. Blue in stanza four represents the cold, null indifference of the sky. In other poems, for example 'The Manor Garden' or 'Ouija', blue is associated with a chill, suffocating mist. The sinister 'red' and 'plum-color' stars of the final stanza signify the planet Mars, associated in classical mythology with war.

'The Colossus' has been read variously in terms of mythology, autobiography, history and female creativity. Judith Kroll proposes a mythological reading, arguing that the poem is a symbolic depiction of a 'mourning Goddess' attending a 'dying God'.[10] A number of critics have read 'The

Colossus' as autobiography. Suzanne Juhasz, for example, suggests that it examines '"very private, very personal experience, her relationship with her dead father"'.[11] Hughes suggests a context for the poem in Plath's experiments with the ouija board and explains that she communicated through this medium with a spirit called 'Prince Otto' (Otto was Plath's father's name), the self-declared servant and mouthpiece of the enigmatically silent 'Colossus' (WP, p. 180). Stan Smith takes a quite different view, arguing of Plath's poetry as a whole that its meaning 'cannot be reduced to spirit messages from the unconscious'.[12] Of 'The Colossus' he contends that the central encounter of the poem represents not only the child/father relationship, but the 'whole relationship between self and history, mediated through the institutions of a patriarchal society' (Smith, *Inviolable Voice*, p. 209).

Steven Gould Axelrod reads 'The Colossus' as an allegory of patriarchal domination of female creativity where the metaphors of destruction and incomprehension exemplified by the incoherent animal voices of stanza one lament the oppressed, silenced voice of the woman poet. Crucially, though, Axelrod finds that the poem demonstrates the undermining of male dominance. While seeming to 'inscribe female defeat', it 'encodes the survival of female difference and the victory of her voice' (*Wound*, pp. 49–50). Certainly the poem traces the determined assertion of the female voice in the face of seemingly insurmountable obstacles; it opens with 'I', and the 'I' insists on its presence by echoing in the 'i' rhymes throughout. Every stanza contains at least one pair of such rhymes (I/ent*i*rely, I/w*i*ser in stanzas one and two), and in the middle section of the poem where we see the speaker in the most intense conflict with the statue the 'I' cries frantically or stubbornly for attention – lysol/I/l*i*ke/wh*i*te/tumul*i*/eyes and sky/Oreste*i*a/Cypress/Acanth*i*ne – thus resisting effacement by the monolithic statue and the culture it represents.

The last line of the poem, though, loses that sound. We might read this as a sign of the success of the Colossus in silencing the speaker. Conversely, we might see her reconciliation with her fate as a kind of personal achievement. Elisabeth Bronfen, thinking about the poem in psychoanalytic terms, sees in it the simultaneous possibility of self-extinction and self-creation. In lamenting the lost father, the speaker finds her own identity.[13] One might also read the poem as an allegory of Plath's self-constitution as a poet, or as a kind of manifesto. The merciless conditions of the first section, which show a struggle with the past, with the father and with an intractable language, are the necessary grounding for the transcendence realized in the final turn towards the stars and the sunrise. If the speaker is no longer seeking a boat to rescue her (the 'scrape of a keel'), this is because she now recognizes that her subject, and the resources she needs to make something of it, are to hand.

A psychoanalytic approach to this and other poems is potentially fruitful. I have already indicated that 'The Colossus' may be read as a study of the female subject's struggle to reconcile herself with, and paradoxically to achieve mature independence from, the lost, feared and desired father. One might also read 'The Colossus' as not simply an account of the father/ daughter relationship (real or abstract) but as a study of the psychoanalytic process itself. It reveals the difficulties of the 'talking cure' and the prolonged effort it takes in therapy to piece together the psyche. The 'talking cure' was first described, and its limitations first made apparent, in Josef Breuer's account of the case of Fraulein Anna O. Arguably there are parallels between this case and Plath's poem; in each we have a narrative about a fraught father/daughter relationship set in a scene which is characterized by incomprehensible language, blindness and disorder.[14]

A slightly earlier poem, ostensibly on the same broad theme, is 'Full Fathom Five'. Here, as Plath explained, the father is cast in the role of 'father-sea-god muse' (*J*, p. 399). Where in 'The Colossus' the geography is bleak and parched and the father austere, monolithic and impenetrable, in 'Full Fathom Five', as the alliterative title intimates, all is fluid and mutable. The ebb and flow of the largely terza rima scheme and the occasional 'homophonic internal rhyme' such as 'come in'/'coming' in line two (Kendall, *Critical Study*, p. 5) accentuate this tidelike rhythm.

'Full Fathom Five', like 'The Colossus', apostrophizes the father, but here the 'I' itself remains implicit, staying hidden until stanza six and reemerging only in the final two stanzas. It is as though the speaker hardly dares to confront her object ('I / Cannot look much') – like Sophocles' Oedipus, she both desires and fears to know the truth. There is a preoccupation in *The Colossus* and *Crossing the Water* with forms of knowledge or insight and a persistent anxiety about sight and sightlessness, about seeming to see but failing (we are reminded of the image of the 'bald, white' and therefore unseeing eyes in 'The Colossus') or of not being seen and therefore barely seeming to exist (see 'Candles' (*CW*)). Throughout 'Full Fathom Five' there is unease about the kind of knowledge or insight it might deliver. This is realized in contradictory images of clarity and obfuscation ('clear' and 'obscurity' are juxtaposed in stanza five, and 'clearness' and 'muddy' in stanza seven) that replicate the larger scene – a mutable seascape in which things are tantalizingly and repeatedly glimpsed beneath, and then hidden by the waves.

The association with Shakespeare's *The Tempest*, from which the poem draws its title, is apt (the specific allusion is to Ariel's speech in I.iii.399–405) and we should also note the poem's engagement with Eliot's and Auden's own meditations on this theme in the 'Ariel' poems and 'The Sea and the Mirror' respectively. H. D.'s 'Calypso Speaks' suggests another possible source. *The Tempest* may be understood as a play about deception and revelation, about tyranny and enslavement – a drama in which family bonds are confused or betrayed and where the magical power of language is used to subjugate and silence as well as to create and to heal. In an addendum to her comments about the 'father-sea-god muse' theme of the poem, Plath explains that in 'Full Fathom Five' 'the pearls and coral [are] highly-wrought to art: pearls sea-changed from the ubiquitous grit of sorrow and dull routine' (*J*, p. 381). What she takes from *The Tempest* is the theme of transformation and specifically of transformation wrought in language. This poem about the speaker's relationship with her father (and by extension, as Al Strangeways has argued, about her relationship with patriarchal literary models such as Shakespeare and Eliot)[15] is also about the speaker's relationship with her art.

As such contradictions demonstrate, there is a complex and finally productive dialectic in these poems. Images of blank unseeing impenetrability in 'The Colossus' and 'The Disquieting Muses', for instance, are contrasted with starlike moments of insight and illumination. Metaphors of rocks, stones and other smooth impenetrable surfaces represent dumb, uncomprehending, unyielding indifference ('Suicide off Egg Rock'), stubborn obstacles to happiness and self-realization ('Man in Black', 'Departure') or the vulnerability of the lone subject ('Hermit at Outermost House'). However, in other poems (such as 'Hardcastle Crags', discussed later) rocks and stones signify latent potential, or the creative spark. In such cases abject or occluded experience is transformed into radiant meaning. In 'The Disquieting Muses' and 'I Want, I Want' (and in *Ariel*'s 'Paralytic') Plath implies a contiguity between bare blank stone and the smooth, impenetrable surface of an egg. In each case the stone/egg, if it can only be fertilized, tapped or ignited, will yield great rewards.

The opening poem of *The Colossus*, 'The Manor Garden', announces these dialectical concerns and embodies this pervasive anxiety about poetic utterance. Written at Yaddo, the writer's retreat, in late 1959 when Plath was pregnant with her first child, the poem contemplates different kinds of productivity – maternal, literary, botanical.[16] In a short note, 'Context', written in 1962, Plath confirms the importance and the contiguity of diverse creative forms: 'the real issues of our time are the issues of every time ... making in all its forms – children, loaves of bread, paintings, buildings'.[17] 'The Manor Garden', though, is mindful of the ever-present threat of stagnation. The poem's first and end-stopped line declares bleakly and emphatically, 'The fountains are dry and the roses over.' Yet in saying this, the poem controverts its own logic; the fountains (a conventional symbol of poetry) in being so described prove that they continue to flow.

This opening ambiguity establishes a sequence of equally fraught images. Into this scene of aridity and decay come images of fertility and fruitfulness, with 'pears' fattening 'like little buddhas' (the metaphor connotes the shape of the growing womb). We are in a Keatsian 'season of mists and mellow fruitfulness' yet Plath's 'blue mist' has more sinister connotations. It drags the lake, as though seeking a drowned body. Here, as in 'The Colossus', 'The Stones', 'Departure' and many other poems of this period, there is a sense of unspecified menace. In 'The Manor Garden' it is the speaker's own creative powers which are under threat. Like a character in some perverse version of a fairy tale – Sleeping Beauty, perhaps – she is able to bequeath the child, or endow the poem, with nothing but a litany of obscure and symbolically confused objects: 'white heather' (traditionally bringing luck), 'two suicides, the family wolves' (suggesting trouble) and 'blackness' (conveying despair and annihilation). 'The Manor Garden' echoes the title poem in its final appeal to the unpromising 'hard stars' for inspiration, yet what it finds is that support and succour come only from the small and apparently meagre; from the 'worms' and 'birds' which, in the final line, 'bring gifts to a difficult borning'. The word 'borning' is itself both 'difficult' ('birth' would have been a simpler choice) and entirely coherent. It maintains the archaic diction of, say, stanza three and it completes the 'ing' rhymes of the preceding two stanzas. Most importantly, it connotes the little-used term 'borning room'. This was a room, familiar in seventeenth-century architecture, built solely for giving birth and – crucially in the context of the persistent ambivalence of this poem – for caring for the dying.

'Black Rook in Rainy Weather' (omitted from the American edition of *The Colossus*) contemplates explicitly the process of poetic inspiration. It, too, takes the image of the star and of sparks of light to signify insight and illumination and it expresses something of the frustrating powerlessness of the poet as she waits for inspiration to strike. This is a determinedly precise and controlled poem whose taut *abcde* rhyme scheme is maintained throughout. The emphatic monosyllables of the opening line displace the speaker's own tension ('stiff[ness]') on to the first object she sees and epitomize her fraught and expectant mood. In a classic Freudian negation where, as Freud explains, 'a repressed image or idea can make its way into consciousness on condition that it is *negated*', the speaker insists, 'I do not expect a miracle.'[18]

The speaker is willing to accept illumination from any source and what she finds is that inspiration may strike from unexpected – and apparently inauspicious – places, from the blackness of a rook's feathers seen in rainy weather, for instance. When it does strike it is a physical, visceral experience: it may suddenly 'seize my senses, haul / My eyelids up' and this – however painful and intimate a process – is a welcome alternative to the dreaded numbness of 'total neutrality'. An earlier poem, 'The Eye Mote', makes a similar point. It establishes an idealized pastoral scene which is shattered by a splinter which suddenly pierces the speaker's vision: 'Abrading my lid, the small grain burns: / Red cinder.' This awful pain is the necessary precondition to elevated insight (we are reminded again of the story of Oedipus and the paradoxical conflation of blindness and understanding) and to a powerful imaginative vision which – although uncomfortable and finally regretted – is effective in transforming the dull white horses of stanza one into the altogether more striking 'double-humped camels or unicorns' of stanza three.

'Hardcastle Crags' circumvents 'Black Rook in Rainy Weather''s 'long wait for the angel' by imagining a speaker capable of sparking her own fire. It describes a lone woman striding through and beyond the streets of a Yorkshire village. With fierce energy the poem combusts into life: 'Flintlike, her feet struck / Such a racket of echoes', igniting 'quick air', 'tinder' and 'firework[s]'. The poem draws on a number of creation myths (Prometheus, Frankenstein) in its depiction of the woman's generative powers. The metaphor of the 'echoes' recalls Ovid's tale of Narcissus where Echo, the wood nymph, cannot speak without someone else making the first utterance.[19] In 'Hardcastle Crags' nothing the subject sees can speak or mean without her interpellation.

In the opening stanza the clanging sound of the feet is registered in the onomatopoeic repetition of the 'ck' and 'k' sounds ('struck', 'racket', 'tacking', 'crooks', 'black', 'quick', 'shake'). Similar horseshoe sounds ring out in two *Ariel* poems, 'Elm' and 'Words'. The woman in every case seeks to dominate her environment, to make her mark. But the exuberant spark of the opening lines of 'Hardcastle Crags' has, by the middle of the second stanza, already begun to fade. Although the 'ck' and 'k' sounds flicker sporadically and gamely later, for example in stanza seven, they are softened by being used silently as at the beginning of 'knelt' or as a weak, falling sound at the end of 'tussocks'.

The preoccupation throughout 'Hardcastle Crags' is with language and the fear is of being outside or beyond it. Away from the social and familiar – the 'steely street' and 'stone-built town' – the woman must recognize that there is no 'word' with which to 'body' her 'blank mood'. Stripped of language, she is stripped of her dreams; shoeless (hence 'footsoles'), she can no longer strike fire. There is a process of effacement or annihilation here which is entirely characteristic of the poems of *The Colossus* and *Crossing the Water*, with the wind 'paring' her down (the word appears again in 'The Beekeeper's Daughter') and the narrow walls of the valley funnelling away to nothing. For Plath, 'funnel' often signifies a process of depletion or diminishment. In 'Parliament Hill Fields' (*CW*) the word is used to convey loss and silence, and in 'Wuthering Heights' (*CW*) the moors attempt to 'funnel my heat away', signalling a move from plenitude to nothingness.

For a number of critics, this and similar poems in *The Colossus* are primarily to be read as explorations of the relationship between the lone self and the natural world. As Bronfen argues, Plath is able to refigure these 'landscapes into scenes of psychic liminality' (Bronfen, *Sylvia Plath*, p. 66). 'Mussel Hunter at Rock Harbor', like 'Hardcastle Crags', figures the subject alone amid an unpeopled and incomprehensible world. Revealing the influence of Marianne Moore in its careful syllabic metre, and of Elizabeth Bishop in its compression and close observation, the poem shows its first-person speaker's close encounter with the other world of a seaside rock pool. Anthropomorphism and careful description (see the repetition of the 'b' and 'u' sounds in stanzas two and three, which onomatopoeically represent the softly bubbling sand and water) are an attempt at possession and set the scene for a finally qualified epiphany.

'Mussel Hunter' opens with competition and conflict. The word 'Hunter' in the title establishes a potential battle between pursuer and prey, and the initial scene is set in images connotative of attack and defence with 'light that scours' and 'smacks beached'. The latent threat of erosion and effacement, of being 'pared' down, which we saw above is here made physical and explicit. Stanzas four and five develop these combative metaphors. The crabs which are the objects of the speaker's vision ready themselves for the fight, putting 'forth claws', camouflage and shields. This is an ancient world (we are reminded of Elizabeth Bishop's 'The Fish') which looks to the long-lived, well-tested resources of the past (the rhetoric of medieval 'knights' and 'mottled mail') to shut out the observer and protect it in the present.

The poem closes with the speaker's discovery of the shell of a fiddler-crab, isolated and exposed on the rim of the pool. This has been 'bleached' by the sun and wind (the word takes us back to the 'beached' boats of stanza one) and is a signally contradictory and self-reflexive metaphor, representing both vulnerability (the crabs 'innards' are exposed) and daring (it is a 'headstrong Columbus crab'). The crab shell thus signifies the choices to be made by the speaker/poet: to risk self-exposure or to recede to safe conformity? Its value, the contemplation of which takes up the climactic final four stanzas, lies in its capacity to remind the living speaker of the aesthetic worth of her own seemingly inauspicious material: the inanimate, the powerless, the dead. One might argue, as does Seamus Heaney, that the discovery of the crab shell provides some kind of 'resolution', a 'certain founding of identity and security', a 'drama of survival'.[20] To which one might answer that the crab's victory is a pyrrhic one; it survives the death-by-drowning of the 'mass-motivated hordes', only to be eroded by the other elements. The 'resolution', then, is equivocal.

## Crossing the Water

'Tilted and disparate, and always unstable': this line from 'Wuthering Heights', the first poem in *Crossing the Water*, gestures towards what follows. These poems are, indeed, 'tilted' (oblique, off-key, disordered) and 'disparate' (ranging widely in theme, form and setting). They are 'unstable', too, in the sense that they feature multiple and mutable voices, are elusive, sometimes abstract and often defy straightforward assessment.

*Crossing the Water* includes elegies for others ('Among the Narcissi'), for the self ('Parliament Hill Fields') and for the past ('The Babysitters'). There are nature and animal poems such as 'Blackberrying' and 'Pheasant'. The former is an ostensibly pastoral scene which only partially veils a sense of natural and personal menace, of failure, hostility and rage. These poems often portray the speaker as alienated or dislocated in a threatening sea or landscape ('Finisterre', 'Sleep in the Mojave Desert'); in 'Whitsun', for example, the speaker watches, horrified, from the margins of a scene which she can barely comprehend and which simultaneously repulses and compels her. Plath often uses metaphors of rings, circles or circumferences to signal the exclusion of the speaking subject from the centre which nevertheless ceaselessly commands her attention. In 'Wuthering Heights' and 'Parliament Hill Fields' the ringed 'horizons' and the 'round sky' frame and limit the speaker's world. In 'A Life' 'A woman is dragging her shadow in a circle', endlessly prowling the peripheries. A number of critics have suggested that *Crossing the Water* traces the move that Plath made as a young woman from the US to Europe and thereby records associated processes of transformation and change. I propose to think about the collection in broader terms, as tracing a ceaseless journey around the edges of something which cannot quite be seized, understood, assimilated. It is a book of perpetual motion.

The collection features a number of dramatic portraits; these are often mocking in tone, and spoken in a variety of first person ('Zoo Keeper's Wife') and third person ('Face Lift') voices. The perspective in 'Face Lift' shifts throughout, connoting the fundamental instability – and duplicity – of subject and object alike. Sardonic in tone, the poem relishes its unveiling of the woman who has just emerged from cosmetic surgery. It delights in 'whipping off' the covers, 'peel[ing] away' the surface and thus exposing her vanity, her folly, her pride. 'The Tour' employs a similarly critical voice, which this time spits out its condemnation in angry short lines and harsh monosyllabic words. The speaker conveys both her own barely veiled hostility to the visiting 'maiden aunt' of the opening line and the aunt's infuriating egotism. The abrasiveness and pace of the language (what Judith Kroll calls a 'maniacal jauntiness' (*Chapters*, p. 242 n. 43)) and the harsh alliteration ('Gecko', 'flick', 'sparkle', 'lipstick') anticipate the vicious 'Ich, ich, ich, ich' rhymes of 'Daddy' (*A*). In the best traditions of the dramatic monologue, it is the attitude of the speaker and not of her object which is exposed. As Tracy Brain has argued, the real object – the 'Aunt Sally', perhaps – of this attack is not so much the unfortunate aunt as the English gentility and conservatism which she represents.[21]

*Crossing the Water*, then, employs a variety of voices in its treatment of 'disparate' subjects. Nevertheless, there is a complex and intriguing network of themes, metaphors and perspectives which weaves its way across and between these poems. Certain images recur, almost obsessively: images of stones and rock, for example, and of alleys and valleys (used in 'Wuthering Heights' and 'Insomniac' to suggest both an escape route and an awful entrapment), of pools and rivers ('The Tour', 'Mirror', 'Crossing the Water') and of bald, glassy, egglike and eyeless faces ('Facelift', 'Zoo Keeper's Wife', 'Parliament Hill Fields', 'Magi' and many others). We find an underlying coherence and unity which belies the confusion of the book's origins and the apparent disparity of its representations. There is also a real sense in the poems of *Crossing the Water* that these are not so much preparatory exercises for the *Ariel* poems which followed as complete, consistent and above all profoundly self-reflexive explorations of Plath's poetics.

Plath's first volume, *The Colossus*, closes with an image of the body in parts. Its final poem, 'The Stones', features multiple shots of dislocated organs and limbs: 'the stomach', the 'mouth-hole' and 'ear', the 'pink torso', 'any limb', 'heads', 'hands', 'hearts' and finally 'ten fingers' – a metonym, surely, for the writing self which seeks desperately to make something of this profound trauma. To Ted Hughes, the poem conveys the positive reconstruction of the female speaker's identity and voice (*WP*, p. 183), but it might equally be read as a narrative of dissociation or autotomy.

*Crossing the Water* is notable for its continued representation of these themes of fragmentation and isolation. 'An Appearance' – a poem which has much in common with Sexton's 'Self in 1958' and 'Housewife' – figures the female body as a domestic machine, alienated from herself and dominated by her environment (the 'iceboxes annihilate ... me', she complains). 'The Surgeon at 2 a.m.' reveals the remorseless dissection of the human body. This time the focus turns away from the suffering and fragmented self and towards the predatory other. Spoken in the voice of the surgeon, the poem refuses to disclose its speaker's or the patient's gender (Brain, *Other Sylvia*

*Plath*, pp. 122–4), thus experimenting with different voices and perspectives and with the authority available to each.

The collection contains many abstract poems which, like the nature and landscape poems, often register a pervasive though unspecified threat. Poems such as 'Small Hours' and 'Apprehensions' turn to the difficulties of reconciling the real and the imagined, actuality and aesthetics; they are about the inconsolations of philosophy. 'Small Hours' is a study in instability. This is signalled, not least, by the uncertainty about the title of the poem – the 'Small Hours' of *Crossing the Water* is known as 'Barren Woman' in the *Collected Poems*. Moreover, as much as this is a poem of complex abstractions, its imagery aligns it with the poetry of domesticity and female creativity found in *Crossing the Water* as elsewhere in Plath's oeuvre.

'Small Hours'/'Barren Woman' opens with a sense of diminishment and failure. The first word is 'empty', the speaker's voice echoes hollowly, and we find successive negatives ('least', 'without', 'sinks', 'dead', 'nothing', 'blank'). Stanza one paints a picture of pure isolation with the 'I' standing alone in a cold, unforgiving frame (the 'museum', which though architecturally ornate, has no 'statues', nothing which recalls human experience or achievement). At the same time, this is a subject who yearns for communication, who dreams of maternal and artistic creativity. In the second stanza she imagines herself as 'Mother of a white Nike and several bald-eyed Apollos' and as the object of a 'great public' (the image invokes the 'peanut-crunching crowd' of 'Lady Lazarus' (*A*)). Her hopes, though, are frustrated. She is provided only with the 'attentions' of the 'dead'. The poem closes in a further ambivalent or contradictory image. The final word, 'nurse', sounds the death knell as – 'Blank-faced and mum' – she silences the speaker. Yet as 'nurse' or midwife to the imagination, she shows a new way forward. From this perspective, 'Blank-faced' depicts not silence and erasure but the archetypal blank sheet of creative freedom.

In a comment on 'Parliament Hill Fields', a key poem in *Crossing the Water*, Plath signals a recognition of the tensions between voice and silence, subject and object, self and other and reality and abstraction. She suggests that the poem – which tells obliquely of a woman's recovery from miscarriage – turns away from numb silence and towards recovery (*CP*, pp. 290–1). The apparent resolution, however, may be less complete and reassuring than at first appears. There is a sense of threat here which only increases as the poem develops. We see blocked escape routes (the cloud or smog-barriered South in stanzas five and six), a knifelike moon and uncanny shapes cast on a child's nursery wall (stanzas eight to ten) and an austerely lit house which compels the speaker's return and closes the poem with a dreadful finality. Even children (the lost foetus, the surviving child, other people's children) are menacing – hence the 'crocodile' of schoolgirls which subsumes her in stanza three.

The real turn in the poem, I would argue, is the declaration in stanza six that the speaker is 'too happy'. What this admits is not necessarily the grief of miscarriage but the inadmissible feeling that while mourned, it is not wholly regretted. There is a liberation in not being perceived as pregnant: 'nobody can tell what I lack', and the images of fluidity (ponds, brimming eyes, gulls, river, snow, clouds, trees), while commemorating the loss of the baby and the flow of foetal blood, also celebrate the possibility of flight and change. The image of the dropped barrette, or hair slide, in stanza four also works two ways in evoking both the lost infant and, if one reads the metaphor as signalling the dropping or removal of a barrier, the restoration of personal freedom. The closing images, which from one perspective herald the glow of new life, also symbolize suffocation, hence the metaphors of the 'cellophane balloon' and the colour blue (the colour of maternity but also of asphyxiation, anaemia and death). The tone here is ambivalent; the speaker has turned her back not on grief but on the potential autonomy that her loss – albeit fleetingly – had seemed to promise.

'Parliament Hill Fields' and 'Small Hours' have much in common with another informal group in *Crossing the Water*, self-reflexive poems such as 'Widow' (the title alludes in part to the women's situation and in part to the typographical terms 'widow' and 'orphan'; both describe errors in setting the page), 'Last Words' and 'Stillborn'. The main preoccupation of these is their own poetic processes, their language, their aims and inadequacies. 'Stillborn', like 'Small Hours', yokes poetic and maternal failure. Clear and clinical in its approach, it begins, 'These poems do not live.' Yet the poem is deceptively complex, first confirming, then resisting, and finally transcending its own 'sad diagnosis'.

'Mirror', too, opens confidently: 'I am silver and exact.' But it then qualifies its own certainty. As the poem unfolds we see that this hermetic autonomy may be a deceptive façade masking the need for communion and dialogue. As Steven Gould Axelrod explains, this 'claim to passive veridicality ... does not accord with the mirror's actual role of dominating and interpreting its world' (*Wound*, p. 210). The poem is catoptric, describing while exemplifying in its own structure (two nine-line stanzas which establish symmetry and thus opposition) the properties of a mirror and the process of reflection. What the second stanza exposes is not simply the woman's need of the mirror but the mirror's need of the woman. Without her, things may be 'exact', 'truthful' and uncomplicated ('unmisted by love or dislike'); with her, a vast and unsettling but nevertheless vivid world comes to life. The duality or separation the poem seems to herald is thus completely undermined – the mirror itself is no longer a boundary but a liminal and penetrable space.

This volume's title poem offers a less explicit contemplation of the mirroring process. 'Crossing the Water' establishes a sequence of binaries, starting with the unspecified points of departure and arrival implicit in its title. Brain argues that this is deliberately enigmatic, making it 'impossible to identify just what water is being crossed'. Nevertheless, she offers a fruitful reading of the poem as an exemplification of Plath's 'mid-Atlanticism' and her 'refusal to choose' between England and the US and the cultural and linguistic identities which attach to each (Brain, *Other Sylvia Plath*, p. 48ff). The poem turns on the conflict or tension between its initial dualities; between the 'two black, cut-paper people', between surface and depth, 'light' and 'dark'. Like the 'Mirror' in the poem of that name, the lake is dependent on the object it reflects to give it identity. It is only in the final stanza, inspired by the night sky, that it at last yields its secrets, offering, as though from its depths, a mirror image of the shining stars above, luminous 'among the lilies'. Kendall emphasizes the blackness of this poem, reading it as a journey into the dark underworld, as the mythical passage across the River Styx to Hades: 'past the "astounded souls" of the dead' (*Critical Study*, p. 83). Certainly the poem stresses the awed silence of the scene. Nevertheless, it also retains faith in 'a little light' and in the power of the lake/mirror – and by extension, perhaps, of the poem – to transform this into something insightful and compelling: 'Stars open among the lilies. / Are you not blinded by such expressionless sirens?' Even, or precisely, out of darkness comes illumination. Significantly, 'Words', the closing poem of the 1965/1966 edition of *Ariel*, returns to this scene, albeit with less optimism about the potential of the mirror/pool (the poem?) to transform its object into something wondrous. In 'Words', in place of the generative mobility of 'Crossing the Water' (note the latter's use of multiple verbs and verb forms), we have only 'fixed stars' which 'govern a life' – the earlier poem shows a proliferation of meanings, the later the closing down of meaning.

## Self-reflexivity

The poems of *The Colossus* and *Crossing the Water* are preoccupied with their own poetic, linguistic and ontological status. They are textually self-reflexive, even narcissistic in the specific sense in which Linda Hutcheon uses that term. Textual narcissism, as she designates it, is writing which is textually rather than biographically 'self-reflective ... auto-referential, auto-representational'.[22] It contemplates and interrogates its own 'narrative and/or linguistic identity', thematizing or mirroring not only the subject ostensibly at its heart (a walk on the moors, say, or memories of the lost father) but its own processes of reconstruction and representation. This is evident throughout these collections and most explicitly in the poems I have just discussed about mirrors, mirroring and other forms of reflection or duplication. 'In Plaster', for example, explores the duplicity and noncoherence of the double image and thereby problematizes the relationship between original and copy. Mirroring, in Plath's poetry, is both strategy (reflection or mimesis as process) and object (the reflection or replication as material subject of enquiry).

It has been posited by Ted Hughes and others that the apparently singular voice of the *Ariel* poems is Plath's true voice; that the immature and transitional voices of *The Colossus* and *Crossing the Water* are false ones which must be shed or sloughed off like the skin of a snake before the resplendent new and authentic identity can be assumed (*CP*, p. 16). My argument is, first, that there are multiple voices, personae and perspectives at play in these collections – sometimes contradictory, often indeterminate, always carefully constructed. Second, that in seeking the 'true' Plath voice, we may be blind to other aspects of the poems which merit attention: their allusiveness and elusiveness, their variety and range, their complexity and above all their sophisticated self-reflexivity.

## Notes

1. See Jo Gill, 'Anne Sexton and Confessional Poetics', *Review of English Studies* 55 (2004), pp. 425–45, on the critical reception of confessional poetry in this period.
2. Anne Sexton, 'Craft Interview with William Packard', in J. D. McClatchy (ed.), *Anne Sexton: The Artist and her Critics* (Bloomington: Indiana University Press, 1978), p. 46.
3. John Berryman, *The Dream Songs* (London: Faber and Faber, 1993), p. vi.
4. T. S. Eliot, *Collected Poems: 1909–1962* (London: Faber and Faber, 1974), pp. 13, 89, 109, 223.
5. W. H. Auden, *Selected Poems*, ed. Edward Mendelson (London: Faber and Faber, 1979), pp. 79, 86.
6. Jacqueline Rose, *The Haunting of Sylvia Plath* (London: Virago, 1991), p. 73 (Rose's emphasis).
7. Linda Wagner (ed.), *Sylvia Plath: The Critical Heritage* (London: Routledge, 1988), p. 1.
8. Tim Kendall, *Sylvia Plath: A Critical Study* (London: Faber and Faber, 2001), p. 24.
9. Helen Hennessy Vendler, *Coming of Age as a Poet: Milton, Keats, Eliot, Plath* (Cambridge, MA: Harvard University Press, 2003), pp. 150–4.
10. Judith Kroll, *Chapters in a Mythology: The Poetry of Sylvia Plath* (New York: Harper & Row, 1976), pp. 54, 82–3.

11. Quoted in Steven Gould Axelrod, *Sylvia Plath: The Wound and the Cure of Words* (Baltimore: Johns Hopkins University Press, 1990), p. 45.

12. Stan Smith, *Inviolable Voice: History and Twentieth-Century Poetry* (Dublin: Gill and Macmillan, 1982), p. 218.

13. Elisabeth Bronfen, *Sylvia Plath* (Plymouth: Northcote House, 1998), p. 80.

14. Josef Breuer, 'The Case of Fraulein Anna O.', in Sigmund Freud and Josef Breuer, *Studies on Hysteria* (PFL3), trans. and ed. James and Alix Strachey (Harmondsworth: Pelican, 1974), pp. 73–102.

15. Al Strangeways, *Sylvia Plath: The Shaping of Shadows* (Cranbury, NJ, and London: Associated University Presses, 1998), p. 168.

16. Grace Schulman, 'Sylvia Plath and Yaddo', in Paul Alexander (ed.), *Ariel Ascending: Writings about Sylvia Plath* (New York: Harper & Row, 1985), pp. 165–77.

17. Sylvia Plath, *Johnny Panic and the Bible of Dreams* (London: Faber and Faber, 1979), p. 92.

18. Sigmund Freud, *On Metapsychology: The Theory of Psychoanalysis* (PFL 11), trans. James Strachey, ed. Angela Richards (Harmondsworth: Pelican, 1984), pp. 437–8.

19. Ovid, *Metamorphoses*, trans. Mary M. Innes (Harmondsworth: Penguin, 1955).

20. Seamus Heaney, *The Government of the Tongue* (London: Faber and Faber, 1988), pp. 158, 159.

21. Tracy Brain, *The Other Sylvia Plath* (Harlow: Longman, 2001), pp. 74, 75.

22. Linda Hutcheon, *Narcissistic Narrative: The Metafictional Paradox* (New York: Methuen, 1984), p. 1.

# 8

CHRISTINA BRITZOLAKIS

## *Ariel* and other poems

*Ariel*, the slim volume of poems published posthumously under Sylvia Plath's name in 1965, has become an iconic document in twentieth-century literary history, a status underlined by the most recently published edition, which restores the selection and sequencing of the poems Plath left at the time of her death in 1963 (*A Rest*.).[1] *Ariel* is closely identified with the disturbing power of a poetic voice whose reverberations were felt to be, from the outset, distinctively, even scandalously, female and embodied.[2] The '*Ariel* voice' seems to trope a return of the repressed, at both the personal and the political level. For the volume's first readers, of course, this voice was marked above all by its proximity to her suicide, and was apprehended as a psychic unleashing or release. Reviews frequently invoked a 'breakthrough' in style: a discovery, or recovery, of a liberating immediacy of feeling. This binary model of Plath's poetic development, grounded in a biographical narrative, was partially undermined by the appearance of the *Collected Poems* in 1981, which revealed the range and extent of Plath's work, and the many continuities between *The Colossus* (UK 1960/US 1962) and *Ariel* (1965/1966).

That Plath's style altered dramatically over the course of her career is undeniable. While she begins by exploring the possibilities and limits of the academic mode promoted by the New Critics during the 1950s, her poems move towards a mode of surrealism, replacing narrative sequence with a series of hallucinatory images, in language marked by a new rhythmic and colloquial freedom. While these stylistic shifts are sometimes described in terms of internalization, even in the early poems a concern with capturing the particularity of the natural object alternates with more allegorical elements such as the poetic 'inscription' to prior visual or verbal texts, or the psychoanalytically inflected address to a parent figure. The concept of the 'breakthrough' also risks occluding the many and varied discursive contexts of her work, which recent critics have gone some way towards recovering.[3] Plath's later poetry emerges from a particularly stark conjuncture between the discredited psychosexual and political discourses of the Eisenhower era, and the emergent feminist, ecological and disarmament movements. The arc of her development as a poet, within the short space of her writing life, represents a devastating critique of the postwar formalist lyric and a recovery of the wider cultural resources of modernism as critique.

Plath's experiments with voice and persona resist the tendency to read her poems as a psychobiographical narrative of self-discovery. What is sometimes known as her 'confessionalism' is more usefully viewed, I shall argue, as a doubled discourse, which, while it may well draw upon autobiographical materials, withholds from both poet and reader any secure identification. For Plath, the psychic is always already a theatrical space, an 'other scene', layered with multiple texts and images. In spite of its apparent centrality, then, the location of the 'I' in these texts is unstable and duplicitous, and this instability or doubleness is often registered by critics as a threat, danger or negativity elided with femininity itself. Plath's figurative language also generates considerable ambivalence among her critics. On the one hand, she is noted for the vividness and ingenuity of her metaphors; on the other, these same metaphors tend to call forth charges of staginess, rhetorical overreaching or manipulative sensationalism. For some readers, she is guilty of metaphoric excess, of irresponsibly exploiting the power of analogy, most notoriously in later poems such as 'Daddy', which yoke together historical and psychic events in highly unstable metaphoric conjunctions. These moments of metaphoric 'conceit' alternate with moments of linguistic regression which foreground the material basis of signification: the acoustic stuff of language such as puns, echoes and nonsense.

In this chapter I shall argue that the organizing trope of Plath's later poems is the return of the repressed, and that this trope is acted out through an interplay of metaphor and sound, of the analogical and the oral dimensions of poetic voice. For Plath, as I suggested earlier, 'voice' is thoroughly embodied, bringing into play the sexual and reproductive potency of the female body, no less than its symbolic and institutional location. Sigmund Freud, in his article 'The Uncanny', points out that the meanings of the German word for uncanny (*unheimlich*) are closely related to, and indeed dependent upon, its apparent opposite, the *heimlich*: the domestic, familiar or homely.[4] The dynamics of the family, and more especially, of what has been repressed within it, preoccupy Plath's writing from the outset. Like many of her poetic contemporaries, she uses the Freudian family romance to explore her relation to wider structures of authority; 'Daddy', for example, famously links the paternal figure with linguistic mechanisms of silencing and the deprivation of speech. A recurrent pattern in *The Colossus* is an attempt to trace a mythic lost moment of origin within or through a scene of parental instruction. In the later poems these oedipalized scenarios are inflected by a more directly politicized engagement, on the one hand with 1950s myths of femininity, and on the other with the geopolitical discourses of the Cold War.

## Codes of estrangement

Plath's childhood memoir, 'Ocean 1212-W', models the pattern of an impossible quest for origins in her work. It constructs a personal myth, in which the resented birth of a sibling marks a loss of the mother, and consequently of the infant's 'beautiful fusion with the things of this world' (*JP*, p. 120).[5] Childhood memories 'stiffen' into 'a fine, white flying myth' (*JP*, p. 124), objectified spatially as a ship-in-a-bottle. Creativity is henceforth premised on a traumatic disjunction between language and subjectivity. Many of Plath's poems are organized around this mythology of a fall or exile into a language and history (including literary history) that is seen as radically other and even inimical to the self. Inspiration, of which the *ur*-metaphor is the 'breathing rhythm' described at the start of 'Ocean 1212-W' (*JP*, p. 120), is preempted by frozen or petrified spatial forms (cast, mould, monument, mannequin, sarcophagus). The 'I' is inscribed within the alienations of a preexisting order. This Romantic mythology of subjection to otherness shapes Plath's representation of the natural world, of femininity and of literary tradition. Images of entombed voice abound: the hearselike 'black boot' of the priest in 'Berck-Plage', the 'black shoe' in which the white foot lives in 'Daddy', the 'black and stiff' suit offered to 'The Applicant' and the 'black phones' of 'The Munich Mannequins'. The poet seems unhappily exiled from an originary moment of voicing, which can only be echoed or parodied through metrical, allusive or conventional devices.

What 'Ocean 1212-W' refers to as the 'awful birthday of otherness' (*JP*, p. 121) blocks aesthetic creativity and freezes imagination, menacing the subject with a dereliction of language itself. It frequently turns the female body, which conventionally signifies life and fertility, into a trope of imprisonment and petrifaction. In 'Barren Woman' the speaker is a 'museum ... with pillars, porticoes, rotundas'; but her fertile counterparts, the 'Heavy Women', also become prisoners of their 'weighty' bodies, merging with the female 'archetypes' of motherhood. The maternal body is represented as a 'mausoleum' ('The Rival'), an allegorical Greek statue and a 'womb of marble' ('The Other'). In 'Medusa' it is a 'Ghastly Vatican', a 'bottle' in which the speaker 'lives' (recalling, yet again, the imagery of encapsulation in glass).

This mythology of estrangement in Plath's poetry is organized, as I have argued elsewhere, around parental objects of frozen or petrified desire, and the polarization of their legacies (Britzolakis, *Theatre of Mourning*, pp. 41–65). The mother is linked with the feminized moral and ideological codes transmitted by domestic and sentimental traditions of writing. Her significance is signalled by a pervasive lunar imagery which lends Plath's psychic landscapes a distinctive bleakness ('The Moon and the Yew Tree', 'Barren Woman', 'Elm', 'Edge'). The lunar/maternal figure, 'staring from her hood of bone' ('Edge'), is both dispirited and dispiriting, a sterile light-borrower and a withholder. This emblem of maternal disempowerment and self-effacement recalls André Green's description of the 'dead mother' as 'a mother who remains alive but who is, so to speak, psychically dead in the eyes of the young child in her care'.[6] The dead moon/mother precipitates a condition of 'blank mourning', which empties meaning from the world.

Whereas the maternal principle is associated with a devalued culture of domesticity and sentiment, the dead father is linked with the formal and mythic qualities of high art (especially of modernism). The display of technical expertise in *The Colossus*, while doing homage to the authority of the literary canon, is accompanied by tropes of dislocation from any vital or sustaining model of the cultural past. The colossus represents a literary history congealed into stone-dead forms; 'tradition' is apprehended as a piling up of fragmentary signifiers of antiquity, within which an obscure loss is lodged. This oedipalized scenario, which recurs in various forms across Plath's writing, draws attention to its own excessiveness and indeed perversity. Literary tradition is constituted through a self-conscious mythologizing of the death of the father; it comes to occupy the status of a fetish, a substitutive and compensatory fiction, forestalling a prior loss, coded as maternal. Writing, then, is seen as the product of polarized maternal and paternal cultural legacies, which can enter into dialogue with each other only indirectly, through the vocabulary of the uncanny.

The stylistic shift evidenced in the *Ariel* poems is the result of Plath's remodelling, from 1961 onwards, of the postwar empirical-formalist lyric, as institutionalized by the New Critics. Plath's considerable investment in these protocols, which insisted on the necessity of form as a sublimatory or distancing mechanism, comes under a range of pressures, including her interest in Freudian psychoanalysis, the example of contemporaries such as Robert Lowell and Anne Sexton, and the breakdown of her marriage to Ted Hughes. Increasingly, the spatial organization of the later poems enables the recovery of an oral/aural, incantatory element at the level of language. In psychic landscapes such as 'Wuthering Heights', 'Blackberrying', 'The Moon and the Yew Tree', 'Little Fugue' and 'Elm', a Gothicized iconography begins to violate the empirical-formalist mode. The natural world tends to alternate between the psychic tropes of projection and incorporation. On the one hand, it takes on an appearance of active malignity, which imperils the inwardness of the subject ('Wuthering Heights', 'Blackberrying'). On the other, it is organized around metaphors of spatial enclosure, and coded as the scene of obsessive rituals ('The Moon and the Yew Tree', 'Little Fugue'), marking a thematic of psychic obstruction and 'the unspeakable'.

In their reading of Freud, the psychoanalysts Nicholas Abraham and Maria Torok identify incorporation as a type of failed or refused mourning whereby the other is secreted within oneself. The emblem of incorporation is, they argue, the crypt, 'an enclave . . . a kind of artificial unconscious lodged in the midst of the ego' which turns the self into a 'cemetery guard'.[7] The architecture of the crypt is that of an archive of texts and images (family history, literary tradition, psychoanalysis, fantasy), within which a lost object (maternal or paternal) is figuratively kept alive as a stranger or 'living dead'. Such rituals of incorporation or encrypting tend to dominate space-time relationships in Plath's later poems. Recurring figurative patterns tend to replace linear sequence with a repetitive or traumatic temporality, producing an occult traffic between familial and public memory. In 'The Moon and the Yew Tree' a highly formal, coded and dualistic scheme of imagery deterministically signals psychic as well as spatial enclosure and a deadlock of creativity. The vaultlike, 'Gothic' yew tree, coded as a medium of transmission for ancestral and paternal voices, is lined up against the moon, token of 'blank' maternal mourning.

Like 'The Moon and the Yew Tree', 'Little Fugue' is dominated by the image of the yew tree as a medium of paternal transmission, and turns on the Gothic and oedipalized motif of the 'unspeakable'. The poem's title suggests an exercise performed under male tutelage, a minor repetition, or mimicry, of Beethoven's 'Grosse Fuge'. The 'fugue' refers both to a contrapuntal form of musical organization and to a hysterical symptom. Plath's highly coded and self-referring use of interwoven sound and image patterns in this poem is mapped on to the structures of the nuclear family, as a form of refused or withheld communication. The perverse father figure of 'Little Fugue', who looks backward to 'Man in Black', and forward to 'Berck-Plage' and 'Daddy', belongs to the hystericized imaginary of Gothic romance. He is the seducer/antagonist whose house contains guilty secrets, and whose counterpart is the figure of the hysteric (the silenced woman *par excellence*), 'arranging' [her] 'morning'/mourning. Plath's 'man in black' is an emblematic figure, signalling a crisis in paternal law, and the failure of the oedipal resolution through which the (male) child, in Freudian terms, enters the symbolic order. He marks the anomalous and enigmatic status of femininity itself within a Freudian paradigm, which occludes the daughter's relation to the mother.

For Plath, then, subjectivity is suspended between tropes of muting or silencing and of unleashed voice. In 'Elm' the tree of the title is described as 'inhabited by a cry', and this 'cry' unfolds as a series of reverberating questions that circle back upon themselves. The poem, which at one point in the *Ariel* manuscripts is entitled 'The Elm Speaks', animistically 'voices' the elm. Through this act of oral projection/impersonation, the speaker gains access to a phantasmatic 'other space', linked with tropes of nightmare, uncanny metamorphosis and gestation, and with incantatory repetition. In the later poems orality marks both the creative-destructive power of the maternal body (as in 'Elm'), and a repressed or stigmatized female sexuality, often signalled through colour. 'Tulips' contrasts the seductively anaesthetic blankness of the hospital setting with the 'sudden tongues' of the red flowers, which 'hurt' the speaker back into life, and implicitly writing. In 'Poppies in July', too, the blood-red colour of the flowers suggests a sexualized wounding, while in 'Poppies in October' the flowers become 'late mouths' which 'cry open'.

For Plath, the sexual politics of voice and voicing is played out on the tabooed oral/aural boundary between the linguistic and the non- or prelinguistic. In the early poems the mimetic use of sound devices such as alliteration, assonance and internal rhyme can be seen as an attempt to incarnate the minute particulars of the natural object, an aural approximation of its density. However, although auditory devices ostensibly serve the cause of mimesis and embodiment of the natural world, they also threaten to become repositories of uncanny experience. The aural level of the text tends to repel closure, imperilling the formalist ideal of the poem as 'a well-steered country / Under a balanced ruler' ('Lorelei'). In the *Ariel* poems the mimesis of sound, which constituted a central project of *The Colossus*, is parodied as an obsessive ritual. Devices such as onomatopoeia and repetition become a form of verbal sympathetic magic, privileging the regressive, incantatory level of language. The compulsive nursery-rhyme rhythms of 'Daddy' provide the most obvious example of this linguistic regression, as does the poem's use of infantile and nonsense words such as 'gobbledygoo' and 'Achoo'.

The linguistic primitivism of the later poems taps into what Freud in *Beyond the Pleasure Principle* calls the 'daemonic' power of repetition.[8] Plath's harnessing of the uncanny power of sound through repetition inscribes at once an 'instinct for mastery', in Freud's phrase, and the limits of the ego's mastery of experience. In 'Words' language is seen as ultimately escaping the speaker's control; the echoes which travel 'off from the center like horses' return as 'riderless' aural or rhythmic traces, as a beat ('the indefatigable hoof-taps'). More generally, noise has the power to infiltrate and to undermine the symbolic order in localized weak spots, particularly in the 1962 sequence that has become known as 'Bee Poems'. The 'din' of imprisoned bees in 'The Arrival of the Bee Box', with their 'unintelligible syllables', reminds the speaker of 'a Roman mob' (compare the staccato of the beekeeper's gunshots in 'The Swarm'). In 'Edge' the moon's 'blacks crackle and drag', disrupting the apparent finality and sculptural self-containment of the poem-as-image. These knots and 'snags' (a recurrent word) in the smooth, controlled flow of meaning announce a subterranean text of orality. As 'The Courage of Shutting-Up' puts it, the tongue 'has nine tails, it is dangerous. / And the noise it flays from the air, once it gets going!' The unleashed tongue recovers a prehistoric era, buried by repression, in the evolution of the 'I'.

## Doubled discourse

Plath's undergraduate dissertation, on Dostoyevsky, cites Freud's view in 'The Uncanny' of the *doppelgänger* as the product of a split between the critical agency or conscience and the rest of the ego.[9] Her own poetic discourse is often caught up in structures of address, which externalize the agency of an antagonistic, ambiguously gendered 'other' or 'rival'. This doubled discourse, marked by a theatricalized, unstable irony, is the product of a certain psychic violence; it travesties modernism's resistance to the domestic, maternal and sentimental. Plath frequently pits the poet against the figure of the domesticated woman: the 1950s 'housewife'/mother. In 'An Appearance' the persecutory double takes the form of a mechanized woman, a cypher of 'efficient' domesticity, whose body is described as 'a Swiss watch'. In 'A Birthday Present' the nameless object of the title appears to the speaker in the kitchen, the site of domestic labour, as a female commodity-body, with 'breasts' and 'edges'.

The play of sexualized masks in the later poetry is enmeshed in a network of competitive identifications, not only between men and women but also between women. It marks an ideological clash between the discourses of postwar femininity and of professionalism, which runs through all Plath's writings. The ironizing of femininity as masquerade, seduction and false representation recalls Joan Riviere's 1929 analysis of oedipalized femininity as a mask 'behind which man suspects some hidden danger'.[10] 'Lesbos', a pseudo-dramatic monologue addressed to a female interlocutor, explores a rivalrous and perversely eroticized relationship between two women (hence the ironic allusion to Sappho's island, dedicated to female love and friendship). The poem is filled with images of domestic space as hell: the 'stink of fat and baby crap', the 'smog of cooking', lit by a migraine-inducing 'fluorescent light'.

The rhetorically volatile voice of the later poems generates aggressive and rebellious scenarios, whose effect is to satirize the discredited mythology of

1950s femininity. It precipitates a melodrama or black comedy of sexual relations, which tends to undo gender identifications ('Stopped Dead'), and which oscillates between victim plots ('The Rabbit Catcher', 'The Jailer') and revenge plots ('Daddy', 'Lady Lazarus', 'Stings'). The revenge plot brings into play a thematic of artifice and perversity, a dizzying circulation of inherited texts and images. 'Purdah' adopts the mask of a veiled Asian woman, as a signifier of submissive femininity, preparatory to releasing 'the lioness, / The shriek in the bath, / The cloak of holes'. The woman is ironically likened to a faceted gemstone, a 'valuable' object whose sole purpose is to mirror the male psyche. Exploiting the theatrical possibilities of suspense and deferral, notably through enjambement, the poem is poised in the moment preceding the denouement of its own narrative: the breaking of purdah, the shattering of formal control and the unleashing of revenge. Its spatial and formal organization parodies an aestheticism which it sees as synonymous with the male fetishizing of the 'appurtenances' of femininity.

Vengeful and castratory scenarios such as those of 'Purdah' exploit the potential threat or aggression associated with female performance, while constantly drawing attention to the cultural production of such fantasies. In the infantile/disciplinary scenario of 'Daddy', a demonic reflexivity harnesses the most regressive aspects of language; this is a graphically schematized, flicker-book world of doubles and puppetlike projections in which father/oppressor and daughter/victim undergo a bewildering series of transformations and role reversals. The tools of the father/oppressor are above all linguistic; Daddy's sign ('Ich') is the form that kills the force, the 'barb wire', which traps and hurts the daughter's 'tongue'. Accordingly, 'Daddy' wreaks its revenge on this figure through parody voodoo rituals, which exploit the linguistic primitivism of the unleashed tongue. The father becomes a scapegoat, ritually dismembered into metonymic body parts (foot, toe, head, moustache, blue eye, cleft chin, bones, heart), and resurrected in a bewildering variety of guises. Pastiche and parody govern the poem's discourse, which recycles nursery rhymes, Gothic folklore, literary (especially modernist) echoes, Freudian texts and historical events. At the same time, language threatens to break down into nonsense, stuttering and aphasia ('the brute / Brute heart of a brute like you').

Although Plath was initially celebrated as a poet of anguished authenticity, her rhetoric can now be read as encoding a spectacular relation between poet and audience, which foregrounds questions of sexuality and power. The later Plath in particular makes her distinctive black comedy by crossing orphic myths of the inspired poet with an ironic deployment of stereotypes of alienated or objectified femininity. As 'Lady Lazarus' demonstrates, the ironic specularity at work in Plath's language is an effect not merely of literary history, or of a gendered literary market, but also of a culture of consumption in which images of women circulate as commodities. Among the personae which appear most frequently in Plath's poetry are those of the prostitute, the female performer and the mechanical woman. In 'Fever 103°', as in 'Lady Lazarus', the speaker occupies all three of these roles, oscillating between the positions of artist and artefact, consumer and commodity-spectacle. Indeed, *Ariel* situates itself as part of a culture in which self-revelation or self-expression has itself become a cliché: what 'Lady Lazarus' calls 'the big strip tease'.

Plath's formation as a poet coincides with the point at which modernism began, in the 1950s, to be canonized and institutionalized within the Anglo-American academy, as the epitome of 'high' (as opposed to 'mass') culture. Her later poems unsettle these cultural hierarchies; their verbal landscape is saturated with visual spectacle and the melodramatic plots of mass culture. The imagery of *Ariel* has an almost compulsively visual, phantasmagoric character. Exotic and brilliantly coloured plants and animals, including spotted orchids, camellias ('Fever 103°'), tiger lilies ('The Night Dances') and sea anemones ('Lesbos') form a decor, a decadent iconography. Many of the poems recycle stock tropes of cinematic horror: the dismembered corpse ('Berck-Plage', 'A Birthday Present', 'The Detective'), the malevolent neighbour ('Eavesdropper'), the psychopath ('Stopped Dead'). Their satirical target, like that of many contemporary thrillers and horror films, is the stifling family-centred and ethnocentric conformity of the 1950s small-town idyll, particularly the sanitized 'normality' of the suburban ideal home ('A Secret', 'The Tour').

## Body language

Although she often models her relation to poetic language through bodily metaphors ('Metaphors'), for Plath the status of the reproductive female body as literary sign is highly unstable, announcing a crisis in femininity itself, as a social, psychic and literary-historical construct. Indeed, although her metaphors are often celebrated for their sensuous power, this sensuousness tends to manifest itself negatively. In 'Ariel' the trope of the horse and rider unfolds an ambiguous celebration of embodied movement ('at one with the drive') as intensely pleasurable, yet self-immolating. In the poem's dual register, images of darkness, earth, blood, orality and the female body give way to those of light, transcendence and disembodiment. The phallic, solar and vertical register is punctuated by the repetition of the 'I', culminating in the image of suicidal flight 'Into the red//Eye'. This passage from the 'nigger-eye' to the 'red//Eye'/'I' traces the emergence of a power structure within the psyche, a movement into the realm of a paternally identified ego-ideal. The Apollonian 'red//Eye', destination of the poem's journey, is an emblem of specularity and surveillance, while the 'cauldron' of morning/mourning invokes an extreme religious imagery of martyrdom and purification; in Isaiah 29:1 Jerusalem is referred to as Ariel, the city destined to be destroyed by fire.

Feminist readings of Plath's later poems have dwelt on their recurrent tropes of woundedness, bleeding and mutilation as signs of an internalized violence.[11] Notoriously, 'Kindness' opposes reproductive maternal 'nature', represented by the allegorical nurse figure, Dame Kindness, to the phallic 'blood jet' of 'poetry', which refuses consolation. In Plath's poetry blood is a trope of bodily excess, of that which violates both aesthetic and ideological closure. Defiling flows such as blood or milk, which transgress the body's 'clean and proper' boundaries, signal, according to Julia Kristeva, a trauma of maternal separation, never quite overcome by the body's social demarcation into zones of cleanliness and pollution. Abjection threatens to return the symbolic to the (feared and desired) inside of the maternal body and to that extent constitutes a 'deviation' from the oedipal triangulation of desire.[12] It marks the abject female body, associated with the rites of childbirth and menstruation, in opposition to the closed, 'perfect' body of woman-as-artefact. In 'Edge' 'the woman is perfected', ironically achieving, in death, the frozen concreteness of an emblem or sculptural object. Inorganic images of petrified stasis alternate with images of organic fluidity (the 'sweet, deep throats of the night flower'). As in 'Kindness', the condition of aesthetic 'perfection' is self-immolating, exacting revenge upon life and maternity.

The exploration of the 'powers of horror' associated with the female (and especially the maternal) body in Plath's work forms part of a broader dialogue with modernism. She tends to figure femininity as abject at points when its social, cultural and literary inscriptions come under the heaviest strain, as in 'Lesbos' and 'Medusa'. 'Medusa' links the maternal body with a repellent, engulfing viscosity, through a series of self-consciously erudite and surreal tropes. In 'Medusa', as in 'Cut' and 'Kindness', metaphoric activity – the analogical intelligence or wit which elicits similarities between apparently unlike objects – becomes an exercise of power which negates and punishes the maternal/reproductive body, and which tends to rebound upon the self.

Plath's poems about motherhood, many of which elegiacally celebrate the mother-infant relation, are no less caught up in these paradoxes. Her exploration of the relation between maternal subjectivity and writing is highly innovative, combining lyrical intimacy and tenderness with a critique of motherhood as a symbolic and institutional discourse. Since Plato, the maternal has been located at the limit of the symbolic order, and aligned with nature and matter as the 'literal' ground of representation, from which both enlightened thinking and figurative language emerge. Plath draws on this philosophical tradition, reflexively exploring the transformative potentialities and limits of metaphor. She presents the maternal body as the repressed ground of figuration, in poems containing some of her most vivid and hallucinatory images ('Nick and the Candlestick', 'The Night Dances'). The Platonic myth of the cave, the womblike space of imprisonment, which allows men to see only flickering shadows or reflections of the truth, informs 'Candles', 'By Candlelight' and 'Nick and the Candlestick' (the latter two composed within five days of each other). These poems reinvent the libidinal, domestic and textual space of the mother-infant relation under the sign of a discredited paternal law.

The maternal body frequently appears in the *Ariel* poems as a symbolic site of resistance to the Enlightenment narrative of technological mastery over nature. Plath draws on aspects of the symbolic and religious discourse of motherhood as a critique of Cold War militarism, what she refers to in a letter to her mother as 'the military-industrial complex' (*LH*, p. 438).[13] In 'Getting There' the train, bearing the speaker through a nightmare landscape of war and carnage, is obstructed by 'the body of this woman' and by 'garlanded children'. 'Brasilia' and 'Mary's Song' adopt the stance of the *mater dolorosa* who laments the sacrifice of her son; 'Brasilia' imagines the coming of a race of 'super-people', while the sacrificial 'holocaust' of 'Mary's Song' references both the Nazi death camps and the threat of nuclear annihilation. 'Nick and the Candlestick' refers to the effects of environmental poisoning, 'Thalidomide' to the birth deformities caused in 1960–1 by the administration of that drug to pregnant women.

Drawing on emergent pacifist and ecological critiques, the later poems tend to associate technology with the historical unfolding of a relentlessly instrumental and dominating rationality. The train is a key image of this oppressive rationality; it is described as 'killing the track' ('Totem') and as 'an animal / Insane for the destination' ('Getting There'). In 'Daddy' the infamous comparison of the speaker to a Jewish victim of the Nazi death camps is initiated via the conceit of the German language as 'an engine, an engine / Chuffing me off like a Jew'. Technological modernity appears as a global discourse of destruction, hyphenating the catastrophes of World War II (especially the Holocaust and Hiroshima), with contemporaneous Cold War threats of nuclear warfare and environmental contamination. Plath's insertion into these debates remains highly ambiguous, even, some have argued, opportunistic. Her invocation of the Holocaust ('Daddy', 'Lady Lazarus', 'Mary's Song'), and of Hiroshima ('Fever 103°', 'Mary's Song') was highly controversial for a generation of earlier critics, such as Irving Howe, who accused her of capitalizing on the collective significance of these events.[14] This has become a different kind of critical issue for contemporary readers, since the parodic movement of poems such as 'Daddy' and 'Lady Lazarus', which cannibalize media reports and historical events, along with Freudian clichés and sexual and racial stereotypes, is now itself a cultural dominant.

Many of Plath's later poems entail an ambiguous identification with figures of victimized racial otherness. These tropes form part of a dialogue with the legacy of modernist primitivism, transposed into the post-World War II moment of global expansion of American influence. The paranoid optic of the Cold War, with its cult of national, familial and racial hygiene, is satirized in *The Bell Jar* and, more obliquely, in poems such as 'The Surgeon at 2 a.m.', 'Letter in November' and 'The Arrival of the Bee Box'. In 'Ariel' the phallic and self-immolating trajectory of the 'I' into the red solar 'eye' subsumes in its course both the 'nigger-eye / Berries' and the 'dew' (with its pun on 'Jew'). While the Nazi/Jew metaphor in 'Daddy' has been much discussed, less often noticed is the adoption in 'Purdah' of the mask of a subjugated and silenced Asian woman in order to stage a symbolic revenge against a patriarchal oppressor. The practice of purdah is thereby turned into a metaphor for a dispossession very different in degree and kind; arguably, the image rejoins a history of Western appropriation of colonized cultures as ethnographic spectacle.

## Mourning and melancholia

Plath's later poems, I have argued, tend to fragment or displace linear sequence, replacing it with the repetitive temporality of trauma. Narrative links are usurped by a series of enigmatic, hallucinatory images, which refract a collective history through privatized rituals of mourning. The phantasmagoria of *Ariel* is not simply the sign of a psychobiographical predicament. It engages in a dialogue with literary history (especially with the legacy of modernism), and with the lyric genre itself as a repository of collective memory. The surrealist logic of Plath's poems is frequently opaque. Her images tend to acquire an emblematic or iconic status, through internal repetition and elaboration, in the manner of a compulsive, magical or Gnostic ritual. This resistance to interpretation can be seen in terms of Freud's distinction between mourning and melancholia. According to Freud, the normative rites of mourning enable the ego eventually to recoup its psychic losses and consolidate itself, whereas melancholia makes mourning an end in itself, turning inwards towards obsessive rituals which are withdrawn from shared reality.[15] In melancholia, mourning, which heals the breach left in the symbolic order by death, has gone wrong, precipitating a disorder of language and subjectivity. It is locked into a logic of spectrality, of the conjuration of the dead, which internalizes threats to the legitimacy of a particular cultural order.

For the melancholic, the status of language is profoundly ambiguous. If on the one hand, as Freud argues in his essay, excessive or pathological mourning produces exacerbated linguistic activity, on the other, it undermines the symbolic order, blocking communication and turning language in upon itself. In 'Berck-Plage' and 'The Munich Mannequins', for example, a surrealist cross-cutting of images, and a hermetic elaboration of the isolated detail, produces a radically estranged landscape of menacing and petrified part-objects. Literary history is also subject to melancholic rituals of incorporation, objectification and display. The mortuary images of 'Death & Co.' invoke a history of allegorical personifications of death, from Romanticism (signalled by allusions to Heine and to Blake's death mask) to the baroque motif of the scheming courtier.

In the 1962 sequence known as the Bee Poems, a surrealist logic of displacement and condensation inserts the dynamics of the oedipal family into a social and historical continuum. Beekeeping is associated for Plath not only with the infantile fantasy of the omnipotent father – bees were the academic specialism of Otto Plath, author of *Bumblebees and their Ways* (1934) – but also with female fertility and reproductive power. In the 1959 poem 'The Beekeeper's Daughter', the beekeeper is the priestlike 'maestro of the bees', moving among the 'many-breasted hives'. The Bee Poems, which draw on Plath's own experience of beekeeping in Devon, are often read as a parable of female self-assertion, or as a narrative rite of rebirth, affirming the integrity of the creative self, and thus furnishing an alternative, more hopeful ending for Plath's career.[16] Yet if on one level they can be seen as forging a personal mythology of survival, on another their surrealism resists the linearity of this biographical narrative. The scapegoating or sacrificial trope, which dominates the sequence, undergoes a number of psychic and narrative permutations. Although the speaker is initially seen as at once pupil and sacrificial victim ('The Bee Meeting'), she subsequently receives a box of bees with which to begin her own hive ('The Arrival of the Bee Box'). In 'Stings' it is the father/beekeeper who is stung by the bees; the threat posed to the protagonist is displaced from the emblematic male figure of the beekeeper to the domestic female collectivity of worker bees, the 'winged, unmiraculous women', or 'drudgers'. In 'The Swarm' the beekeeper is likened to a dictator who uses the bees as instruments of imperialist self-aggrandisement. In 'Wintering' the final poem of the sequence, he disappears, leaving the speaker alone, 'wintering in a dark without window', with the harvest of her beekeeping.

The beehive, with its highly structured division of labour, is a classical trope of the hierarchically ordered, industrious collectivity. Yet it is also a rich source of paradox and contradiction. For example, it is a matriarchal society of female producers, a detail which is crucial to Plath's reflection on power. It is also, of course, an authoritarian society. The hive allows the poet to assume multiple and constantly changing points of identification – including those of beekeeper, queen and worker-drudge. This mobility of identification is signalled by a pervasive imagery of clothing and disguise. For example, the villagers' protective beekeeping gear in 'The Bee Meeting' turns them into participants in a sinister rite, while the speaker's lack of 'protection' casts her in the role of sacrificial initiate/victim. In 'The Arrival of the Bee Box' she dreams of escape from vengeful forces through metamorphosis and disguise, assuming the 'petticoats of the cherry' or a 'moon suit and funeral veil'. The Bee Poems are fascinated by expert, technical or specialized knowledges as coded forms of power and pleasure. They work variations upon the familiar scenario of the daughter's initiation into the mysteries of writing by a father whose power she both desires and repudiates. In 'The Arrival of the Bee Box' the speaker hesitates on the brink of assuming her ownership of the potential hive, torn between terror of its 'dangerous' powers and fantasies of absolute control. The box of bees becomes a metaphor of the unconscious itself, linked with the threat of racial and class otherness ('the swarmy feeling of African hands', 'black on black', the 'Roman mob'). It also suggests a linguistic primitivism; the 'unintelligible syllables' of the bees threaten the speaker with loss of sovereign control over words and meaning.

Feminist readings of the Bee Poems in the 1970s and 1980s placed a particular stress on the climactic moment in 'Stings' when the queen bee escapes from her enclosure in 'the mausoleum, the wax house'. Her triumphant flight recalls the apocalyptic-destructive power of other iconic female apparitions in Plath's work: the Clytemnestra figure in 'Purdah', the red-haired demon in 'Lady Lazarus' and 'God's lioness' in 'Ariel'. Yet the Queen Bee is a highly equivocal totem of female power; she is a mere instrument of the hive's survival, and to that extent reinforces a mythic view of femininity as grounded in unchanging laws of nature. It is a masculine figure, the beekeeper, who exploits and regulates the labour and raw materials of the hive, and the fertility of the queen bee, for the production of a commodity, whether as surgeon, technocrat, emperor or totalitarian leader ('The Arrival of the Bee Box', 'The Swarm').

In the Bee Poems equivocal attempts to imagine a female collectivity are intercut with fantasies of individual martyrdom, usurpation and revenge. The last poem of the sequence, 'Wintering', celebrates the female hive's powers of survival and its expulsion of 'the blunt, clumsy stumblers, the boors', once they have performed their limited function. But the protofeminist trope of the matriarchal community remains essentially tentative and undeveloped. Rather, Plath's use of beekeeping as the unifying metaphor of the sequence insists on the materiality of writing as social practice. The text appears as the product of social as well as individual energies. In an ironic rewriting of her New Critical apprenticeship (which saw the poem as self-referring verbal microcosm or autotelic object), what emerges from the Bee Poems is a view of the poetic text as at once psychically and historically overdetermined. At the same time, all myths of power, whether individual or collective, are seen as fissured by internal contradictions and therefore as ultimately self-defeating.

It might be objected that the 'melancholic' reading of *Ariel* which I have been proposing cannot account for the anger which has given her poems an iconic status, particularly for feminist criticism. Yet it is, perhaps, merely the reverse side of that reading. The violence which the melancholic inflicts on herself is, according to Freud, a form of aggression directed originally against a loved object; 'a mental constellation of revolt ... has ... passed over into the crushed state of melancholia' (Freud, 'Mourning', p. 257). The dejection of the melancholic is unstable; it has a tendency to alternate with states of exultation or triumph. The fragmented and often inward-turning narratives of the *Ariel* poems articulate an ambiguous 'constellation of revolt'. Their critique of the nuclear family, for example, as the conduit of the sexual and political discourses of the Cold War, is obviously circumscribed by their introjection of patriarchal authority; the exorcism of the oppressive parent almost inevitably rebounds on the self. Similarly, despite her proto-feminist response to war and her attack on patriarchal discourse, Plath remains notably ambivalent towards the reproductive body. Such paradoxes, marking her location on the cusp of second-wave feminism, made her work pivotal to psychoanalytically inflected debates about gender and subjectivity during the 1980s and 1990s. Plath's cultural legacy remains difficult to disentangle from her suicide, continuing to serve as a key reference point for the depressive internalization of political anger. For many readers, however (and particularly for writers whom she has influenced), her testament is one not of defeat but of an active struggle against, and refutation of, a despairing voicelessness.

## Notes

1. On Ted Hughes's editing of the 1965 edition, see Marjorie Perloff, 'The Two *Ariels*: The (Re)making of the Sylvia Plath Canon', *American Poetry Review* 13 (November–December 1984), pp. 10–18; Steven Gould Axelrod, 'The Second Destruction of Sylvia Plath', *American Poetry Review* 14 (March–April 1985),

pp. 17–18, reprinted in Linda Wagner (ed.), *Sylvia Plath: The Critical Heritage* (London: Routledge, 1988), pp. 313–19.

2. Plath herself characterized the style of her latest poems, in a 1961 BBC interview, as more 'spoken' than 'written' (*PS*, p. 170).

3. See, for example, Jacqueline Rose, *The Haunting of Sylvia Plath* (London: Virago, 1991); Al Strangeways, *Sylvia Plath: The Shaping of Shadows* (Cranbury, NJ: Associated University Presses, 1998); Christina Britzolakis, *Sylvia Plath and the Theatre of Mourning* (Oxford: Clarendon Press, 1999); Renée Curry, *White Women Writing White: H. D., Elizabeth Bishop, Sylvia Plath and Whiteness* (Westport, CT: Greenwood Press, 2000); Deborah Nelson, *Pursuing Privacy in Cold War America* (New York: Columbia University Press, 2001); Tracy Brain, *The Other Sylvia Plath* (London: Longman, 2001); Robin Peel, *Writing Back: Sylvia Plath and Cold War Politics* (Madison: Fairleigh Dickinson University Press; London: Associated University Presses, 2002).

4. Sigmund Freud, 'The 'Uncanny'', in Angela Richards and Albert Dickson (eds.), *Art and Literature* (PFL14) (Harmondsworth: Penguin, 1985), pp. 335–76.

5. References are to the English edition of *Johnny Panic and the Bible of Dreams* (London: Faber and Faber, 1977).

6. André Green, 'The Dead Mother', *On Private Madness* (London: Hogarth, 1986), p. 142.

7. Nicholas Abraham and Maria Torok, 'The Topography of Reality: Sketching a Metapsychology of Secrets', in Nicholas T. Rand (trans. and ed.), *The Shell and the Kernel*, 2 vols. (Chicago: University of Chicago Press, 1994), I, p. 159.

8. Sigmund Freud, 'Beyond the Pleasure Principle', in Angela Richards and Albert Dickson (eds.), *On Metapsychology* (PFL11) (Harmondsworth: Penguin, 1984), p. 293.

9. Sylvia Plath, 'The Magic Mirror: A Study of the Double in Two of Dostoyevsky's Novels', Smith College undergraduate dissertation, 1955, Lilly Library mss.

10. Joan Riviere, 'Womanliness as Masquerade', in Victor Burgin, James Donald and Cora Kaplan (eds.), *Formations of Fantasy* (London and New York: Methuen, 1986), p. 43.

11. For feminist readings of this motif, see Margaret Homans, *Women Writers and Poetic Identity: Dorothy Wordsworth, Emily Brontë and Emily Dickinson* (Princeton: Princeton University Press, 1980), pp. 219–25; Alicia Ostriker, *Stealing the Language: The Emergence of Women's Poetry in America* (London: Women's Press, 1987), p. 103; Joanne Fiet Diehl, *Women Poets and the American Sublime* (Bloomington: Indiana University Press, 1990), pp. 126–41; Rose, *Haunting*, pp. 114–64; and Britzolakis, *Mourning*, pp. 157–91.

12. Julia Kristeva, *Powers of Horror* (1980), trans. Leon S. Roudiez (New York: Columbia University Press, 1982), p. 96.

13. Plath's pacifist response to the Cold War is a recurrent motif in *Letters Home*. In 1961, after reading an article in *The Nation* entitled 'Juggernaut, the Warfare State', she writes, 'I began to wonder if there was any point in trying to bring up children in such a mad, self-destructive world' (*LH*, p. 438). See also Plath's comments on McCarthyism (*LH*, p. 163); Britain's attack on the Suez ('this flagrant nationalism and capitalism' (*LH*, p. 282)); germ warfare laboratories (*LH*, p. 402); the fallout shelter craze and the radioactive poisoning of the environment (*LH*, p. 434).

14. Irving Howe, 'The Plath Celebration', in Edward Butscher (ed.), *Sylvia Plath: The Woman and the Work* (London: Peter Owen, 1979), p. 233. See also George Steiner, 'Dying is an Art', in Charles Newman (ed.), *The Art of Sylvia Plath: A Symposium* (Bloomington: Indiana University Press, 1970), p. 216; Joyce Carol Oates, 'The Death-Throes of Romanticism', in Butscher, *The Woman and the Work*, p. 209; Richard Allen Blessing, 'The Shape of the Psyche', in Gary Lane (ed.), *Sylvia Plath: New Views on the Poetry* (Baltimore: Johns Hopkins University Press, 1979), p. 67; and Calvin Bedient, 'Sylvia Plath, Romantic', in Lane, *New Views*, p. 6.

15. Sigmund Freud, 'Mourning and Melancholia', in Richards and Dickson (eds.) *On Metapsychology* (PFL11), p. 253.

16. See Perloff, 'The Two *Ariels*', pp. 10–18; Susan R. Van Dyne, 'More Terrible Than She Ever Was: The Manuscripts of Sylvia Plath's Bee Poems', in '*Stings: Original Drafts of the Poems in Facsimile*, reproduced from the Plath Collection' (Northampton: Smith College, 1982), reprinted in Linda Wagner (ed.), *Critical Essays on Sylvia Plath* (Boston: G. K. Hall, 1984), pp. 154–69.

# 9

JANET BADIA

## *The Bell Jar* and other prose

Perhaps because it is Plath's only published novel, *The Bell Jar* has assumed iconic significance in literary and popular culture.[1] One might even say that *The Bell Jar* enjoys its own celebrity, having made cameo appearances in American films as different as *10 Things I Hate About You* (1999) and *Natural Born Killers* (1994). In the first, the novel appears in the hands of the film's central character, Kat Stratford, a cynical, depressed and angry teenage feminist who, in one early scene, defends Plath's status within the literary canon against what she calls 'the oppressive, patriarchal values that dictate our education'.[2] In the latter, the novel can be glimpsed lying face down on the bed next to a sleeping Mallory (née Wilson) Knox just moments before she and her boyfriend Mickey murder her abusive parents and subsequently set off on their cross-country murder spree.[3] References to the novel – and to Plath more generally – are common in television as well, especially those shows that centre on young adult women, such as *Freaks and Geeks* and *The Gilmore Girls*. Nor are such cameos limited to Hollywood. The novels *Sleepwalking* by Meg Wolitzer and *Seven Moves* by Carol Anshaw both depict female characters who, as part of important plot developments within the stories, read *The Bell Jar*. Indeed, there is a certain variety of entertainment in which one just expects to encounter a young woman reading or referencing *The Bell Jar*. One would hardly be surprised to find *The Bell Jar* in the hands of Clare Fisher from the current HBO drama *Six Feet Under* or any of the central characters who plot female revenge in the film *The Smokers* (2000), to name just a couple of examples.

The image has become so common, in fact, that it has even been parodied in an episode of the American cartoon *The Family Guy*. The episode, entitled 'Fish Out of Water' (2001), centres on two parallel plots: Peter, the father of the Griffin family, loses his job, buys a boat and decides to become a fisherman; meanwhile, Meg, Peter's teenage daughter and, according to her, 'the only one in school without plans to go on spring break', sulks about the house, arms crossed in disgust, until her mother, Lois, drags her along for a week at a spa. One early scene in particular sets the stage for an episode about teen angst and ostracism and, of course, a cameo appearance by *The Bell Jar*. In the scene Peter approaches his wife and daughter as they are about to leave on their trip and tells them he will see them in a few days, to which Meg responds, 'Not if I strangle myself with seaweed wraps and die.' Commenting on the obvious, Peter replies in kind: 'Oh, you are dark.' Needless to say, mud baths do nothing to ameliorate Meg's image of herself and the pair leave the spa earlier than planned so that Meg, as she puts it, can 'go home and spend the next three days in solitary confinement where I belong'. On their way home, however, Lois spots a sign for a 'Spring Break Blowout' and, while Meg sleeps, detours to the beach to surprise her pouty teenager daughter. Once at the blowout, it is Lois who enjoys the parties while Meg, disgruntled as ever, struggles to fit in. After one particularly gruelling night of rejection, Meg returns to her hotel room and finds solace in (what else?) *The Bell Jar*.[4]

Because images like this might suggest that Plath, as a writer, need not be taken seriously, most Plath scholars would probably prefer to ignore the fact that Plath and *The Bell Jar* have become fodder for cartoons. Yet the image of the novel in *The Family Guy* should not be overlooked, for it can provide us with an interesting opportunity not simply to consider the fact of the novel's iconic status, but also to think about why the novel has assumed the meaning it has in literary and popular culture. While one's first inclination may be to take the image of Meg reading *The Bell Jar* at face value – that is, as a depiction meant to signal a melodramatic, though no less recognizable, teenage pathology – it is important to remember how much of *The Family Guy* is satire and rather sophisticated satire at that. When placed in this larger context, the image of Meg reading *The Bell Jar* becomes something more than the straightforward depiction of the young adult angst and depression one sees in films like *10 Things I Hate About You* and *Natural Born Killers*.

Consider, for instance, that here we have a cartoon character who is miserable simply because she has been excluded from typical spring-break festivities and who later, when given the chance to participate in the festivities, apparently finds more pleasure sitting in her hotel room reading a novel Plath had once titled 'Diary of a Suicide'.[5] In other words, Meg might be a mopey teenage girl but her gloominess is hardly commensurate with Esther Greenwood's descent into deep depression. Because of this gulf in expectation, one cannot help but wonder just what the show's creators are spoofing with this image of Meg Griffin as a Plath reader. Is the object of the parody the young adult angst that presumably draws Meg to *The Bell Jar*, or is the object of the parody something more original, like the very idea that *The Bell Jar* can function metonymically as a symbol of young women's depression? That is to say, perhaps *The Family Guy* uses the comical image of Meg reading *The Bell Jar* to pose a serious question about whether it is fair to diagnose a young woman's mental state from the book she chooses to read.

However one interprets the image of Meg reading *The Bell Jar*, it does make one point clear: the question of who reads *The Bell Jar* and why they read it has been the focus of much attention within literary and popular culture throughout the novel's history. One could further argue that images of *The Bell Jar*, insofar as they are tied to the question of who reads Plath's writing and why, have been central to determining everything from the novel's literary and cultural value, to Plath's status within the literary canon, to acceptable modes of reading the story the novel tells. Indeed, thinking about the novel's cameo roles in such pop culture arenas as film and television can provide a helpful starting point for examining not only *The Bell Jar*'s association with young adult female angst but also its layered themes and the various lenses that critics have used to interpret those themes since the novel's earliest reception.

## *The Bell Jar*'s reception

In thinking about the reception history of *The Bell Jar*, it is important to keep in mind its unusual publication history. Released just one month before Plath's suicide, the novel was published in England on 14 January 1963 by William Heinemann. Fearing perhaps that it might harm people only thinly disguised therein, Plath chose to publish *The Bell Jar* under the pseudonym Victoria Lucas. While many in literary London knew that Plath was the novel's author when it was released in 1963, her name would not appear on the cover page until 1966 when Faber and Faber published another edition. It would be another five years before *The Bell Jar* would be made available in the US, a delay that resulted, in part at least, from Aurelia Plath's strong belief that the novel's often unkind portraits of those people Plath knew and loved would be injurious not only to those portrayed but to Plath's growing reputation as a serious poet. When the novel did finally appear in the US in 1971, it arrived to a much different reception from its UK reception, one greatly impacted by both the publicity surrounding Plath's death and the posthumous publication of *Ariel* in 1966. In the years between the novel's original publication in England in 1963 and its US release eight years later, Plath had been transformed from a poet well known in London's literary circles to a writer in demand among general and literary readers alike on both sides of the Atlantic. When we talk about the reception of *The Bell Jar*, then, it is probably more appropriate to speak of three reception histories: the

British reception of the novel in 1963 when it was first published under the pseudonym Victoria Lucas, the British reception of the novel in 1966 when the new cover named Sylvia Plath as the author, and the American reception of the novel in 1971.[6]

The 1963 reception of *The Bell Jar* by England's literary scene is perhaps best described as a small, tempered one. Almost twenty magazines and newspapers, many of them local, reviewed the novel. Most early reviewers seemed to agree that *The Bell Jar* was a promising, even 'clever first novel', as Robert Taubman put it in his review for the *New Statesman*.[7] One even called it a 'brilliant and moving book'.[8] But generally speaking, praise for the novel was not so enthusiastic. Simon Raven's review for the *Spectator*, for example, finds *The Bell Jar* to be an 'unpleasant, competent, and often very funny novel' but advises readers 'to stick to home produce' since Lucas is 'by no means as unpleasant, competent, or funny as her English counterpart, Miss Jennifer Dawson'.[9] Of course, since *The Bell Jar*'s initial reception is so limited in scope, one is hesitant to invest the early reception of the novel with too much significance. It is probably true that Plath fared no worse than most first-time novelists. Nevertheless, the initial reception is a good starting place for thinking about the novel within Plath's oeuvre. This is especially true given the relative vacuum in which the novel is first published and reviewed. As Taubman's review in the *New Statesman* makes clear, the novel's identity in 1963 is that of a first novel by a literary newcomer, rather than the work of a literary icon known widely and equally for both her poetry and her suicide.

The extent to which this contextual vacuum exists is evident when one looks at the later reviews of 1966 and 1971, many of which attempt to shed light on the novel's literary merits by drawing evaluative comparisons between the novel and *Ariel*, which, until *Crossing the Water* and *Winter Trees* were published in the early 1970s, was the only volume of Plath's poetry to have been published since *The Colossus* (UK 1960/US 1962). Two 1966 reviews – one in the *Spectator* by M. L. Rosenthal and one in the *New Statesman*, again by Robert Taubman – place the novel in the new context of *Ariel*, which having been published in England in 1965 was, of course, fresh in critics' minds. Taubman found that the novel 'suffers in comparison with [Plath's] poems',[10] while Rosenthal spoke to the greater difference the intervening three years had made, explaining, 'I very much regret missing [*The Bell Jar* in 1963], for now it is impossible to read without thinking of [Plath] personally and of the suicidal poems in *Ariel*'. Such regrets seem to feed Rosenthal's larger assessment that while the novel has its 'magnificent sections whose candour and revealed suffering will haunt anyone's memory', it is nonetheless 'an inexpert, uneven novel'.[11]

In turning to the novel's reception in the US in 1971, one frequently encounters the same sentiment expressed again and again, with only some minor variation. In a review in *Prairie Schooner*, Linda Ray Pratt calls *The Bell Jar* a 'small novel distinguished primarily by those occasional images which find their proper expression in the poems',[12] while the reviewer for *Newsweek* magazine more subtly asserts that the novel 'has a special interest because it was written by a very, very, very special poet'.[13] Taking the comparison one step further, Christopher Lehmann-Haupt prescriptively recommends in his review for the *New York Times* that 'perhaps [the novel] ought best to be read, not as fictional art, but as a corollary to her two collections of poetry'. Underlying Lehmann-Haupt's recommendation is his stated assumption that the publication of the novel in the US is good not because it has literary merits but because 'it will be welcomed by Plath's already large and still growing American audience'.[14] It is an assumption that also seems to shape Guy Davenport's review for *National Review*, in which he concludes that the novel is 'scarcely worth recommending except to readers of [Plath's] anguished poetry who will want to read everything she wrote'.[15] But Davenport would take his assessment even further, arguing that the book's republication under Plath's name was a clear ploy to use the poet's fame to disguise the novel's literary flaws.

While such plain dismissals of the novel's general literary value are more the exception than the rule throughout the reception of the 1971 American edition of *The Bell Jar*, it is clear that one of the major preoccupations among critics at this stage was whether the novel could stand on its own as a literary achievement and thus deserved the fame it had gained in the eight years since it was first published in England. Calling it a 'deceptively modest, uncommonly fine piece of work' in her review for the *Saturday Review*, Lucy Rosenthal argues that the novel is 'more than a posthumous footnote to [Plath's] career as poet'. 'The novel', she goes on, 'is in its own right a considerable achievement. It is written to a small scale, but flawlessly.'[16] Mason Harris's assessment for the *West Coast Review* echoes the sentiment: 'In its forceful linking of private to public madness *The Bell Jar* not only adds a new dimension to the poetry but deserves to be considered a major work in its own right.'[17]

For other critics inclined to value *The Bell Jar* as an independent work, as Rosenthal and Harris were, there was still the issue of the book's popularity and even, as one review put it, its 'reputation', to contend with (Lehmann-Haupt, 'American Edition', p. 35). A clear measure of the demand for the book created by the eight-year delay in publication, upon its release in the US *The Bell Jar* quickly made its way on to the *New York Times* bestseller list. According to Plath biographer Paul Alexander, '*The Bell Jar* became so popular that, when Bantam Books brought out an initial paperback edition in April 1972 – a run of 375,000 copies – it sold out that printing, plus a second and a third, in one month.'[18] Indeed, by the time some reviewers got round to reviewing the novel, it had already been on the *New York Times* bestseller list for, in some cases, as many as twenty-four weeks. As often happens in the literary world, the fact that the novel sold well with general readers was a potential mark against it as a piece of serious literature. As a reviewer for *Publishers Weekly* put it, while *The Bell Jar* is a 'finely written novel, full of truth', it is also 'a best seller – one hopes, although dimly, for reasons of literary merit, rather than the circumstances of the author's life and death'.[19] In his review for the *Washington Post Book World*, Clarence Peterson took on the problem more directly, offering an explanation for the book's market success that attributes it to the publicity surrounding the Plath family's protests against the novel's publication in the US. Admitting that the controversy 'no doubt helped [*The Bell Jar*] become a best seller' and thereby offering a nonliterary reason for the novel's popularity, Peterson redirects the conversation back to literary merit and concludes that 'the book is well worth its fame on merit alone'.[20]

Peterson's attempts to redefine the book's fame as the result of true literary merit, rather than its popularity among general readers, becomes more significant if one understands that by the early 1970s Plath was perhaps as well known for her readership as she was for her writing. At the very least, it is clear that for some critics Plath's readers had become as interesting a subject as Plath herself. Helen Dudar's 1971 article on *The Bell Jar* for the *New York Post* provides one of the earliest examples of this phenomenon. Entitled 'From Book to Cult', the article opens:

> If you tuned into [*The Bell Jar*] early, you got a cooperative aunt to buy it for you on her trip to England in 1964. A while later, you found your way to the two book stores in New York that imported the $1.75 paperback and acquired one before they ran out of the latest shipment. You feel slightly superior to the late-arrivals who read it only last month in the American edition. But for those who respond to it with the same intensity the book evoked from you, what you feel most of all is kinship.[21]

Using this image to set the stage, Dudar goes on to describe the 'fan-club atmosphere' ('Book to Cult', p. 38) that began with the poetry, took root with the gossip surrounding the novel's autobiographical sensationalism and grew vigorously as the novel became a staple of freshman reading lists in universities increasingly being shaped by the women's liberation movement. Dudar even offers a term for the adulation, naming it 'Plath cultism', a term meant to describe how the novel and author had become a 'cult object and cult figure for several generations of young and over-30 readers, many of them women' ('Book to Cult', p. 3).

In defining readers of *The Bell Jar* in this way, Dudar presumably aims to expose the damage caused to the author by 'Plath cultism', at least this is what the final paragraph of the article suggests with its emphasis on how Plath would probably have looked upon the cultlike tendencies of her readers with disapproval. At the very least, one can certainly locate anxiety in the term she opts to use. Associated with those who are misguided in belief or adulation, the word 'cult' minimizes, if not erases, the central act performed by those in the so-called Plath cult, namely, the act of reading or of critically engaging with the work in question. According to this logic, Plath fans perpetuate an injustice against Plath, the novel and even themselves by failing to read *The Bell Jar* critically. In his review of *The Bell Jar* for the *Christian Science Monitor*, Melvin Maddocks explains the perceived problem more bluntly: 'Perhaps Plath readers should keep in mind that, while living in "the rarified atmosphere under a bell jar," what Sylvia Plath wanted, above all, was to *get out*.'[22]

## Reading *The Bell Jar*

As this overview of the reception histories of *The Bell Jar* suggests, the debate about the novel's merits – that is, whether it is a 'good' or a 'bad' novel – is not simply a debate about whether the book is worth reading. It is also a debate about how the novel is best read. Is the novel a thinly disguised autobiography, or is it best read as fiction? Is it concerned primarily with the psychological and therefore the intensely personal existence of its narrator, or does it emphasize Esther Greenwood's historical situatedness in 1950s America? If one does foreground history when reading the novel, should the British context of *The Bell Jar* matter as much as the American context, since Plath was after all living in England at the time she wrote the novel? Are the social, sexual and clinical experiences Esther narrates endemic mainly in women's lives, or do these experiences raise questions more universally relevant to both genders? Is the novel's narration stylistically uneven and thus flawed, or does the possibility of unevenness indicate Plath's talents as a novelist who set out to capture the world as seen through the distorting glass of a bell jar?

For many critics, both past and present, how one answers these questions impacts on an even more important issue: is *The Bell Jar* the work of a mature, accomplished novelist that should therefore be thought of as serious 'literature' in the highbrow sense, or is it best remembered as a popular novel by an author whose true literary gift was her poetry – a novel, therefore, mostly of interest to scholars of Plath's poetry and to those young adult readers who can ostensibly identify with Esther Greenwood's plight?

All these questions have been treated extensively by Plath scholars, many of them contributors to this companion. Linda Wagner-Martin's critical study of the novel, *The Bell Jar: A Novel of the Fifties*, offers several approaches, including a compelling reading of the book's narrative structure that centres on the claim that 'the prose style ... is meant to convey the mental anguish of the protagonist, so disoriented that she grasps at pieces of information, races to another topic, returns to the first and then breaks any rational profession into fragments by inserting her own highly personal ... and sometimes intentionally comic reactions between the sentences that express her thoughts' (p. 26). Pat MacPherson's *Reflecting on The Bell Jar* usefully situates the novel alongside the intertwined historical discourses of the 1950s, including Cold War politics, suburban structures and normative heterosexuality, while Tracy Brain and Robin Peel position the novel in British literary and cultural contexts, respectively.[23] Arguing against the common categorization of the novel as autobiography,[24] Lynda K. Bundtzen understands *The Bell Jar* as an allegory about femininity, specifically 'the woman's place in society; her special creative powers; and finally, her psychological experience of femininity'.[25]

Even more interesting than the approaches contemporary critics have used is the concern with appropriate reading methods that often governs them. While the construction of modes of reading is always integral to literary criticism – after all, it is the goal of literary criticism to provide models and methods of interpretation – discussions of *The Bell Jar* are often unusually preoccupied with correcting previous modes of reading, particularly those that approach the novel as autobiography. While present in the early reception of the novel, this kind of prescriptive interpretation is especially evident in more recent criticism and it stems, in part at least, from a desire to sever the connection between Plath and the young woman reader depicted so often in the images that began this chapter. These readers, the argument goes, have been reading the novel all wrong, or, if not wrong, then for all the wrong reasons. The corollary of this argument requires Plath to be rescued from her readers and from certain reading practices that might diminish the importance of her work. Because so much of Plath criticism begins from these assumptions, it is perhaps not surprising that criticism of *The Bell Jar* sometimes asserts a way of reading the novel that claims to be better than the way young women have ostensibly been reading it, as if the critical discourse surrounding the novel needs to be controlled lest it cause damage to Plath's reputation as a writer. Such critics seem reluctant to consider the alternative: namely that the very fact that the novel has remained so valued by young women readers could actually be read as a sign of the novel's strengths.

Certainly, for many young adult readers – especially women – the appeal of the novel now lies in its reputation. That is to say, reading *The Bell Jar* has become a teenage rite of passage, one frequently initiated by other adolescents and, increasingly today, by mothers and teachers eager to share the novel that had been influential in their own adolescences. But while the novel's reputation might explain why some new readers pick up the novel in the first place, it does not explain the appeal of what those readers find within its pages. If one does seriously entertain the question of this appeal, some interesting avenues emerge.

For example, the apparent desire among critics to control how the novel is read is especially interesting when one considers Esther's own preoccupation with control and self-determination. From her relationship with Buddy Willard and her mother, to her experimentation with suicide methods, to her fight to escape the bell jar, nearly all the plot episodes within the novel reveal Esther's struggles to gain control over her own life, to determine her own choices, rather than merely to accept those that society presents to her. In fact, one could argue that it is Esther's desire and search for control that threads together the many identities Esther struggles with, including her identity as a young woman, a patient, a daughter, a successful student, an aspiring writer and, of course, a potential wife and mother.

In the very first scene of the novel, Plath introduces readers to the general loss of control that Esther experiences as a young woman new to New York City and the publishing world of women's fashion magazines. The narrative of the 1950s middle-class American dream tells Esther that, having won a scholarship to Smith College and now a guest editorship at a fashion magazine, she is supposed to be 'the envy of ... other college girls just like [her] all over America' (*BJ*, p. 2). The girl in this narrative, Esther explains, is supposed to end up 'steering New York like her own private car'. This kind of control is not, however, what Esther experiences during her stay in the city. As she puts it, 'I wasn't steering anything, not even myself. I just bumped from my hotel to work and to parties and from parties to my hotel and back to work like a numb trolley-bus' (*BJ*, pp. 2–3). Later, when faced with the options of going to a fur show with Betsy and the other guest editors, going to Coney Island with Doreen, or staying in bed by herself, Esther experiences a similar paralysis: 'I wondered why I couldn't go the whole way doing what I should any more. This made me sad and tired. Then I wondered why I couldn't go the whole way doing what I shouldn't ... this made me even sadder and more tired' (*BJ*, p. 30).

Underlying Esther's feeling of paralysis is her inability – or, if one prefers, her rebellious refusal – to make choices about her life. Unlike many women of the 1950s who did not have access to the relative social mobility Esther enjoys, she does have many life choices before her; a result, in part at least, of her success as a student, which, as she herself acknowledges, has prepared her to take any number of career paths. In one of the central metaphors of the novel, Esther imagines these choices in her life as a green fig tree branching out before her, with one fig representing 'a husband and a happy home and children', another fig representing 'Europe', others representing an academic career, publishing, poetry; and 'beyond and above these figs were many more figs [she] couldn't quite make out' (*BJ*, p. 77).

Because Esther's fear of her own inadequacy constantly overwhelms her, she cannot see the fig tree and the choices each branch represents in a positive light. She is simply crippled by such choices: 'I saw myself sitting in the crotch of this fig tree, starving to death', she says, 'just because I couldn't make up my mind which of the figs I would choose ... choosing one meant losing the rest and, as I sat there, unable to decide, the figs began to wrinkle and go black' (*BJ*, p. 77). Reminding us of the way her last name, Greenwood, reflects the fig tree, Esther's damaged self-image turns the once-green branches into rotten, dreadful choices that fall, spoilt, to her feet.

While many readers today might wish to find themselves faced with so many promising options, Esther's frustration is not unreasonable given the societal constrictions regarding women's roles in mid-century America and what Plath once described as 'The great fault of America', namely, its 'expectancy of conformity' (*J*, p. 411). As her description of the withering figs makes clear, the problem is not that she lacks choices or even that none of the options appeals to her; the problem lies in her desire to have what society tells her is impossible, 'two mutually exclusive things at one and the same time' (*BJ*, p. 94). Just as importantly, Esther is told again and again that her choices, while hers to make, will have repercussions she cannot control. She might opt to be both a mother and a poet, for example, but the state of marriage and motherhood in mid-century America, as Buddy Willard tells Esther, dictates that 'after [she] had children [she] would feel differently, [she] wouldn't want to write poems any more' (*BJ*, p. 85). At best, then, the process of choice for Esther has been circumscribed by societal rules and expectations – rules and expectations that tell her to be one, and only one, thing, despite her own inclinations. At worst, the process of choice is completely denied her.

This is perhaps nowhere more clear than in Esther's struggle with her sexuality and the possibility of pregnancy. In the chronological time of the narrative, one of the first examples of this struggle occurs in her relationship with Buddy. On a visit to his room at Yale, Buddy introduces the topic of sex by asking Esther if she would like to 'see' him naked (*BJ*, p. 68). Esther indulges him, but then dismisses him when he asks her to reciprocate by letting him 'see' her. The thought of standing naked in front of Buddy does not appeal to her at all, but the invitation prompts her unexpectedly to ask Buddy if he has 'ever had an affair with anyone' (*BJ*, p. 69). Because Buddy has presented himself as sexually inexperienced throughout their relationship, Esther expects him to say 'no'. After all, as her mother tells her, Buddy was 'a nice, fine boy ... the kind of person a girl should stay fine and clean for' (*BJ*, p. 68). But, of course, Buddy has had an affair and when he discloses the extent of his relationship with the waitress, Esther quickly reexamines their sexual interaction. As she explains, 'from the first night Buddy Willard kissed me and said I must go out with a lot of boys, he made me feel I was much more sexy and experienced than he was' (*BJ*, p. 70). Clinging to her pride, Esther is forced to bottle her indignation, an indignation that springs not so much from Buddy's transgression as from her realization that she has never had control over her own sexual identity in her relationship with Buddy. As she explains, it was not the thought of Buddy's previous relationship that concerned her: 'What I couldn't stand was Buddy's pretending I was so sexy and he was so pure, when all the time he'd been having an affair with that tarty waitress and must have felt like laughing in my face' (*BJ*, p. 71). As these passages make clear, not only does Esther discover that she has been made the butt of Buddy's joke, she also realizes that she is subject to societal double standards that understand a young man's sexual experiences as 'sowing wild oats' but then judge a young woman's sexual experiences as 'promiscuity'. In other words, what she realizes is that Buddy can construct his own sexual identity while she cannot.

Dismayed by this sexual double standard (*BJ*, p. 81), Esther attempts to seize control over her sexuality by losing her virginity to someone other than Buddy. But as we know from the scene of sexual assault she has already narrated by this point in the novel, even her virginity – or rather her decision to lose it and to whom – is potentially subject to the control of men like Marco, the Cuban 'woman-hater' (*BJ*, p. 160) who spits, '"Sluts, all sluts" ... "Yes or no, it is all the same"', after Esther successfully fights off his attempt to rape her (*BJ*, p. 109). Furthermore, Esther can never have complete control over her sexuality because, while the choice to lose her virginity to Irwin is finally her own, the possibility of pregnancy, like the bell jar, always looms over her. This fact is one her mother tries to impress upon Esther by giving her the *Reader's Digest* article 'In Defense of Chastity', which, as Esther characterizes it, attempts to compel young women to choose chastity until married, out of fear of rejection by a future husband and because there is 'no sure way of not getting stuck with a baby' (*BJ*, p. 81). To someone as adamant about not wanting to have children as Esther is at this stage, the possibility of pregnancy makes the decision to lose one's virginity a perilous choice at best. For Esther especially, the risk is 'a baby hanging over her head like a big stick, to keep her in line' (*BJ*, p. 221). It is perhaps no wonder then that Esther, in her determination to gain control by losing her virginity, tries to convince herself that the thought of pregnancy 'hung far and dim in the distance and didn't trouble [her] at all' (*BJ*, p. 80).

It is also important to remember that when Esther does finally sleep with Irwin, she does so only after she has been fitted for a diaphragm, an act that underscores why birth control is such an apt synonym for contraception. Yet even the moment of her fitting for the birth control device ironically reveals the limited control that society actually allows Esther to exercise over her own sexuality. As Esther explains, birth control is illegal in Massachusetts at this time and it is only with Dr Nolan's help that she is able to see a doctor who can fit her for the diaphragm. Nor does she have the money herself to pay for the medical service. She must rely instead on the money that Philomena Guinea has given her as a get-well present, money that would surely have been denied Esther had her benefactress known how it would be spent. But despite the obstacles of access and money, Esther sees birth control as her path to self-determination. In her words, 'Whether she knew it or not, Philomena Guinea was buying my freedom' (*BJ*, p. 221). Perhaps for the first time in the novel, Esther expresses full self-possession: 'I am my own woman', she says to herself as she rides back to the asylum with her purchase (*BJ*, p. 223).

### Plath's prose and the question of value

While it is true that *The Bell Jar* has become the iconic work of Plath's oeuvre, a metonym even of Plath herself, the question of the novel's place within Plath studies remains very much unanswered. On the one hand, the fact that new editions of the novel seem to arrive perennially on bookstore shelves would seem to support the claim that *The Bell Jar*, like *Ariel*, is a major piece of Plath's oeuvre, at least in the minds of general readers whose interest presumably generates the republication of the novel in its various forms, including a 25th Anniversary edition and an Everyman's Library edition. On the other hand, the work still receives less scholarly attention than the poetry. Perhaps the difficulties in deciding the novel's value lie with Plath herself, who, in ways she could not have anticipated, established a framework for the evaluation of her own work. While in a letter to her mother she described the poems that would eventually form the volume *Ariel* as the 'best poems of [her] life' – poems that would 'make [her] name' – she instructed her mother to 'Forget about the novel and tell no one of it. It's a potboiler and just practice' (*LH*, pp. 468, 477). The implication of words like 'potboiler' and 'just practice' suggest, of course, that Plath saw her novel as inferior to her poetry. Yet on another occasion, Plath described her poetry as 'an evasion from the real job of writing prose' (*JP*, p. 3).

These seeming contradictions in Plath's own descriptions of her prose and poetry point to her complex ambitions as a writer, a writer who wished to have the cash rewards that went with successful story writing but whose talents seemed to be better suited to poetry. In the end, perhaps it is this tension between her professional drive and her talents that produces the reluctance among scholars to isolate *The Bell Jar* as an independent work whose value does not depend on its relation to the poetry. Or perhaps the reluctance more complexly reflects the anxieties that generally surround Plath's prose writing.

As the publication of *Johnny Panic and the Bible of Dreams* in England in 1977 makes clear, the question of how Plath's prose writing might affect her literary reputation is central to evaluations of her work. Published in a slightly different edition in the US in 1979, *Johnny Panic and the Bible of Dreams* includes a small selection of the more than seventy stories that Plath had written in the decade before her death, as well as examples of her journalism and narrative sketches excerpted from her journals. Given Ted Hughes's admission in the 'Introduction' to the collection that some pieces contain 'obvious weaknesses', it is not at all surprising that most reviewers also found *Johnny Panic and the Bible of Dreams* to be generally lacking in literary quality. Perhaps because their own jobs as reviewers had been pre-empted by Hughes's disclaimers about the quality of the work included, many reviewers zeroed in on the question implied in the disclaimers themselves: with the collection's flaws so readily apparent, who exactly would want to buy the book? Even Plath had asked, '"Who would want to read them?"', when considering her ability to get some of her short stories published (quoted in *JP*, p. 4). Of course, Plath's own question is rhetorical, but for those reviewing the work the question required an answer. While some reviewers conceded that the book would have value to Plath scholars, many assumed that the book's main audience would be Plath's 'devotees',[26] those quick to ingest what Carol Bere calls the latest 'chunk of Plathiana'.[27] Others could not even imagine this much of a readership. As Simon Blow wrote, 'even Plath addicts cannot have grown so indiscriminate as to swallow these writings whole'.[28]

The publication and reception of *Johnny Panic and the Bible of Dreams* transformed what was perhaps simply a mild worry over *The Bell Jar*'s popularity with general readers into a full-blown anxiety attack about Plath's readers and the challenges they posed to her status as a serious writer. For some critics, in fact, it seemed as though the body of Plath's work had been taken over by reader demand and a desire among those handling Plath's manuscripts to offer Plath up 'for popular consumption' (Bere, '*Johnny*', p. 358). Perhaps because critics could not control the publication of Plath's work, some of them, apparently opting for the next best thing, set out to control the terms by which the newly published prose writings could be understood. As one reviewer cautioned, if *Johnny Panic and the Bible of Dreams* is valuable, it is 'as an instructive guide to Plath's more realized work – but certainly no measure of the writer herself' (Bere, '*Johnny*', p. 359). Such heavy-handedness in directing readers about how to approach the material was not, of course, a phenomenon peculiar to the reception of *Johnny Panic and the Bible of Dreams*. It occurred, though perhaps to a lesser degree, throughout the reception of *The Bell Jar*. It can be heard especially in Melvin Maddocks's assertion, quoted earlier in this chapter, that readers would do well to 'keep in mind that, while living in "the rarified atmosphere under a bell jar," what Sylvia Plath wanted, above all, was to *get out*'.

That so much of our understanding of *The Bell Jar* and Plath's other prose writing has become entangled with anxieties about readers seems both inevitable and ironic. In the end, it might be that the anxieties speak not to the quality of Plath's prose but to a larger desire among critics to protect Plath, who, after all, had no opportunity to reflect on the place of her prose within her entire published oeuvre. Whatever the explanation, the reasons for the anxieties matter less than what the anxieties themselves can teach us about Plath's prose writing, particularly *The Bell Jar*. No matter how much critics might wish to divorce the novel from its popularity among young women especially, there is no getting around *The Bell Jar*'s iconicity. The best we can do as we approach *The Bell Jar* is be mindful of its association with Plath's most devoted readers and the ways it unavoidably seeps into our interpretations of the novel's meanings and value.

## Notes

1. References throughout are to the American editions of *The Bell Jar* (New York: Harper & Row, 1971) and *Johnny Panic and the Bible of Dreams* (New York: Harper & Row, 1979).
2. *10 Things I Hate About You*, directed by Gil Junger (Touchstone Pictures, 1999).
3. *Natural Born Killers*, directed by Oliver Stone (Warner Brothers, 1994).
4. Seth MacFarlene, 'Fish Out of Water', *The Family Guy* (Fox, 2001).
5. Robin Peel, *Writing Back: Sylvia Plath and Cold War Politics* (Madison: Fairleigh Dickinson University Press; London: Associated University Presses, 2002), p. 66.
6. For an alternative overview of *The Bell Jar*'s reception, see Linda Wagner-Martin, *The Bell Jar: A Novel of the Fifties* (New York: Twayne, 1992), pp. 10–14.
7. Robert Taubman, 'Anti-Heroes', *New Statesman* 65 (25 January 1963), p. 128.

8. Laurence Lerner, 'New Novels', *Listener* 69 (31 January 1963), p. 215.
9. Simon Raven, 'The Trouble with Phaedra', *Spectator* 217 (15 February 1963), p. 203.
10. Robert Taubman, 'Uncles' War', *New Statesman* 72 (16 September 1966), p. 402.
11. M. L. Rosenthal, 'Blood and Plunder', *Spectator* 217 (30 September 1966), p. 418.
12. Linda Ray Pratt, 'The spirit of blackness is in us ...', *Prairie Schooner* 47 (Spring 1973), p. 87.
13. Geoffrey Wolff, '*The Bell Jar*', *Newsweek* 77 (19 April 1971), p. 120.
14. Christopher Lehmann-Haupt, 'An American Edition – At Last', *New York Times* (16 April 1971), p. 35.
15. Guy Davenport, 'Novels in Braille', *National Review* 23 (18 May 1971), p. 538.
16. Lucy Rosenthal, '*The Bell Jar*', *Saturday Review* 54 (24 April 1971), p. 42.
17. Mason Harris, '*The Bell Jar*', *West Coast Review* 8 (October 1973), p. 56.
18. Paul Alexander, *Rough Magic: A Biography of Sylvia Plath* (New York: Penguin, 1991), p. 348.
19. '*The Bell Jar*', *Publishers Weekly* 201 (28 February 1972), p. 74.
20. Clarence Peterson, '*The Bell Jar*', *Washington Post Book World* (30 April 1972), p. 8.
21. Helen Dudar, 'From Book to Cult', *New York Post* (2 September 1971), p. 3.
22. Melvin Maddocks, 'A Vacuum Abhorred', *Christian Science Monitor* (15 April 1971), p. 11.
23. Pat Macpherson, *Reflecting on The Bell Jar* (London: Routledge, 1991); Tracy Brain, *The Other Sylvia Plath* (London: Longman, 2001); Peel, *Writing Back*.
24. See, for example, Eileen Aird, *Sylvia Plath: Her Life and Work* (New York: Harper & Row, 1973), p. 98.
25. Lynda K. Bundtzen, *Plath's Incarnations: Woman and the Creative Process* (Ann Arbor: University of Michigan Press, 1983), p. 113.
26. '*Johnny Panic and the Bible of Dreams and Other Prose Writings*', *Publishers Weekly* 214 (6 November 1978), p. 71.
27. Carol Bere, '*Johnny Panic and the Bible of Dreams and Other Prose Writings*', *Southern Humanities Review* 13 (Fall 1979), p. 358.
28. Simon Blow, 'Sylvia Plath's Prose', *Books and Bookmen* 23 (June 1978), p. 42.

# 10

TRACY BRAIN

# Sylvia Plath's letters and journals

There are many reasons why Sylvia Plath's letters and journals matter. They are strewn with the sharp writing and observations of a poet and novelist, as we see in Plath's descriptions of people she knew: 'I'm having Mrs. Hamilton, the wife of the dead coffee plantation owner and local power, to tea today. She is old, booming, half-deaf with a dachshund named Pixie' (*LH*, p. 432). 'Linda is ... nondescript as an art gum eraser. Her eyes are nervous and bright like neurotic goldfish' (*J*, p. 38). Plath writes honestly and subversively about the body:

> A delicate, pointed-nailed fifth finger can catch under dry scabs and flakes of mucous in the nostril ... a heavier, determined forefinger can reach up and smear down-and-out the soft, resilient, elastic greenish-yellow smallish blobs of mucous ... sometimes there will be blood ... God, what a sexual satisfaction! (*J*, p. 165)

In her explicit anatomization of the grotesque, Plath breaks the rules of decorum. She looks at the body as if through a magnifying glass, and does so with wry humour.

By providing evidence of Plath's concerns with larger political, historical and environmental matters – about nuclear fallout, McCarthyism and social inequality (*LH*, p. 434; *J*, pp. 46, 32) – the letters and journals point readers away from the solipsism in which Plath has so often been accused of indulging. They record her impressions of what have since become recognized as key encounters in twentieth-century literary history, for example, of attending a cocktail party at Faber and Faber where Ted Hughes was photographed with other Faber poets – T. S. Eliot, W. H. Auden, Louis MacNeice and Stephen Spender (*LH*, p. 386). The photograph Plath here describes was to become famous and much printed.

Plath's letters and journals offer information about the books, films, art and sculpture (for example *J*, pp. 406–8) that might have influenced her work. She writes on 29 November 1962 about her review of a new

biography, *Lord Byron's Wife* (*LH*, p. 483), the story of Anne Isabella
Milbanke, a mathematician and intellectual to whom Lord Byron was
briefly married and with whom he had a daughter. The relationship soon
descended into angry violence and Byron ditched England, and his marriage,
for Europe. Linda Wagner-Martin writes that 'Lyonnesse' and 'Amnesiac'
(21 October 1962) 'continue the description of [Plath's] estranged husband'.[1] However, the tale of Lord Byron's sour marriage could easily
be a source for these two poems, which are about male abandonment
and fear of family life. In 'Amnesiac' the male character's desire for 'the
red-headed sister he never dared to touch' is as likely to be the product of
*Lord Byron's Wife* as it is a confession of any personal animosity Plath might
have felt.

Anybody who is interested in Plath's own story will find her letters and
journals a fascinating source of information, though not necessarily more
'true' or reliable than the multitude of literary biographies about her. They
are dotted with Plath's comments on her own work and frequently express
what to her were key points about given texts. Thus the 1955 short story
'Superman and Paula Brown's New Snowsuit' (*JP*) is characterized by
'images fused of the superman ... of shame and exultation' while the 1959
poem 'Point Shirley' is 'Oddly powerful and moving to me in spite of the rigid
formal structure' (*J*, pp. 328, 463).

I have begun by establishing just a few of the reasons for the significance of
Plath's letters and journals, because what I will go on to talk about in this
essay is the history of their publication, the archival sources on which these
publications are based, and the severe limitations of the published editions.
In brief, the publication history went like this. Plath's *Letters Home:
Correspondence 1950–1963* was published in the US in 1975 and in the
UK in 1976. The letters were selected and edited by Plath's mother, Aurelia
Plath. Plath's journals were first published in the US only, in an abridged
edition edited by Ted Hughes and Frances McCullough (1982). In 2000 a
relatively complete edition of Plath's journals, edited by Karen V. Kukil, was
published in the US and the UK under slightly different titles and, as I will
explain below, with small variations within the texts.

## Publishing Plath's letters and journals

On the photocopy of a letter in which Plath tells her mother about an
argument she had with Ted Hughes's sister Olwyn during Christmas of
1960, Aurelia Plath makes a note that she must donate or sell all her
daughter's letters, and ensure they are placed where the public can read
them.[2] In 1977 she did sell the letters her daughter had been writing to her

throughout her life, to the Lilly Library at Indiana University.[3] In 1981 Ted Hughes sold to Smith College many of the handwritten volumes, typed sheets and fragments that constitute Plath's adult journals (*J*, p. ix).[4]

To date, *Letters Home* is the only published edition of Plath's letters, and it is far from complete. The incompleteness stems partly from omissions in the text (these are rarely indicated and thereby distort Plath's meaning or context) and partly from the limited chronological range of the selection. *Letters Home* begins with the first letter Plath wrote from Smith College on 27 September 1950, one month before her eighteenth birthday, and ends with excerpts from a letter written on 4 February 1963, one week before she died (the last letter by Plath in the Lilly Library's holdings). The unpublished letters that are in the public domain span a larger timeframe than this. Although they may not change the face of Plath scholarship, the Lilly Library holds a letter that the eleven-year-old Plath wrote to her hospitalized mother in 1943,[5] and a sheaf of others that Plath wrote from camp each summer from 1945 to 1948.[6]

In the years since Plath's death, two editions of her *Journals* have been published. The first appeared in 1982. A 'docked text'[7] that was notorious for its 'omission marks and ellipses',[8] this abridged edition of the *Journals* made Marni Jackson feel that 'Plath's husband, mother and editor' were 'peering over [her] shoulders as she read'[9] and prompted Nancy Milford to ask, 'who is doing the cutting? And why?' ('The Journals', p. 83). These are the questions that Jacqueline Rose explored nine years later in *The Haunting of Sylvia Plath*. Rose argues that what is removed from the abridged *Journals* – or severely reduced – are references to Plath's politics, references to sex, 'selective' references to real people, Plath's 'experiments with popular fictional forms', and passages where she expresses happiness.[10]

Erica Jong remarks that literary history is 'strewn with examples of "well-meaning" relations and friends suppressing great works for their seemingly altruistic motives'.[11] In the case of the abridged edition of the *Journals*, Ted Hughes must surely bear some responsibility for the cuts. In the case of *Letters Home*, Aurelia Plath is largely responsible, but Hughes also made his own demands. While Aurelia Plath then owned the physical papers that constituted her daughter's letters (now in the Lilly Library), Hughes held the copyright, and had a final say about what could go into the book. According to Rose, what Aurelia Plath removes from the letters are 'signs of hostility towards her mother, demands for autonomy and separation' and allusions to Plath's 'constant physical ailments' (*Haunting*, p. 78). What Hughes removes from *Letters Home* are 'the most negative representations of him by Plath', as well as those moments where 'her idealisation sets him up ... as super-human' (*Haunting*, p. 87).

Sylvia Plath's own omissions from the journals are also revealing, a point made by Karen Kukil, who observes that Plath omits any account of her wedding or her drive with Hughes across the US in the summer of 1959.[12] Even the reader who goes to the archives to look at the originals of the letters will not be able to read every word. There are a few occasions where Aurelia Plath took a black marker to score out portions of her daughter's letters, particularly the angry letters that Plath wrote after her marriage grew troubled. In one instance Plath's mother crosses out seven and a half lines in three different places, addresses future readers of the manuscript with an annotation that the blocked material is personal to her only, and then initials the comment.[13]

Jo Brans has remarked that the 'devices' of Plath's letters ('exclamation marks', 'parenthetical asides' and 'cute closings') are 'mercilessly banished from the poetry'.[14] Carol Bere has noted 'discrepancies between the Sivvy of the letters "singing" her "native joy of life" and the violent, destructive poet of *Ariel*'.[15] For Martha Duffy, the letters 'show a capacity for wonder and joy unreflected in her work'[16] (as if the letters are not part of Plath's work). Views such as these miss the talky informality of many of Plath's poems – 'The Applicant', 'Daddy' and 'Lady Lazarus', to name but a few – which owe a debt to the direct appeal and address that is a feature of letter writing and do in fact contain the odd exclamation mark ('there goes the stopper! // Watch out!' ('A Secret')) and aside ('Seven years, if you want to know' ('Daddy')). There is a danger here of erecting false and overly rigid boundaries between Plath's different types of writings, of believing that the poems could not possibly share qualities with, or even arise from, her epistolary practices.

Critics of the journals have echoed many of the assumptions made by those early reviewers of the letters. Never mind *The Bell Jar* or *Johnny Panic and the Bible of Dreams*, the inside front cover of the 1982 abridged *Journals* asserts that the journals are 'in fact her best prose', and that they reveal Plath's 'deep psychic crack that left her open to frequent depression, anxiety, and panic – as she described in *The Bell Jar*'. The message seldom varies. Plath's poems are a ceaselessly repeated personal monologue about her own frightening and lonely experiences, and are fodder for biographical readings of Plath as a confessional writer.

While Erica Wagner, Jacqueline Rose and Tim Kendall have written careful, thought-provoking reviews of Karen Kukil's 2000 edition of the *Journals*, others have greeted it in similar terms to those with which the 1982 edition was received.[17] Michael Sheldon sees the new *Journals* as 'evidence of' Plath's 'hopelessly deranged thinking'. For him, they are 'a thousand pages of Plath's self-incriminating testimony', 'her own suicide note'.[18] For Allison Pearson, the new *Journals* reveal Plath as a 'tortured specimen preserved in her bell jar ... forever young, forever anguished, forever betrayed by her man' and trapped within her 'cast-iron solipsism'.[19]

Plath used her journals as a writer's notebook where she tried out various tones and emotions. As journals so often are for writers, Plath's were a place to play with and store material that she would later use. Rose's contention that Plath's journals 'were never intended for publication' and were written, 'above all ... for herself' ('So Many Lives') does not convince me. A writer as self-consciously ambitious as Plath is likely to have written her journals with a continual fantasy and even occasional conviction that some day they would be read by a larger audience. Plath pores over Virginia Woolf's diary and alludes to doing so in her own (*J*, p. 269). There is too large a gap between Plath's 'real' experiences and the mediation of writing for us to use the *Journals* as simple documentary evidence of her mental state or emotions. Nancy Milford's view is that Plath's journals should not be used 'as a key to the poetry, but to know about the life from which the poems sprang'. Yet, as Milford warns, the 'revelations' in journals 'are not to be confused with fact. Hidden, shaped, toyed with and mercilessly reworked, fabricated even ... journals tell only a kind of truth – taken on run, or when the mood is foul' ('The Journals', p. 81). Nonetheless, it is easy to imagine that those who wish to 'own' Plath, to stake their claims for knowing the 'truth' about her, will find ways to justify their views through her journals and letters: 'evidence can be found within them to support every single theory that has ever been produced about Sylvia Plath' (Rose, 'So Many Lives'). For many, this will be the most powerful inducement to read them.

The incomplete and fragmentary nature of the Plath archive means that it can be difficult to halt these arguments. A later letter which gives the 'truth' back to the other side may not be in the public domain, or it may have once existed but since been lost or destroyed. Plath's letters – and possibly even some sections of the journals – are dispersed between different archives and the numerous people who possess them. For some of the latter, this possession may for ever remain a private matter, and the materials therefore never come to light. In a few cases this may be because individuals have come by the papers illegally. Diane Middlebrook quotes a letter from Ted Hughes to his sister-in-law Joan, in which he complains that '"everything that had her or my signature, her manuscripts, towels, sheets, tools – whenever I wasn't actually on watch, something was pinched."'[20] Carolyn Steedman is rightly sceptical about the way that in 'the practices of history and of modern autobiographical narration, there is the assumption that *nothing goes away*; that the past has deposited all of its traces, somewhere, somehow'. Some things – letters or journals, for instance – disappear or are lost to any public record. At the same time, the fact that certain things are not discovered 'doesn't mean they weren't – aren't – there to be found' (to use Steedman's phrase).[21]

Jacqueline Rose describes one of the most useful things we can do with these materials: 'Put the poem and the journal entry together, plus the letters which she is writing to Aurelia Plath at the same time, and you get an extraordinary instance of intertexuality' (*Haunting*, p. 89). Rose subsequently engages in a psychoanalytic reading of Plath's epistolary and journalistic accounts of the beginning of her relationship with Hughes, and her 1956 poem 'Conversation Among the Ruins', but other approaches can be taken. While working on Plath's 'Nick and the Candlestick', written in late October 1962, I wondered if any specific article or visit to a nearby cave might have prompted the poem's allusion to white newts, but if there ever was anything in her journal about this, we cannot know it. This leads us to one of the most frustrating, and notorious, circumstances surrounding Plath's journals: their patchiness. There are no journals for the last three years of her writing life, and the absence of any full version of what letters there are is doubly frustrating.

## *The Journals of Sylvia Plath: 1950–1962/The Unabridged Journals of Sylvia Plath*

On 14 September 1998, a few weeks before his death, Ted Hughes unsealed sections of Plath's journals that he had originally planned to keep locked until 2013, or for as long as Plath's mother and brother remained alive (Aurelia Plath died in the mid-1990s). Once unsealed, these sections were published in Karen Kukil's 2000 edition of the *Journals*. Kukil has provided a scholarly transcription of all of Plath's personal papers that Smith College holds. She has preserved Plath's spelling, syntax, capitalization and punctuation, and refrained from interrupting Plath's text with her own.[22] She has kept each journal separate, and used her endnotes to describe the formats of the sources from which the transcribed material was taken.

Given the variety of forms that Plath's physical papers take, this must have been no small challenge. The word 'journals' itself might be put in scare quotes. Plath's 'journals' include handwriting in bound and spiral notebooks, typing on miscellaneous pieces of paper, and scrawls on sheets of varying sizes, colours, types and formality. Some of these are difficult to date precisely, or even to narrow to a reasonable range of years. While the 'journals' are officially lodged in Smith College's Rare Book Room, the Lilly Library also possesses papers and small calendars in which Plath jotted her thoughts. These might also, legitimately, constitute Plath's 'journals'.

So, too, might the large numbers of Plath's papers that are entwined with Hughes's own in the archives at Emory University. We must accept that there will never be a 'complete' edition of Plath's *Journals*.

Even Kukil's relatively authoritative edition of the *Journals* is authoritative to different degrees in the US and UK editions. The first and most obvious difference between the two is the title. The American edition is known as *The Unabridged Journals of Sylvia Plath*, while the English is the rather ungainly *The Journals of Sylvia Plath: 1950–1962*. While the English edition has 'no omissions, deletions, or corrections of Plath's words', 'twelve sentences' have been omitted from the US edition and some names have been disguised ( *J*, p. x). It is peculiar, then, that this edition should be called 'unabridged'. The deleted sentences concern Plath's speculations about the possible infertility or impotence of some of her acquaintances; when a name is disguised, it tends to be because Plath is speculating about somebody's medical or sexual problems.[23]

Kukil herself implicitly acknowledges some aspects of the *Journal's* incompleteness. She tells us that Plath 'began keeping diaries and journals at the age of eleven and continued this practice until her death at the age of thirty. It is her adult journals from 1950 to 1962 that comprise this edition' (*J*, p. ix). In terms of the period of time covered, however, not much has changed since the publication in the US in 1982 of the expurgated journals which, as Nancy Milford remarked, 'do not cover the period 1959–1963, when her major work got written' ('The Journals', p. 81). Kukil's edition really ends on 15 November 1959. All we get from 1962 in the 2000 *Journals* are notes Plath made about her neighbours. Plath typed these on loose, extra long, lined sheets of paper that were certainly not part of the supposedly destroyed or lost journal ledgers. From 1961 we get some notes that Plath titled 'The Inmate', in which she writes about her stay in hospital in February of that year. In this light, the UK edition's full title, *The Journals of Sylvia Plath: 1950–1962*, does appear odd.

Hughes has made contradictory and famous statements about the last, unpublished volumes of Plath's journals. In particular, he has spoken of two 'maroon-backed ledgers ... from late '59 to within three days of her death'. Hughes says of the last of these ledgers that he 'destroyed it' in order to protect the children, and tells us that the penultimate one 'disappeared' ( *J Abr.*, p. xv). Referring to these same two journal volumes in another 1982 piece, Hughes writes, 'the second of these two books her husband destroyed, because he did not want her children to have read it ... The earlier one disappeared more recently (and may, presumably, still turn up)' (*WP*, p. 177).

While similar, Hughes's two accounts of what happened to the last ledger nonetheless differ in important ways. First, as Janet Malcolm has observed, there is Hughes's shift from first person to third person. The distancing effect of his rhetorical pose suggests that he has no personal involvement in this.[24] To Malcolm's point we can add Hughes's equally strange attachment of the children to Plath alone. He uses the pronoun 'her' before 'children', where we would expect 'our'. Syntactically, he has nothing to do with the couple's daughter and son. The other significant difference between the two accounts of what happened to the journals is Hughes's parenthetical note that they may still 'turn up' (WP, p. 178). One feels that Hughes, within the parentheses that imply relative unimportance, is dryly teasing the Plath scholars or 'crazy club' whom he sees as the enemy (WP, p. 163). Hughes dangles hope that, as Malcolm puts it, 'the journal is in fact . . . in his hands' (Silent Woman, p. 5). Yet Hughes can also write, maddeningly (because with a tone of innocence), 'we certainly have lost a valuable appendix to all that later writing' (WP, p. 178). Again the pronoun shift is revealing; it is as if Hughes suffers the loss with us, and had nothing to do with its cause.

Hughes himself has admitted his fallibility in accounting for Plath's missing work. In his 'Introduction' to Johnny Panic and the Bible of Dreams, he speaks of stories that he 'remembered her having written', stories that he assumed she had 'lost or destroyed as failures', only to find they had turned up at the Lilly Library, 'acquired . . . from . . . the writer's mother' (JP, p. 11); he also speaks of the absent journals in the present tense, as if they still exist (JP, p. 13).[25] He suggests that some parts of Johnny Panic have been 'selected', as though from a matrix of other work from the same period. You cannot select if all other options have been lost or destroyed. Anne Stevenson tells us in Bitter Fame that 'an entry Olwyn remembers from Sylvia's lost journal strikes a poignant note: "We answer the door together. They step over me as though I were a mat, and walk straight into [Ted's] heart."'[26] Does Hughes's sister remember word for word a text that supposedly no longer exists? Is she paraphrasing – and doing a plausible job of mimicking words that Plath wrote during the spring of 1962? Does the journal still exist, so that Olwyn Hughes was able to dip into it in the late 1980s and bring along the quotation for Stevenson?

In April 2000 Emory University opened its archive of Hughes's personal papers. In this collection is a sealed trunk that Hughes stipulated must remain locked for twenty-five years after his death.[27] It is tempting to hope that the missing journals are in it, though Hughes's literary agent, who packed the sealed trunk, insists that they were not there.[28]

### Letters Home: Correspondence 1950–1963

No controversy of quite such notoriety and mystery touches Plath's letters – at least so far. Despite its deficiencies, Letters Home provides a great deal of valuable material. Yet *Letters Home* is not a writer's 'selected letters' in the traditional sense: we are largely given Plath's letters to her mother, but only a handful from Plath to any other correspondents. Virginia Woolf, whose novels were so important to Plath ('[they] make mine possible', she wrote (*J*, p. 289)) said in a letter to Gerald Brenan, 'It is an interesting question – what one tries to do, in writing a letter – partly of course to give back a reflection of the other person. Writing to Lytton or Leonard I am quite different from writing to you.' Here is Woolf in a letter to Vita Sackville-West: 'With Lytton I talk about reading; with Clive about love; with Nessa about people; with Roger about art; with Morgan about writing.'[29] The implication of Woolf's comments is that we are all of us different people, depending on who we are talking to. *Letters Home* really gives us only the version of Plath that arose when she spoke to her mother.

'We have little evidence of how Aurelia Plath responded to the letters,' wrote Rose Kamel.[30] However, if we take Woolf's point that letters try to 'give back a reflection of the other person', and if we assume that Plath was a skilled letter writer, it could be said that *Letters Home* gives us a very vivid picture of Aurelia Plath. Moreover, even without the latter's side of the correspondence, there is one source that offers us a great deal of information about how she responded to her daughter's letters. That source is Aurelia Plath's own annotations on the originals. These, though seldom discussed, are worth examining in detail because they allow us to see Plath's letters and their history from a fresh angle.[31] The annotations are not merely of private significance to Aurelia, but give us a skeleton of the principles upon which *Letters Home* was formed. In many cases the annotations are actually addressed to future readers. They are a sort of invisible ink, undetectable in the published book, but revealed by a visit to the Plath archives.

Some of Aurelia Plath's annotations seem to have been made soon after she received her daughter's letters, perhaps even as she read them for the first time, and to have been used by her to make quick notes of any questions or points she wanted to raise in response. When Plath discusses her plans and worries about raising enough money to buy a house, for example, Plath's mother wonders in the margin whether Plath and Hughes can claim that Hughes is an employee of the BBC for mortgage purposes.[32]

A fair number of her annotations are not so contingent upon the moment. Many of them take the form of brief notes on envelopes that she made while selecting the material for *Letters Home*. These annotations tend to describe the contents of the envelopes, a sort of filing system for subject matter. Typically earmarked are references to people who played, Aurelia Plath thought, an important part in her daughter's life, such as Olive Higgins Prouty, who sponsored Plath's scholarship to Smith.[33] Also highlighted is Plath's allusion to the fact that Aurelia Plath is a wonderful mother[34] and that she misses her family, who mean so much to her.[35]

Sometimes it is difficult to determine whether Aurelia Plath's annotations were made at the time she received a letter, or years later. Sometimes, though, it is clear that the latter was the case. In the margin of a letter that Plath wrote on 6 February 1961, in which she tells her mother that she had a miscarriage (*LH*, p. 408), her mother writes the date 14 February 1963. This date is two years after Plath wrote the letter, and three days after her death. On the same letter Aurelia Plath makes a loving reference to her daughter and annotates her regret that Plath felt she could not write about the difficult aspects of her life because she was chary of her mother's overidentification with her.[36] What this shows is a layering of the annotations at different dates, as the recipient rereads and returns to the letters and builds up her own narrative upon them.[37]

But to whom is Aurelia Plath speaking? To whom is she confiding her regret that Plath could not write frankly of her difficulties? Herself? Plath? Future readers of the manuscripts? All of these at once? In a self-conscious annotation for posterity, Aurelia Plath states that she uses annotations to draft her responses to letters.[38] This explanation is the antithesis of Carolyn Steedman's assertion that 'the Historian who goes to the Archive must always be an unintended reader, will always read that which was never intended for his or her eyes' (*Dust*, p. 75). Many of her annotations are written specifically for other people's eyes: those of the researchers who use the archive.

From the point in time where the Plath/Hughes marriage foundered, Aurelia Plath's underlinings of her daughter's letters grow in number, focusing on Plath's negative comments about Hughes while ignoring the many positive remarks Plath makes about him even after they have separated. Plath's mother begins to use these underlinings in an attempt to manipulate the reader's attention in ways that were not possible in the published version of *Letters Home*. It would be misleading, however, to suggest that this was her only emphasis. The letters in the Lilly Library continue from Plath's death until 1977 and consist of a large number of letters to Aurelia Plath from other correspondents. Her annotations are not reserved for her daughter's letters alone.

While Aurelia Plath's annotations of the *Letters Home* typescript itself are largely businesslike, concerning, for instance, pagination, line spacing or the insertion of footnotes,[39] she does in a few places use the typescript as a place to record what she has had to take out. For instance, she notes that the excerpt in *Letters Home* from Plath's letter of 1 January 1961 omits her daughter's account of a severe argument she had with Hughes's sister.[40]

In his study of Samuel Richardson's eighteenth-century epistolary novel *Clarissa*, Terry Eagleton argues that letter writing is tied to power and sexual politics, to questions of who can say what to whom, and to an erosion of boundaries between the private and the public. The tussle between Aurelia Plath and Ted Hughes over what letters, and parts of letters, could be printed in *Letters Home* turned upon tensions between Hughes's desire for privacy and the mother's wish for her daughter's correspondence to have a public audience. Aurelia Plath had power of a particular emotional kind over Hughes: as a grieving mother who was distressed by the sudden publication of *The Bell Jar* in the US, when she had been promised by Hughes that this would not happen. And Hughes had a very practical power over Plath's mother as the copyright holder with a right to veto all or any of her selection of letters; for her to publish *Letters Home* at all was entirely in his gift.

Eagleton reminds us that letters can be 'waylaid, forged, stolen, lost, copied, cited, censored, parodied, misread, rewritten, submitted to mocking commentary, woven into other texts which alter their meaning, exploited for ends unforeseen by their authors'.[41] What Eagleton describes in *The Rape of Clarissa* has been true of Plath's writing, and continues to be so. Critics and scholars comment upon and weave Plath's texts into their own, using them in ways that Plath could never have predicted. Owing to the practical demands of publishing a selection of letters, and Aurelia Plath's dual role as editor and mother, *Letters Home* necessarily excerpts, selects, misinterprets (what mother could perfectly interpret her child's letters?) and attempts to manipulate and control the reader's interpretation through its commentary. Aurelia Plath's writing *upon* Plath's letters, though unpublished, is perhaps the most immediate example of a commentary that weaves Plath's text into another and uses her letters in a way that she could not have foreseen. As Eagleton says of *Clarissa*, and we might say of Plath's own correspondence, 'As one letter spawns another ... the impulse to protect and control writing grows accordingly sharper' (p. 50).

Aurelia Plath arguably uses her annotations to justify or defend herself, either in her planned response to her daughter's letter, or to us. Alongside Plath's query as to why her mother does not see the advantages Plath would gain by living abroad, Aurelia Plath answers that it was because Plath had never told her, and declares that she is glad to know it at last. Aurelia Plath addresses these points to her daughter using the second person. In the same letter, when Plath worries that her comments will anger her addressee, Mrs Plath switches to the third person and protests that Plath is making hasty assumptions. These annotations were probably made in 1973, as they are written in the same pencil in which Aurelia Plath notes that she has successfully excerpted the letter for *Letters Home*, an act which she dates as 17 September 1973.[42] Ten years after Plath's death, her mother appears to be having an argument with a correspondent who cannot reply. She does this first through a second person 'you' that mimics the conventions of conversation, but without the possibility of being interrupted or challenged. She then changes to a third person 'she' in a gesture that resembles the act of talking behind someone's back. This impulse seems public as well as private. There is something uncanny about writing that is deeply personal, but also intended for the audience of strangers who will read it in the archive.

Aurelia Plath's letters may have influenced Ted Hughes's famous collection of poetic letters to Plath, *Birthday Letters* (1998). She notes in an annotation that she must retain a birthday letter that her daughter wrote to her brother Warren in 1956.[43] She also records on an envelope which she received in 1962 that it encases the last birthday letter her daughter was to send her.[44] Was the term 'birthday letter' originally Aurelia Plath's, passed to Ted Hughes via her daughter, or discovered by Hughes himself when he came across these annotations?[45] Was it a coincidence that both of them used the phrase? For them both, birthday letters are not just the letters that are written to you to mark your birthday, or that you write to somebody to mark theirs. Birthday letters are the letters that you reread on the subsequent birthdays of both the writer and the addressee, as well as the mixture of written (whether in the form of an annotation or a poem) responses to those letters – and the absent person who wrote them – as the years go on.

One of the most important conditions of reading letters is dramatic irony, the fact that in many cases the reader knows what will happen, while the person who wrote the letter did not. Dramatic irony does not allow for textual freedom, because to move away from the story of a life is to throw away dramatic irony. On 11 February 1960 a heavily pregnant Plath wrote to her brother and mother a letter full of excitement, describing how she had signed the contract for her first book, *The Colossus*, met her editor at Heinemann and then celebrated over lunch with her husband. The letter is full of her plans for decorating the apartment and buying a rocking chair for her baby.[46] Aurelia Plath annotates the letter by pointing out that her daughter wrote it exactly three years before her death. With this annotation, she makes us feel how extraordinary it is that the joy and excitement expressed in the letter could give way to the events of that terrible morning in 1963.

The experience of reading *Letters Home* can often leave the reader feeling as if he or she is watching a car crash that is about to happen. When Plath casually mentions that she and Hughes especially 'liked' the 'young Canadian poet' and his 'German-Russian' wife to whom they have decided to let their London flat (*LH*, p. 423), when she innocently alludes to the fact that the couple (Assia and David Wevill) will be 'coming down' to visit her and Hughes in Devon for the 'weekend' (*LH*, p. 454), or when she writes that she has made 'the final arrangements for a gas stove' to be installed in the Fitzroy Road flat in which she was to kill herself (*LH*, p. 487), the effect of hindsight can be chilling.

Eagleton observes that there is a 'troubling gap ... between "experience" and "expression"' (*Rape of Clarissa*, p. 41). By this he means that however intense the immediacy of a letter may seem, the act of writing can never be contemporaneous with the experiences it recounts. Whatever the mixture of spontaneity and calculation that prompts Aurelia Plath's annotations, her annotations, no less than Plath's original letters, are subject to what Eagleton describes as the capacity of writing to 'exceed and invert' the writer's 'precise meaning' (*Rape of Clarissa*, p. 42): that is, to expose more than they mean to, or say the opposite of what they intend. The sentiments and actions described in Mrs Plath's notes can at times appear to be the antithesis of positive and helpful as they unwittingly reveal her anxiety about what she feared was her daughter's unconventional marriage, lifestyle and vocation. This may not have been the impression Mrs Plath wished to leave with her repeated marginal cheers of approval. Such cheers are elicited by Plath's assertion of her joy at being a woman who loves her man and celebrates nature.[47] Similarly pleasing to Mrs Plath is her daughter's exhibition of feminine values through a desire to teach and give something to others.[48]

Mrs Plath explains in the 'Introduction' to *Letters Home* that she saved Plath's correspondence because she 'had the dream of one day handing Sylvia the huge packet of letters. I felt she could make use of them' (*LH*, p. 3). Despite her explanations as to why she saved them, Mrs Plath's very possession of the letters (particularly love letters written to Plath by early boyfriends and by Ted Hughes) is another instance of where matters 'exceed and invert' her meaning. Why would Plath give such letters to her mother? Jacqueline Rose has addressed this question in psychoanalytic terms: love letters in the mother's hands become a symptom of the blurring of the 'distinctions ... between mother and lover' (*Haunting*, p. 80). Sometimes, however, the banal explanation is the most probable: perhaps Plath gave her lovers' letters to her mother just as many students, while young and travelling or at university, leave them in storage with their parents rather than tote them around the world.

## A happy ending?

I have written elsewhere about the need for publishing an edition of Plath's poems that gives us the variant versions of all her poems, and considered some of the ways this might be accomplished.[49] Thirty years have elapsed since the publication of *Letters Home*, and it seems important that a new edition of Plath's letters be published. As in the case of Plath's poems, the letters present special difficulties and opportunities. Ideally, any new edition would include not just her letters to her mother, but also those she wrote to other correspondents. Certainly to produce such a volume would present challenges on many fronts (practical and copyright) but it does seem inevitable that, in time, a fuller, more reliable version will appear.

If we return to the question of the missing journal volumes, however, a happy ending is less certain. In a funny way, it is a kind of cliché: that sealed trunk that may or may not contain the missing journals; those ledgers that were probably lost or destroyed, but offer just the barest possibility that they might one day be discovered. Plath's readers so want them to exist; they so want them to be found. Sometimes I wonder if the lost journals are a 'McGuffin', the plot-enabling device in a movie or the object of desire that sets off a mystery. The only real value of a McGuffin is that people think it is valuable. It is like the 'government secrets' that motivate the action in the film *North by Northwest* but are never explained, and, in the end, not important anyway; or the Maltese Falcon that gets the characters together but turns out to be worthless. The situation has parallels with Lacan's reading of Poe's 'The Purloined Letter', with Hughes in the situation of the Minister, and then of Dupin, controlling documents by withholding them.[50]

Even if, once that trunk at Emory is finally opened, there are no journals in it, the quest will continue. The 'lost' journals will always be an absent object of desire, prompting the idea that if they are not in that trunk, they must be somewhere else, a McGuffin to take the story on. We know very little about the contents of the absent journals, yet so much of what critics do – and do not do – with Plath's writing is affected by them. Important pieces of Plath's body of work are missing: the very pieces, so the thinking goes, that might just make sense of it. To believe that the lost journals are merely a McGuffin could bring solace, because it is a way of telling yourself that nothing that mattered, nothing that would change anything, was ever there.

## Notes

Unless otherwise indicated, material referred to at the Lilly Library is from the 'Plath mss. II Correspondence' collection. Grants from the British Academy and from Bath Spa University financed research visits to the Lilly Library.

1. Linda Wagner-Martin, *Sylvia Plath: A Biography* (New York: Simon & Schuster, 1987), p. 219. It is clear from Plath's letter of 29 November (*LH*, p. 483) that,

from extensive broadsheet coverage, Plath was aware of the book before preparing her own review.

2. SP to Aurelia Plath, 1 January 1961, January–May, Box 6, Lilly. Annotation not dated.
3. 'Guide to the Sylvia Plath Materials in the Lilly Library'. The Lilly Library also holds some of Plath's early poetry and prose manuscripts, many of Plath's books, some of her artwork, diaries and calendars, and letters that Plath wrote to others.
4. Smith College also holds some of Plath's calendars and diaries, the manuscripts of many of her late poems, typescripts from *The Bell Jar*, and some of her artwork.
5. SP to Aurelia Plath, 1943, Box 1, Lilly.
6. SP to Aurelia Plath, 1944–5. 1947. 1948, July 16–December, Box 1, Lilly.
7. Nancy Milford, 'The Journals of Sylvia Plath', in Linda Wagner (ed.), *Critical Essays on Sylvia Plath* (Boston: G. K. Hall, 1984), p. 78.
8. Steven Gould Axelrod, 'The Second Destruction of Sylvia Plath', in Linda Wagner (ed.), *Sylvia Plath: The Critical Heritage* (London and New York: Routledge, 1988), p. 314.
9. Marni Jackson, 'In Search of the Shape Within', in Wagner, *Critical Heritage*, p. 305.
10. Jacqueline Rose, *The Haunting of Sylvia Plath* (London: Virago, 1991), pp. 64, 72, 82, 91. Aurelia Plath's annotations of the letters make clear the importance with which she regarded her daughter's engagement with the larger world, even if many of Plath's allusions to this did not make it into the final edition of *Letters Home*.
11. Erica Jong, 'Letters Focus Exquisite Rage of Sylvia Plath', in Wagner, *Critical Heritage*, p. 205.
12. Bill Kirtz, 'The Unabridged Journals of Sylvia Plath – Literary History or Invasion of Privacy?' *Trinity Reporter* (Spring 2001) http://www.trincoll.edu/pub/reporter/Spring%202001/Karen%20Kukil%2077.shtml (Accessed 23 December 2004).
13. SP to Aurelia Plath, 22 November 1962, August–December, Box 6a, Lilly.
14. Jo Brans, 'The Girl Who Wanted to be God', in Wagner, *Critical Heritage*, p. 213.
15. Carol Bere, '*Letters Home: Correspondence 1950–1963*', in Wagner, *Critical Heritage*, p. 222.
16. Martha Duffy, 'Two Lives', in Wagner, *Critical Heritage*, p. 218.
17. See Erica Wagner, 'Love That Passed All Understanding', *The Times* (18 March 2000), p. 21; Jacqueline Rose, 'So Many Lives, So Little Time', *Observer* (2 April 2000), p. 11; and Tim Kendall, 'Showing Off to an Audience of One', *Times Literary Supplement* (5 May 2000), p. 12.
18. Michael Sheldon, 'The "Demon" that Killed Sylvia', *Daily Telegraph* (13 March 2000), p. 9.
19. Allison Pearson, 'Trapped in Time: Sylvia Plath', *Daily Telegraph* (1 April 2000), pp. A1, A2.
20. Diane Middlebrook, *Her Husband: Hughes and Plath – A Marriage* (New York: Viking; London: Little Brown, 2003), pp. 236, 337n.
21. Carolyn Steedman, *Dust* (Manchester: Manchester University Press, 2001), pp. 76, 168.

22. While acknowledging that the impulse to provide a 'corrective' to Hughes's previous editing of the journals is understandable, Joyce Carol Oates regards the fidelity even to Plath's errors as a kind of idolatry by an 'adulatory' editor. Oates feels that the 'wholly unedited version' with no abridgement makes for too much 'repetition'. See 'Raising Lady Lazarus', *New York Times* (5 November 2000). http://query.nytimes.com/search/restricted/article?res = F60711F835550C768CDDA80994D8404482 (Accessed 26 December 2004).

23. The omitted sentences appear on pp. 358 and 444–5 of the English edition (the pagination of the US and UK editions is the same). See also p. 468 for the abbreviation of names in order to protect privacy.

24. Janet Malcolm, *The Silent Woman: Sylvia Plath and Ted Hughes* (New York: Knopf, 1994), pp. 5–6.

25. References are to the English edition of *Johnny Panic and the Bible of Dreams* (London: Faber and Faber, 1979), pp. 11, 13.

26. Anne Stevenson, *Bitter Fame: A Life of Sylvia Plath* (London: Viking, 1989), p. 241.

27. See Erica Wagner, 'At Last, Justice for Hughes', *The Times* (10 April 2000), p. 6, and James Bone, 'Hughes Papers Reveal Devotion to Plath', *The Times* (8 April 2000), p. 10.

28. Roy Davids, 'Plath's Missing Journal', *The Times* (11 April 2000). http://www.times-archive.co.uk/news/pages/tim/2000/04/11/timopnolto1003.html (Accessed 2 January 2005). Davids argues that Hughes possessed an appreciation of 'archival integrity' that 'would have led him to have offered [the missing journal] to Smith where it would have joined Sylvia Plath's working papers and other journals'.

29. Virginia Woolf, *Congenial Spirits: The Selected Letters of Virginia Woolf*, ed. Joanne Trautmann Banks (London: Hogarth Press, 1989), pp. 256, 216.

30. Rose Kamel, '"Reach Hag Hands and Haul Me In": Matrophobia in the Letters of Sylvia Plath', in Wagner, *Critical Heritage*, p. 223.

31. The evolution of *Letters Home* can be read through Aurelia Plath's papers in the Lilly Library. At one point she planned to subtitle the book *A Testament of Love* and to organize it around titles such as 'A New Life in the Old World', 'Return to the Promised Land', 'The Other Side of the Desk', and 'The Song of Frieda Rebecca'. Plath mss. II. Writings *Letters Home* – Notes. Box 9, folder 11, Lilly.

32. SP to Aurelia Plath, 14 April 1961, January–May, Box 6, Lilly.

33. SP to Aurelia Plath, 1950, 16–31 October, Box 1 (postmarked 2 November), Lilly.

34. SP to Aurelia Plath, 1950, December, Box 1, 10 December (Aurelia Plath's dating, but postmarked 6 December), Lilly.

35. SP to Aurelia Plath, 1950, November, Box 1, 26 November (Aurelia Plath's dating), Lilly.

36. SP to Aurelia Plath, 6 February 1961, January–May, Box 6, Lilly.

37. As a corrective to an unspecified epistolary assertion of Hughes's that Plath exaggerated the extreme conditions of her last winter in England, Mrs Plath notes on a photograph of towering snow drifts that Hughes went to Devon a few days before the great storm hit. She initials this note and dates it 28 February 1977. Plath mss. II. Miscellaneous. Box 15, f.67 Miscellany, Lilly.

38. SP to Aurelia Plath, 24 September 1962, August–December, Box 6a, Lilly.

39. Plath mss. II. Writings. *Letters Home* – Part Six. Box 9, f.9, Lilly.
40. Plath mss. II. Writings. *Letters Home* – Part Seven. Box 9, f.10, Lilly. See Anne Stevenson's very different version of the argument (*Bitter Fame*, pp. 203–4).
41. Terry Eagleton, *The Rape of Clarissa: Writing, Sexuality and Class Struggle in Samuel Richardson* (Oxford: Basil Blackwell, 1982), p. 50.
42. SP to Aurelia Plath, 10 February 1955, February, Box 5, Lilly.
43. 23 April 1956, March–April, Box 6, Lilly.
44. SP to Aurelia Plath, 25 April 1962, January–April, Box 6a, Lilly.
45. Hughes quotes from letters Plath received from her mother and her analyst Dr Ruth Beuscher in the title poem of his limited edition collection *Howls & Whispers* (1998), now available in his *Collected Poems* (2003).
46. SP to Aurelia Plath, 11 February 1960, January–April, Box 6, Lilly.
47. SP to Aurelia Plath, 8 October 1956, 1–15 October, Box 6, Lilly.
48. SP to Aurelia Plath, 28 January 1957, January–February, Box 6, Lilly.
49. See Tracy Brain, 'Unstable Manuscripts: The Indeterminacy of the Plath Canon', in Anita Helle (ed.), *The Unraveling Archive: Essays on Sylvia Plath* (Ann Arbor: University of Michigan Press, forthcoming).
50. Jacques Lacan, 'Seminar on "The Purloined Letter"', reprinted in Robert Con Davis and Ronald Schleifer (eds.), *Contemporary Literary Criticism* (New York and London: Longman, 1989), pp. 308–11.

# I I

DIANE MIDDLEBROOK

# The poetry of Sylvia Plath and Ted Hughes: call and response[1]

The first syllables Sylvia Plath ever spoke to Ted Hughes were lifted from a poem that he had written and that she had memorized. "'I did it, I'", she called to him over the dance music at a crowded party at Cambridge University – a launch party for the first issue of a college literary magazine, *St. Botolph's Review*, in which Hughes's work appeared prominently. 'You like?' he responded, and led her into a quieter room where they could say more.[2]

That playful exchange was an overture to the distinctive creative partnership they established soon afterwards. Working side by side, they developed a dynamic of mutual influence that produced the poems we read today. This aspect of their bond can be tracked in their poetry from the months of their courtship through the years of their marriage and separation. And it can also be found in the poetry Hughes published in the year he died, in two volumes addressed to Plath: *Birthday Letters* and the limited edition *Howls & Whispers*.

## Courtship poems

The impact on Sylvia Plath of reading Ted Hughes and of meeting Ted Hughes was instant and permanent, partly owing to its timing in her life. She was a recent graduate of Smith College, attending Cambridge University on a Fulbright Fellowship, studying literature and hoping to establish herself as a writer. Her poetry and stories had appeared in such American magazines as *Seventeen*, *Harper's Magazine*, *Mademoiselle*, *The Nation* and *Atlantic Monthly*; she was now ambitious about finding venues in which to introduce herself to English readers. In January 1956 two of her poems had appeared in *Chequer*, one of the small literary magazines at Cambridge, and, to her acute distress, had been dismissively criticized in another student publication that was widely read in the literary community. Plath viewed the launch party for *St. Botolph's Review* as an opportunity for disarming her critic and impressing the local writers. Hughes's poetry had already captivated Plath before she met him; along with the poems she had found in *St. Botolph's Review*, she had seen poems he published in *Chequer* titled 'The Jaguar' and 'The Casualty'. In her journal she praised the lack of sentimentality she observed in his work.

The poem Plath had quoted to Hughes at the party, 'Law in the Country of the Cats', opens with a cool observation about male aggression. The poem explains that when men meet they often hate one another at first sight, by animal instinct ('their blood before / They are aware has bristled into their hackles'); and this provokes them to acts of sudden violence. The poem closes with a depiction of the consequences of this, with 'one man bursting into the police station / Crying ... "I did it, I"'.[3] Hughes was not the first to have written the phrase that Plath quoted to him in her opening gambit; he was alluding to an anonymous English folksong: '"Who killed Cock Robin?" "I", said the Sparrow, / "With my bow and arrow, I killed Cock Robin."' Hughes had embedded this bloodthirsty theme in a poem completely saturated by the influence of D. H. Lawrence and Sigmund Freud. Specifically, Hughes was drawing upon Lawrence's concept of 'blood consciousness', an idealization of irrational impulses. Blood, Hughes writes, is 'aware' before the men can think.

Plath would almost certainly have recognized all these sources. Although she and Hughes had gone to school on opposite sides of the Atlantic, they had both been deeply influenced by the same modernist texts. But Plath and Hughes were not discussing books that night, they were sampling one another's pheromones: 'bang the door was shut ... he kissed me bang smash on the mouth', she wrote in her journal the next day. 'I bit him long and hard on the cheek ... blood was running down his face. His poem "I did it, I". Such violence, and I can see how women lie down for artists' (*J*, pp. 211–12). Later, Hughes would write, in the poem 'St. Botolph's', that his kiss and her bite constituted the ceremony in which 'the solar system married us / Whether we knew it or not' (Hughes, *Collected Poems*, p. 1051).

In the days immediately following this party, Plath wrote 'Pursuit', a poem that commemorated their meeting, and exemplifies the way Plath's contact with Hughes's writing would work in her own poetry thereafter. Her journal provides a detailed view of the process. She was supposed to be writing a paper on the theme of 'passion as destiny' for a tutorial on Racine's *Phèdre*, but she was completely distracted by her own aroused passion (*J*, p. 214). The influence of Hughes on the poem is quite specific, at two different points. From the poem she had called out to Hughes at the party, 'Pursuit' echoes the theme that human animals are possessed by the violent instincts of animals in the wild.

In Plath's poem the aggression is expressed not between man and man but between a man and women. She gave 'Pursuit' an epigraph from Racine: '*dans le fond des forêts votre image me suit*'; the speaker is being stalked by a (male) panther whose violence ignites (or 'kindle[s]') female sexuality. In 'Law in the Country of the Cats' Hughes had written of the animals' blood rising instinctively. In 'Pursuit' the word 'blood' appears four times, pertinently as in stanza two, as a metaphor for instinct. More overtly, Plath has taken from Hughes's 'Jaguar' the image of an enraged animal deafened by the pounding 'bang of blood in the brain deaf the ear' (Hughes, *Collected Poems*, p. 20). Plath responded by positioning herself as prey of such an animal: 'Blood quickens, gonging in my ears: // The panther's tread is on the stairs.'

'Pursuit' displays the kind of influence that would typify Plath's creative relationship to Hughes's poetry: his words activate her own distinctive poetic method. In those days Plath was a rigorous formalist. In 'Pursuit' she has absorbed and remade the image she found in his poem about blood consciousness, and the flow is entirely Plathian with intensely felt emotion compressed into carefully managed verse. 'Pursuit' is structured in twelve-line stanzas which are actually composed of three four-line rhymed stanzas *abba-cddc-egge fggf-hiih-jkkj*, etc. The rhymes are half-rhymes and the rhythms seem more generated by an obsessive emotion than by counting beats; the rhythm is loosely iambic, four beats in eight syllables per line. The sound of the poem does not highlight this complexity of structure, though, for Plath was very skilled in this mode.

But it was not long before Plath began experimenting as well with the form of her verse, by adopting a mode of archaic diction and extreme terseness that typified Hughes's style at the time, as in his poem 'Bawdry Embraced' with its 'Great farmy whores,' 'buttocks like / Two white sows' and 'no dunghills for Bawdry's cock' (Hughes, *Collected Poems*, p. 13). One of Hughes's literary acquaintances explained that such work displayed the Jacobean style of 'masculine toughness' that appealed to young Cambridge poets in those days.[4] The first evidence of this influence on Plath occurs in her 1956 poem 'Bucolics', where some Hughesianly clotted sound-effects appear: 'Mayday: two came to field in such wise: / "A daisied mead", each said to each, / So were they one; so sought they couch.' Other stylistic influences came into Plath's poetry early in their relationship through their intensive discussions of writers Hughes admired, especially Dylan Thomas, Gerard Manley Hopkins and W. B. Yeats. Hughes read his favourite poems aloud to Plath; she ventriloquized them back in poems that she bragged were 'drunker than Dylan, harder than Hopkins, younger than Yeats' (*LH*, p. 243). Most evident are the influences in Plath's courtship poems, of Dylan Thomas in 'Ode for Ted', 'Faun' and 'Wreath for a Bridal'; of Hopkins in 'Firesong'; and of Yeats in 'Strumpet Song', 'Tinker Jack and the Tidy Wives', 'Street Song' and 'Recantation'.

## Marriage poems

Plath and Hughes had known each other for only four months when they married on 16 June 1956 – Bloomsday, as they were both aware, the 'day' commemorated in James Joyce's novel *Ulysses*. In June 1957, at the end of Plath's Fulbright Fellowship, the couple moved to Massachusetts where Plath took up a faculty position in the English Department at her alma mater, Smith College, and Hughes accepted a faculty position near by at the University of Massachusetts at Amherst. In 1958 they made the important decision together not to continue teaching, but to devote themselves to writing. They moved to Boston for a year. The transition was difficult for Plath; she experienced a bout of writer's block which she tried to vanquish by auditing Robert Lowell's poetry seminar at Boston University, and by working at a job in a psychiatrist's office. Eventually she decided to undertake psychotherapy herself, with the psychiatrist who had treated her during an earlier mental breakdown and suicide attempt. One outcome of the therapy was a decision to have a baby right away, rather than waiting until she and Hughes had established themselves as writers.

Plath wrote relatively little poetry of lasting interest between 1956 and late 1959, though it is arguable that the journal she produced during those years of struggle is one of her major contributions to twentieth-century literature. She emerged from her dry spell at the very end of 1959, when she and Hughes spent six weeks in residence at Yaddo, an artists' colony situated in a mansion in upstate New York. At Yaddo she found a copy of Theodore Roethke's Pulitzer Prize-winning *Words for the Wind*, which she read avidly (Middlebrook, *Her Husband*, p. 109). Roethke, like Plath, had suffered a severe mental illness for which he had been hospitalized; in 1959 he published a book of poems in which he experimented with representing the experience from the inside, in fragmented, surreal imagery shaped in language drawn from childhood memories.

Roethke's example excited Plath, who had not yet found an artistic medium for the expression of her own experience of breakdown and treatment. By adopting Roethke's approach, Plath was able to avoid the normalizing, conversational mode of other confessional poets who wrote about their mental illnesses – specifically, her friends Robert Lowell and Anne Sexton. Plath's sequence 'Poem for a Birthday', written at Yaddo in a style heavily influenced by Roethke, marks the point at which Plath's suicidal ideation and her horror of shock treatment became available to her as literary subjects. A few months later, abandoning the Roethkean voice, she wrote 'The Hanging Man', which displaces the experience of shock treatment into the visual image of one of the cards in a tarot deck.

Plath and Hughes left the US at the end of their stay at Yaddo, to settle in England where the cost of living was lower and writers found work more easily. They moved into a London flat so small that it could not even accommodate a writing desk; they wrote in bed or sitting at different ends of the living-room sofa, until Hughes put a card table in the cramped entry foyer. However, Plath, who was pregnant when they moved, did very little writing until after their first child, a daughter, was born in this flat in April 1960. They named her Frieda, after the wife of D. H. Lawrence (Middlebrook, *Her Husband*, p. 141).

A new surge of creative energy was released in each of them by observing Frieda's development. One inspiration, for both Plath and Hughes, was watching the baby acquire language. In letters to friends Hughes commented on her progress. After two months, he noted, her babble was expanding daily by one new sound;[5] at six months she could make a raspberry, thanks to Plath's assiduous coaching;[6] by Christmas, he observed, she was producing one out of every three syllables while inhaling (Middlebrook, *Her Husband*, p. 142). In a radio interview shared with Plath the following January, Hughes compared the baby to an 'aerial' (possibly 'Ariel') that conducted into the household a repertory of emotions that seemed to originate in another universe.[7]

The fascination that the new parents felt towards their baby issued in a flow of calls and responses that can be tracked from Plath's poems about her pregnancy ('Metaphors', 'You're') through Hughes's celebration of the infant's safe arrival ('Lines to a Newborn Baby'), into Plath's poem about breastfeeding ('Morning Song'), and on to Hughes's lyric about the toddler's self-delighting use of a new word ('Full Moon and Little Frieda').

The initiating calls were from Plath: 'Metaphors for a Pregnant Woman', dated March 1959 when she was wishing to conceive, and 'You're', dated January/February 1960, when she was pregnant with Frieda. These poems are simple, similar, even repetitious; each is merely a playful list of the foetus's attributes. In 'Metaphors' the speaker likens herself to 'a means, a stage, a cow in calf'; 'You're' depicts a 'traveled prawn', a 'sprat in a pickle jug. / A creel of eels'.

Hughes, in response, began drafting a poem titled 'Lines to a Newborn Baby' on the back of a typescript of 'Metaphors for a Pregnant Woman'. He picked up on Plath's metaphors from the animal kingdom (in both 'Metaphors' and 'You're') using images of 'limpets' and 'snails' to characterize the instinctual life of an infant, or 'an instant // Coiled caul shell of comprehension' (Hughes, *Collected Poems*, pp. 96–7). Hughes was ambitious about 'Lines to a Newborn Baby'. In the course of making many drafts, he eventually developed a 62-line poem in three parts, each with a different form and theme threaded together by foreboding.[8] This vulnerable newborn animate life will be subject to all the indifference of accident, of history, 'casual / As some cloud touching a pond with reflection'. The brutal murder of Holofernes by the militant Judith comes to his mind (stanzas ten and eleven). And the parents will be helpless to forestall or prevent such catastrophe.

Once the child has come into this world, Hughes warns, it 'dispossesse[s]' the progenitors who can only hang over the child like unneeded 'masks' after a show (Hughes, *Collected Poems*, pp. 97–8). There is a sense of foreboding in the language of 'To F. R. at Six Months': 'among the *magi* / That crowd to your *crib* with their gifts … / Some *star* glared through' (my emphasis). Precisely the ominous phrases, italicized above, elicited Plath's poem 'Magi'. The three-line stanza of part II of Hughes's poem gave Plath the verse form, and his closing simile of useless masks prompted Plath's opening image: 'The abstracts hover like dull angels: / Nothing so vulgar as a nose or an eye / Bossing the ethereal blanks of their face-ovals.' From the outset Plath counters Hughes's grim prognostications about the fateful star that hovers over the crib by insisting on the infant's own preoccupation with physical life. His abstract sense of evil means less to the baby than a 'belly ache'. In the words of Plath's poem, 'They mistake their star, these papery godfolk. / They want the crib of some lamp-headed Plato.'

Plath's 'You're' and 'Magi' were published during the same spread of months that saw Hughes's 'Lines to a Newborn Baby' published. But Plath was not yet finished with 'Lines'. When baby Frieda was ten months old (in February 1961), Plath had a miscarriage; three weeks later she had an appendectomy and was hospitalized for over a week (*J*, p. 531). This pair of events intensified her already acute awareness of her body, and mourning stimulated her imagination. During the period spanned by grieving and recuperation that winter, Plath wrote a handful of highly accomplished poems, including 'Morning Song', 'In Plaster' and 'Tulips'. In those poems Plath's mature female body entered her art as a direct subject for poetry.

'Morning Song' is about a woman's gradual acquisition of an emotional bond with her newborn. The opening lines express the parents' feelings of anxious alienation from the infant, an emotion Plath expresses by rewriting two images in Hughes's 'Lines' and 'To F. R. at Six Months'. In the latter Hughes compares the parents to two 'masks hung up unlit' (Hughes, *Collected Poems*, p. 98). Plath writes, 'We stand round blankly as walls.' In 'Lines', as we have seen, Hughes employs the metaphor of 'some cloud touching a pond with reflection' (Hughes, *Collected Poems*, p. 96). Plath writes, 'I'm no more your mother / Than the cloud that distills a mirror to reflect its own slow / Effacement at the wind's hand.' 'Our voices echo, magnifying your arrival', as Plath put the case in 'Morning Song', perhaps acknowledging how tightly her emotions clung to that alienation which Hughes had asserted in 'Lines' and 'To F. R.'

Midway through Plath's poem the emotional frigidity and dread expressed at the opening gives way to another complex of emotions entirely. In the key image of 'Morning Song', the infant's cry activates the involuntary response of the mother's endocrine system, releasing her milk: 'One cry, and I stumble from bed, cow-heavy.' By the poem's end, this biological connection has created between mother and infant the possibility of another kind of exchange as the child begins to acquire language, to 'try' her 'handful of notes' and 'clear vowels'. 'Notes' are not cries, they are differentiating elements in a prosody; and vowels are not cries either: they are particles of what will become language after many 'tries'. For the mother, the infant has ascended from mere animate existence into human being she can recognize – whom she can love. Now she becomes a mother.

Hughes later pointed out to a critic that his 'Lines to a Newborn Baby' had been the stimulus to Plath's 'Morning Song', which he regarded as the better poem.[9] He did not add that 'Morning Song' had prompted his own 'Full Moon and Little Frieda', which is another poem on Frieda's acquisition of language. The child is older: now the rising vowels are enclosed in syllables, now she cries out in words '"Moon! Moon!"' (Hughes, *Collected Poems*, pp. 182–3). Echoes of Plath's 'Morning Song' in 'Full Moon' are unmistakable when the poems are examined together:

| 'Morning Song' | 'Full Moon and Little Frieda' |
|---|---|
| bald cry | you cry |
| set you going | going home |
| distills a mirror | still and brimming – mirror |
| moth-breath | wreaths of breath |
| I wake to listen | and you listening |
| cow-heavy | cows are going |
| swallows its dull stars | tempt a first star |
| one cry | 'Moon!' you cry |
| like balloons | 'Moon! Moon!' |

Moreover, it seems significant that Hughes drafted 'Full Moon' on the verso of a typescript of Plath's poem 'Tulips', which she drew from her hospitalization for an appendectomy following her miscarriage. 'Tulips' rejects the burden of intimacy, of the family. 'I am sick of baggage', the speaker declares, 'I have wanted to efface myself.' The poem seems to reflect the depressive mood that often follows surgery, and Plath's choice of 'efface' looks back to the anxiety of 'effacement' in 'Morning Song'. Hughes's 'Full Moon and Little Frieda' affirms the attentiveness of parental love.

It is impossible to know how many of the call-and-response transactions among these poems were intentional. Perhaps Plath and Hughes engaged in the practice with self-conscious awareness – as a kind of game. If so, their rivalry does not seem to have been rancorous. The period of sixteen months between their daughter's birth in April 1960 and their move to a larger house, in Devon, in early autumn 1961, turned out, in retrospect, to be a pinnacle of satisfaction in their creative partnership. They devised an egalitarian work schedule, relieving each other so that Plath had the morning, Hughes the afternoon free for writing while the other looked after Frieda. Hughes summarized Plath's progress to a mutual friend, shortly before the move from London. The poems she had written since their move to England, he reported, were far superior to those about to appear in *The Colossus*, and he particularly praised 'You're'.[10] Plath had also written *The Bell Jar*, in a mere three months (March through May 1961). Hughes, meanwhile, had published his second book of poems, *Lupercal*, and been awarded a major literary prize for it; he had also been commissioned to write a play.

In all these enterprises, each provided the other with enthusiastic encouragement and shrewd critical judgement. The quality of their relationship during this London phase was captured in a radio interview for the BBC. The interviewer asked whether their different backgrounds made for difficulty in getting along. Hughes claimed that, to the contrary, their empathy was so complete that each could enter the other's mind by telepathy. When the interviewer wondered whether they were not perhaps too closely allied, and in danger of imitating one another, Plath bristled. Their work was quite different, she insisted. Hughes backed her up. They were utterly compatible, he claimed; but their imaginations were quite independent. Thus their different temperaments as artists never came into conflict.[11]

This complex dynamic of sameness and difference is vividly demonstrated on the manuscripts they were producing at the time. When Hughes, for example, pulled the sheet of discarded typescript containing Plath's poem about her pregnancy, 'Metaphors', and flipped it over to begin drafting 'Lines to a Newborn Baby', he was apparently practising a kind of magic thinking in which both of them indulged. Often the 'used' side of the paper contains subject matter that is startlingly relevant to the new work underway on the other side. Hughes's 'Lines', for example, went through many drafts – possibly he began writing the poem before the baby was delivered – and an attentive reader can see that a significant number of the apparently random sheets of scratch paper he selected have a loosely common subject: they refer to his own childhood home in Yorkshire. Several pages are typescript of an autobiographical story that deals with a Yorkshire family ('The Courting of Petty Quinnett'). One page contains his sketches of two horoscopes, annotated 'Ma's attack, Ma's Natal?' Two are from Plath's poem 'Hardcastle Crags', written shortly after her first visit to Hughes's family home. Another is a discard from *The Bed Book*, a story Plath was writing for children. And at some point when they wrote, together, 'Billy Hook and the Three Souvenirs', the manuscript carried the name 'Sylvia Hughes' but it was published in *Jack and Jill* as a story by Ted Hughes.[12] In the archives that now contain their papers, just such sheets offer example after example of the '"shared mind"' (quoted in Middlebrook, *Her Husband*, p. 274) that Hughes attributed to them at their most compatible.

## Separation poems

Plath and Hughes left London in early autumn 1961 to make their home in a small village in Devon. Plath was pregnant again; their tiny flat could no longer contain them. London real estate was unaffordable, but they were able to buy a large rundown house, a former rectory called Court Green, that could accommodate both their expanding family and their need for ample separate workspaces. Plath's writing underwent another hiatus while they resettled and made their home habitable. Their second child, a son, was born in mid-January 1962. In early March Plath resumed her routine of working in her study every morning; between March and December that year she wrote the poems that have lifted her name into the canon of poetry in English.

Apparently, the first piece of work she finished, in March, was *Three Women*, a thirty-minute script for the BBC (later, *Three Women: A Poem for Three Voices*). It seems unlikely that Plath would have undertaken such a project without the example of Hughes's relative success in this medium. Ever since their move to England, Hughes had been earning the greater part of their meagre income by writing for the BBC, and in January his play *The Wound*, was produced; Plath wrote to her mother that he received a large fee for two broadcasts – large in comparison to the payments they collected from book reviews and poems.[13] Receiving a commission of her own from the BBC made Plath a contributor again to the family bank account, which pleased her very much. But artistically Plath's radio play did not resemble Hughes's plays in the slightest. *Three Women* is not a drama at all, but a suite of monologues for noninteracting voices. The setting is a maternity ward, where the women reflect on their experiences of pregnancy. 'First Voice' gives birth to a son and contentedly takes him home to the country; 'Second Voice' has a miscarriage and is wracked by depression; 'Third Voice' delivers an illegitimate daughter and abandons her at the hospital after taking a last look, through a glass barrier, at the baby whose 'cries are hooks that catch and grate like cats'.

Moreover, those three voices may well be semi-conscious emanations of Plath's disquiet regarding the emotional reconfiguration that had developed after her own miscarriage and the birth of Nicholas. By the time Plath went back to her desk, the house held two couples: Plath and a placid, nursing baby boy; Hughes and a precocious, high-strung little girl. Plath's engrossment with the new infant was a predictable outcome of breastfeeding, and likely to be temporary, but that did not make it any less influential as a disturbance in her creative partnership with Hughes. For when Sylvia Plath chose, at this moment of postpartum reentry into her professional life, to write about experiences that were distinctively specific to women, she had begun loosening the hold of her lifelong dependence on mentors: the male teachers she had striven to please, the male writers that had formed her literary taste, and the man she had married believing his prowess would always put him miles ahead of her as an artist.

These developments produced a shockwave in Plath's work, at the deepest level. Thematically, her poems were increasingly focused on the instability of love, and emotionally they were saturated with dreadful knowledge into which the speaker of the poem is forced to travel, as to a destination. 'I know the bottom', Plath wrote that April in 'Elm'; 'It is what you fear. / I do not fear it: I have been there.' Some of her dread was expressed in her creative responses to Hughes's work that spring. To pursue just one significant example: a source for the ominous poems 'Crossing the Water' and 'Event' that Plath wrote in April and May 1962 can be found in drafts of Hughes's play *The Calm*, which he had been working on in London around the time of Frieda's birth in April 1960 (Middlebrook, *Her Husband*, pp. 137–9). The manuscript survives only on scattered typescript pages that Hughes and Plath repurposed for drafting other work, but the action of *The Calm* seems to be taking place on the banks of the River Acheron (from classical myth, the river in the underworld where spirits gather after death). The characters are a band of five survivors attempting to merge their memories in order for each to recover a sense of self, under the leadership of a superior being called 'The Helper'. A baby is discovered and brought into their midst at some point, supplying the possibility of a new start.

Hughes never completed the play, but he cannibalized one of its speeches for a poem titled 'The Rescue' which was published in the London *Observer* in October 1961 and then in Boston's *Atlantic Monthly* in March – the month Plath took up writing again. Some of these lines fermented in Plath's imagination that spring, specifically the lines describing the delusion that the survivors would be rescued and returned undamaged to normal life. Hughes wrote, in 'The Rescue' of an approaching 'shipful of strangers' with 'all the sailors white / As maggots waving at the rail' (Hughes, *Collected Poems*, p. 157). In Plath's 'Crossing the Water' the drama of expectation and disappointment depicted in 'The Rescue' is reimagined from the perspective of the dumb survivors in the rowboat, silently watching as what looks like a 'valedictory, pale hand' emerges from the water. In Plath's 'Event' a wakeful woman paces the floor of a moonlit bedroom where her husband is perhaps feigning sleep. The sight of their infant son, lying near by in his white crib, prompts a strange metaphor that emerges from 'The Rescue': 'A black gap discloses itself. / On the opposite lip / A small white soul is waving, a small white maggot.' Black gap; opposite lip with a soul waving on the other side; a valedictory pale hand: Plath is identifying with the fate of the lost souls in 'The Rescue' and fitting the future of 'us' to their hopelessness. And *The Calm*, from which 'The Rescue' was drawn, continued to reassert itself in Plath's work after her explosive separation from Hughes in October. She used typescripts of *The Calm* as drafting paper for some of the bitterest poems that would later be published in *Ariel*: 'Eavesdropper', 'Medusa', 'A Secret', 'The Applicant', 'Lesbos', 'Fever 103°', 'Amnesiac'. And 'Daddy'.[14]

On the same day that Plath finished writing 'Event', she finished another poem that is not at all ambiguous about the anxiety she was feeling regarding her marriage: 'The Rabbit Catcher'. A woman is walking on a violently windy day, perturbed, and enters a quiet thicket, where she discovers a line of snares set for trapping rabbits. An image comes to mind, of the man who set them, and as stanza five explains in sexual and sadistic metaphors ('those little deaths! / They waited like sweethearts'), she is repulsed. Plath has fetched this image and its disturbing eroticism out of a couple of poems by D. H. Lawrence, 'Rabbit Snared in the Night' and 'Love on the Farm'.[15] In 'Rabbit Snared in the Night' Lawrence's first-person speaker has removed a live rabbit from the snare and is holding it on his knees:

> It must have been your inbreathing, gaping desire
> that drew this red gush in me …
> It must be *you* who desire
> this intermingling of the black and monstrous fingers of Moloch
> in the blood-jets of your throat.

In 'Love on the Farm' the point of view is that of a wife who has observed that her husband is sexually aroused by hunting game; when he returns with the corpse of a rabbit, she, too, is aroused:

> He flings the rabbit soft on the table board …
> And caresses me with his fingers that still smell grim
> Of the rabbit's fur! God, I am caught in a snare!
> I know not what fine wire is round my throat;
> I only know I let him finger there
> My pulse of life.

Some background is helpful here. Plath's college journals show that she, like many of her generation, had acquired a sexual ideology by reading the novels and poems of D. H. Lawrence. Her Cambridge journals and letters home show that she identified Ted Hughes as a Lawrentian hero. During 1958–9, the first year that Plath and Hughes allocated to becoming professional writers, Plath was attempting to write their romance into a novel, and she turned repeatedly to Lawrence for inspiration – to be 'itched and kindled' as she put it. 'Why do I feel I would have known & loved Lawrence – how many women must feel this & be wrong!' She spent a whole day reading *Lady Chatterley's Lover*, 'with the joy of a woman living with her own gamekeeper' (*J*, p. 337).

In her own poem, 'The Rabbit Catcher', Plath puts her speaker in the wife's position and arrives at a despairing identification of D. H. Lawrence with her addressee, caught in a relationship with 'Tight wires between us, / Pegs too deep to uproot'. From the outset of their love affair, Plath seems to have been drawn to the potential for cruelty in Hughes ('Such violence, and I can see how women lie down for artists' (*J*, p. 212)). The end of 'The Rabbit Catcher' acknowledges her female complicity with the kind of literary masculinity she used to idealize in Lawrence and Hughes, and has begun to outgrow. She, like the rabbit, has been snared by this man with a 'mind like a ring / Sliding shut' around her own throat.

'The Rabbit Catcher' elicited from Ted Hughes the most direct criticism of Plath that he ever made in public, in a letter he wrote to one of Plath's biographers: 'The only thing that I found hard to understand was her sudden discovery of our bad moments ('Event', 'Rabbit Catcher') as subjects for poems.'[16] He could still feel the blow years afterwards. In the version of *Ariel* that Hughes found carefully assembled in a spring binder, Plath had included 'The Rabbit Catcher'. He left it out. Years later, he published a refutation in a poem he titled 'The Rabbit Catcher' in *Birthday Letters*.

Plath did not live to see these responses to her 'The Rabbit Catcher', of course. What she did live to see, or hear, was a much more subtle countertext by Ted Hughes, a radio script titled *Difficulties of a Bridegroom*. The title refers to one of Hughes's favourite esoteric texts on alchemy, *The Chemical Wedding of Christian Rosencreutz*, in which 'bridegroom' is the name for an initiate. Hughes characterized the plot as a man's conflict with his propensity for being seduced.[17] The longest section of *Difficulties* is almost impenetrably surreal, involving a kind of dream vision in which the male protagonist, Sullivan, is confronted by manifestations of an antagonistic and irresistible female principle called 'She'. But the drama opens with a realistic event: Sullivan is driving his car to a sexual assignation with his mistress, his thoughts preoccupied with the woman who has triggered a hidden circuitry in his brain.[18] Suddenly a hare darts into the road, and Sullivan hits it accidentally; at the end of the story he sells the hare's body and spends the money on two roses for his mistress. The BBC's typescript of *Difficulties of a Bridegroom* is dated 19 December 1962, and arguably reflects Hughes's bewitchment by Assia Wevill, the wife of another poet with whom the Hugheses were acquainted. In July that year, Plath had learnt that Hughes and Wevill were having an affair. Efforts at reconciliation had failed, and in October Plath required Hughes to move out of Court Green (Middlebrook, *Her Husband*, pp. 171–2).

During the ensuing months Plath wrote many of her finest poems. Some were direct responses to the misery of her marriage breaking down. But some were direct responses to Hughes's work, none more evidently than 'Kindness', a poem that contains unmistakable echoes of *Difficulties of a Bridegroom*. Plath's 'Kindness' appears to have been prompted by listening to the broadcast of Hughes's play on 21 January. Hughes wrote, in one of Sullivan's internal monologues, about the terrible scream a hare would make when wounded.[19] Plath wrote, in 'Kindness', of the wildness of 'a rabbit's cry'. Then, reverting to her earlier identification of Hughes with D. H. Lawrence in 'The Rabbit Catcher', Plath ends 'Kindness' with a jab from Lawrence's 'Rabbit Snared in the Night'. Lawrence wrote of 'the blood-jets of your throat'. Plath writes: 'The blood jet is poetry . . . / You hand me two children, two roses.'

'Kindness' is one of many poems in which Plath is conducting the equivalent of a subliminal custody battle with Hughes. Here she appropriates the gift of two roses that Sullivan gives his mistress as metaphors for the rosy children in her own possession, a message that Hughes would have ears to hear. Many other examples of Plath's territoriality towards the children abound in the manuscripts of poems she wrote during their separation. For instance, Plath again pulled typescripts from Hughes's 'Lines to a Newborn Baby' when she began drafting her triumphal poem 'Stings'. In this, the fiercest of Plath's sequence of 'Bee Poems', a woman is lifting combs from the hive while a man looks on; suddenly the bees attack him. He is chased off the property as the queen bee rises into the sky 'More terrible than she ever was', shedding the corpses of the drones as she ascends. The presence of Hughes's 'Lines' on the 'used' side of 'Stings' suggests that Plath was intent on finding a way to satirize Hughes's claims to fatherhood – in other poems of that period Plath consistently images the 'other woman' as barren ('The Other', 'Amnesiac', 'The Fearful', 'Childless Woman'). In contrast, Plath's poems about the children designate herself as their protector, by implication their *only* protector: 'For a Fatherless Son', 'By Candlelight', 'Nick and the Candlestick', 'The Night Dances', 'Child', 'Balloons', 'Edge'.

By far the most significant example of Plath's communications about her bonds with the children are two poems, 'By Candlelight' and 'Nick and the Candlestick', in which a woman is nursing a baby by the light of a candle held in an ornamental candlestick: a kneeling brass god wearing an animal hide. In a note on 'Nick and the Candlestick', Hughes said that the god was Hercules and his cloak was a lion's pelt (*CP*, p. 294, n. 192). But Plath's poem says that the kneeling god was Atlas and that he was wearing the skin of a panther, a detail that links the poems about her infant son to 'Pursuit', the first poem Plath wrote after meeting Hughes. In 'Pursuit' she wrote of a predatory panther with 'bright' and dangerous claws. In the poems about nursing, that avid phallic animal has shrunk to the scale of a table ornament; 'Where his phallus and balls should be, / A panther claw'.[20] The boy-child in the mother's arms now occupies all the emotional space in the poem: 'You are the one / Solid the spaces lean on, envious.'

In the poems she was writing after their separation, Plath's antagonist was the side of Hughes that expressed itself in *Difficulties of a Bridegroom* – the man with a switch in his brain that could be tripped by the biological imperative of sexual attraction. The switch in her own brain was tripped by rage, equally primitive: womanly rage at being displaced by a sexual rival, maternal rage at being deserted by the father of their children. The ironic title she gave to 'Kindness' points to the experience of establishing a life separate from Hughes, where, in daily life, the kindness of friends was balm to her self-esteem, but where rage was the lifeblood of her poetry.

One aggressive activity she continued to pursue was the creative appropriation that had distinguished their working method at their most compatible. Before Hughes moved out of Court Green, Plath had apparently taken from his desk a number of typescripts, which Hughes found lying on her desk after her suicide. The poems were 'The Road to Easington', 'Out', 'The Green Wolf', 'New Moon in January', 'Heptonstall', 'Full Moon and Little Frieda', plus a few versions of poems by José Garcia Lorca that Hughes had underway. Plath had been using them for her own purposes, Hughes later told a friend (Middlebrook, *Her Husband*, p. 219). He recognized immediately what Plath had taken from 'The Road to Easington' in her poem 'The Bee Meeting', written shortly before their separation. Hughes's poem opens, 'Is there anything along this road, are there answers at the road's end? ... / Murmuring, trying to add village to village' (Hughes, *Collected Poems*, pp. 101–2). Plath's poem closes, 'The villagers are untying their disguises, they are shaking hands. / Whose is that long white box in the grove, what have they accomplished, why am I cold.' Plath had arguably coded a message into the very cadences of 'The Bee Meeting', imitating the prosody of 'The Road to Easington' to tell Hughes that his longing to get away would kill her.

One of the very last poems Plath wrote before her suicide imagines that death. Titled 'Edge', its simple imagery depicts the corpses of a mother and two children laid out in a moonlit garden. The poem was written in the aftermath of a bitter disappointment Plath had suffered late in January 1963, when her novel *The Bell Jar* received a lukewarm review in the London *Observer* on the same page that carried a poem by Hughes: 'Full Moon and Little Frieda' (Hughes, *Collected Poems*, pp. 182–3). Plath was, perhaps, crushed by what she saw as an ominous sign that Hughes, not she, was destined to receive the world's approval and rewards. Her acute distress may be read as an overreaction; for one thing, Plath had published *The Bell Jar* under a pseudonym, so her name did not even appear in the newspaper review. But when writing 'Edge', Plath was already experiencing the descent into breakdown that preceded her suicide, and it appears that some of the poem's imagery, specifically that of the milk – a full bucket in Hughes's poem, an empty pitcher in Plath's – and the moon, may have been a response to the call she heard in 'Full Moon and Little Frieda'.

'Edge' was among the poems awaiting Hughes's discovery when he moved into Plath's London flat to look after the children. He later recalled the sleepless nights he spent there, listening to the wolves howling from their cages in nearby Regent's Park. The wolf-howls eventually gave Hughes the closing image of a poem in *Birthday Letters*, 'Life after Death'. Here 'wolves are singing in the forest' lamenting two 'orphans / Beside the corpse of their mother' (Hughes, *Collected Poems*, pp. 1160–1). Hughes's image beautifully integrates the ancient legend about Romulus and Remus, the founders of Rome – abandoned in the wild, the children of Rhea Silvia were suckled by a she-wolf – with the iconography of 'Edge', where the children lie dead next to the mother's body alongside her breasts, 'pitcher[s] of milk, now empty'. In Hughes's poem the singing wolves forecast the children's rescue by a lupine caretaker, himself.

'Life after Death' is only one of many poems that indicate how profoundly Plath's work continued to call for Hughes's response throughout his lifetime as a poet. Only months before his death in 1998, Hughes brought out the two books of poems addressed to Plath – *Birthday Letters* and *Howls & Whispers* – that, he acknowledged, he had been working on for twenty-five years. And in 1997 Hughes sold a large archive of his papers to Emory University in Atlanta, papers that have already begun to reveal to scholars how wide-ranging and subtle were the influences of Plath's work on his own both before and after her death. As Hughes put it, in a metaphor, it was the solar system that had married them the night they met, and in many of the works that flowed from that heavenly creative partnership, they are indissoluble.

# Notes

1. For extensive assistance with the manuscript evidence on which this essay is based, I wish to thank Karen V. Kukil, Associate Curator of Rare Books at the Sylvia Plath Collection, Mortimer Rare Book Room, Smith College, and Naomi L. Nelson, Head of Research Services, Special Collections and Archives, Robert W. Woodruff Library, Emory University.

2. Diane Middlebrook, *Her Husband: Hughes and Plath – A Marriage* (New York: Viking, 2003), pp. 3–4.

3. Ted Hughes, *Collected Poems* (London: Faber and Faber, 2003), p. 41.

4. Karl Miller, 'Poetry from Cambridge, 1952–1954', in Nick Gammage (ed.), *The Epic Poise: A Celebration of Ted Hughes* (London: Faber and Faber, 1999), pp. 3, 6.

5. TH to Aurelia Plath, 30 May 1960, Lilly.

6. TH to W. S. Merwin, nd (late October 1960), Emory.

7. 'Two of a Kind: Poets in Partnership', Ted Hughes and Sylvia Plath interviewed by Owen Leeming, 19 January 1961, broadcast 31 January 1961 transcript and tape (British Library catalogue NP 7400).

8. 'Lines to a Newborn Baby' was published in two parts, and appears in Hughes's *Collected Poems* under two titles: part one as 'Lines to a Newborn Baby' (pp. 96–7), parts two and three as 'To F. R. at Six Months' (pp. 97–8).

9. TH to Keith Sagar, 13 March 1981, British Library.

10. TH to Lucas Myers, nd (September 1961), Emory.

11. 'Two of a Kind'. See also Ted Hughes, 'The Art of Poetry LXXI', *Paris Review* 134 (1995), pp. 55–94 (p. 77).

12. I am indebted to Stephen Enniss, Director of Special Collections and Archives at the Woodruff Library, Emory University, for pointing this out in his unpublished article 'Sylvia Plath, Ted Hughes, and the Myth of Textual Betrayal'.

13. SP to Aurelia Plath, 24 February 1962, Lilly.

14. Karen Kukil, email to the author, 19 August 2004.

15. D. H. Lawrence, *The Complete Poems of D. H. Lawrence*, ed. Vivian de Sola Pinto and Warren Roberts (New York: Penguin, 1977), pp. 240–2, 42. Marjorie Perloff identified 'Love on the Farm' as a source for Plath's 'The Rabbit Catcher' in 'The Two *Ariels*: The (Re)making of the Sylvia Plath Canon', *Poetic License: Essays on Modernist and Postmodern Lyric* (Evanston, IL: Northwestern University Press, 1990), p. 186.

16. Ted Hughes to Anne Stevenson, quoted with Hughes's permission in Janet Malcolm, *The Silent Woman* (New York: Vintage Books, 1995), p. 143.

17. Ted Hughes, BBC interview with Anthony Thwaite (16 January 1963), transcript, British Library. See also Middlebrook, *Her Husband*, pp. 138–9, 170–1.

18. *Difficulties of a Bridegroom*, transcript, British Library.

19. Ibid.

20. These lines are printed without lineation in Stephen Tabor (ed.), *An Analytical Bibliography* (London: Mansell, 1987), p. 143; they occur on all drafts of the poem except the last draft in the Plath archive at Smith College.

# SELECTED READING

For primary sources, please see the List of abbreviations at the front of the book. The booklist below is not exhaustive but it does reflect the diversity of approaches to Plath's writing since her earliest publication. Three bibliographies provide fuller details of Plath's publications and of subsequent scholarship: Cameron Northouse and Thomas P. Walsh, *Sylvia Plath and Anne Sexton: A Reference Guide* (Boston: G. K. Hall, 1974); Stephen Tabor, *Sylvia Plath: An Analytical Bibliography* (Westport, CT: Meckler; London: Mansell, 1987); and Sheryl Meyering, *Sylvia Plath: A Reference Guide, 1973–1988* (Boston: G. K. Hall, 1990).

Extensive archives of Plath material are held at the Lilly Library, Indiana University, and in the Rare Books Room at Smith College. Emory University Rare Books Room holds Ted Hughes's papers.

Aird, Eileen. *Sylvia Plath: Her Life and Work*. New York: Harper & Row, 1973.
Alexander, Paul (ed.). *Ariel Ascending: Writings about Sylvia Plath*. New York: Harper & Row, 1985.
Alexander, Paul. *Rough Magic: A Biography of Sylvia Plath*. New York: Viking, 1991.
Alvarez, A. *The New Poetry*. Harmondsworth: Penguin, 1962; revised edition 1966.
    *Beyond All This Fiddle: Essays 1955–1967*. London: Allen Lane, 1968.
    *The Savage God: A Study of Suicide*. London: Weidenfeld & Nicolson, 1971; New York: Random House, 1972.
Annas, Pamela J. *A Disturbance in Mirrors: The Poetry of Sylvia Plath*. Westport, CT: Greenwood, 1988.
Axelrod, Steven Gould. *Sylvia Plath: The Wound and the Cure of Words*. Baltimore: Johns Hopkins University Press, 1990.
Bassnett, Susan. *Sylvia Plath: An Introduction to the* Poetry. 2nd edition. Basingstoke and New York: Palgrave Macmillan, 2005.
Bennett, Paula. *My Life a Loaded Gun: Dickinson, Plath, Rich and Female Creativity*. Urbana: University of Illinois Press, 1986.
Bere, Carol. '*Johnny Panic and the Bible of Dreams and Other Prose Writings*'. *Southern Humanities Review* 13 (Fall 1979), pp. 358–60.
Bertram, Vicki (ed.). *Kicking Daffodils: Twentieth Century Women Poets*. Edinburgh: Edinburgh University Press, 1997.
Bloom, Harold (ed.). *Modern Critical Views: Sylvia Plath*. New York and Philadelphia: Chelsea House Publishers, 1989.

Brain, Tracy. *The Other Sylvia Plath*. London: Longman, 2001.

Brennan, Claire. *The Poetry of Sylvia Plath: A Reader's Guide to Essential Criticism*. Cambridge: Icon, 2000.

Breslin, Paul. *The Psycho-Political Muse: American Poetry since the 1950s*. Chicago: University of Chicago Press, 1987.

Britzolakis, Christina. *Sylvia Plath and the Theatre of Mourning*. Oxford: Clarendon Press, 1999.

Broe, Mary Lynn. *Protean Poetic: The Poetry of Sylvia Plath*. Columbia and London: University of Missouri Press, 1980.

Bronfen, Elisabeth. *Sylvia Plath* (British Council Writers and their Work). Plymouth: Northcote House, 1998.

Bundtzen, Lynda K. *Plath's Incarnations: Woman and the Creative Process*. Ann Arbor: University of Michigan Press, 1983.

   *The Other Ariel*. Amherst: University of Massachusetts Press, 2001.

Butscher, Edward. *Sylvia Plath: Method and Madness*. New York: Seabury Press, 1976.

Butscher, Edward (ed.). *Sylvia Plath: The Woman and the Work*. New York: Dodd, Mead, 1977; London: Peter Owen, 1979.

Churchwell, Sarah. 'Ted Hughes and the Corpus of Sylvia Plath'. *Criticism* (1998), pp. 99–132.

Cox, C. B. and A. R. Jones. 'After the Tranquillized Fifties: Notes on Sylvia Plath and James Baldwin'. *Critical Quarterly* 6.2 (1964), pp. 107–22.

Curry, Renée R. *White Women Writing White: H. D., Elizabeth Bishop, Sylvia Plath and Whiteness*. Westport, CT: Greenwood, 2000.

Easthope, Antony. 'Reading the Poetry of Sylvia Plath'. *English* 43 (1994), pp. 223–35.

Forbes, Deborah. *Sincerity's Shadow: Self-Consciousness in British Romantic and Mid-Twentieth Century American Poetry*. Cambridge, MA: Harvard University Press, 2004.

Ford, Karen Jackson. *Gender and the Poetics of Excess: Moments of Brocade*. Jackson, MS: University Press of Mississippi, 1997.

Gilbert, Sandra M. and Susan Gubar (eds.). *Shakespeare's Sisters: Feminist Essays on Women Poets*. Bloomington: Indiana University Press, 1979.

Giles, Paul. 'Double Exposure: Sylvia Plath and the Aesthetics of Transnationalism'. *Symbiosis* 5.2 (2001), pp. 103–20.

Hall, Caroline King Barnard. *Sylvia Plath*. Boston: Twayne, 1978.

Hardy, Barbara. 'The Poetry of Sylvia Plath'. *Women Reading Women's Writing*. Ed. Sue Roe. Brighton: Harvester, 1987, pp. 209–28.

Helle, Anita (ed.). *The Unravelling Archive: Essays on Sylvia Plath*. Ann Arbor: University of Michigan Press, 2006.

Holbrook, David. *Sylvia Plath: Poetry and Existence*. London: Athlone Press, 1976.

Hughes, Ted. 'Notes on the Chronological Order of Sylvia Plath's Poems'. *Tri-Quarterly* 7 (1966), pp. 81–8.

   'The Art of Poetry LXXI'. *Paris Review* 134 (1995), pp. 54–94.

   *Collected Poems*. London: Faber and Faber, 2003.

Juhasz, Suzanne. *Naked and Fiery Forms: Modern American Poetry by Women, a New Tradition*. New York: Harper & Row, 1976.

Kaplan, Cora (ed.). *Salt and Bitter and Good: Three Centuries of English and American Women Poets*. New York and London: Paddington Press, 1975.

Kendall, Tim. *Sylvia Plath: A Critical Study*. London: Faber and Faber, 2001.

Kroll, Judith. *Chapters in a Mythology: The Poetry of Sylvia Plath*. New York and London: Harper & Row, 1976.

Lane, Gary (ed.). *Sylvia Plath: New Views on the Poetry*. Baltimore: Johns Hopkins University Press, 1979.

Lant, Kathleen Margaret. 'The Big Strip Tease: Female Bodies and Male Power in the Poetry of Sylvia Plath'. *Contemporary Literature* 34.4 (1993), pp. 620–69.

Lowell, R. 'Sylvia Plath's *Ariel*' (1966). Reprinted in Robert Giroux (ed.), *Collected Prose*. New York, Farrar, Straus & Giroux, 1987.

Macpherson, Pat. *Reflecting on The Bell Jar*. London: Routledge, 1991.

Malcolm, Janet. *The Silent Woman: Sylvia Plath and Ted Hughes*. London: Picador, 1994; New York: Vintage, 1995.

Middlebrook, Diane. *Her Husband: Hughes and Plath – A Marriage*. New York: Viking, 2003.

Middlebrook, Diane Wood and Marilyn Yalom (eds.). *Coming to Light: American Women Poets in the Twentieth Century*. Ann Arbor: University of Michigan Press, 1985.

Nelson, Deborah. *Pursuing Privacy in Cold War America*. New York: Columbia University Press, 2002.

Newman, Charles (ed.). *The Art of Sylvia Plath: A Symposium*. Bloomington: Indiana University Press, 1970.

Ostriker, Alicia. *Stealing the Language: The Emergence of Women's Poetry in America*. Boston: Beacon, 1986; London: Women's Press, 1987.

Peel, Robin. *Writing Back: Sylvia Plath and Cold War Politics*. Madison: Fairleigh Dickinson University Press; London: Associated University Presses, 2002.

Perloff, Marjorie. 'The Two *Ariels*: The (Re)making of the Sylvia Plath Canon'. *Poetic License: Essays on Modernist and Postmodern Lyric*. Evanston, IL: Northwestern University Press, 1990, pp. 175–97.

Ramazani, Jahan. *Poetry of Mourning: The Modern Elegy from Hardy to Heaney*. Chicago: University of Chicago Press, 1994.

Rose, Jacqueline. *The Haunting of Sylvia Plath*. London: Virago, 1991; Cambridge, MA: Harvard University Press, 1992.

  *On Not Being Able to Sleep: Psychoanalysis and the Modern World*. London: Chatto & Windus, 2003.

Rosenblatt, Jon. *Sylvia Plath: The Poetry of Initiation*. Chapel Hill: University of North Carolina Press, 1979.

Rosenthal, M. L. *The New Poets: American and British Poetry Since World War II*. New York: Oxford University Press, 1967.

Smith, Stan. *Inviolable Voice: History and Twentieth-Century Poetry*. Dublin: Gill and Macmillan, 1982.

Stevenson, Anne. *Bitter Fame: A Life of Sylvia Plath*. London: Viking; Boston: Houghton Mifflin, 1989.

Strangeways, Al. *Sylvia Plath: The Shaping of Shadows*. Cranbury, NJ, and London: Associated University Presses, 1998.

Van Dyne, Susan, R. *Revising Life: Sylvia Plath's Ariel Poems*. Chapel Hill: University of North Carolina Press, 1993.

Vendler, Helen Hennessy. *The Music of What Happens: Poems, Poets, Critics*. Cambridge, MA: Harvard University Press, 1988.

*Coming of Age as a Poet: Milton, Keats, Eliot, Plath*. Cambridge, MA: Harvard University Press, 2003.

Wagner, Linda (ed.). *Critical Essays on Sylvia Plath*. Boston: G. K. Hall, 1984.

*Sylvia Plath: The Critical Heritage*. London and New York: Routledge, 1988.

Wagner-Martin, Linda. *Sylvia Plath: A Biography*. New York: Simon & Schuster, 1987.

*The Bell Jar: A Novel of the Fifties*. New York: Twayne/Macmillan, 1992.

*Sylvia Plath: A Literary Life*. New York: St Martin's Press; Basingstoke: Palgrave Macmillan, 1999; 2nd edition 2003.

Whitehead, Kim. *The Feminist Poetry Movement*. Jackson: University Press of Mississippi, 1996.

# INDEX

# CAMBRIDGE COMPANIONS TO LITERATURE

## CAMBRIDGE COMPANIONS TO CULTURE

Printed in the United States
75933LV00002B/19-30